Auto Accident Survivor's Guide for British Columbia

About the author

Jill Franklin grew up in New York and was educated at Brown University and Sarah Lawrence College. She lived in India for many years before moving to British Columbia in 1985 and becoming a Canadian citizen. Her books have been published throughout the world in many languages. She's also been a U.S. presidential candidate's speechwriter and has worked as a para-legal, run therapy groups, lectured at universities and professional conferences, set up the first debit card system in North America, and managed a large food service facility.

The author's experiences after a serious auto accident in Vancouver in 1990 led her to research and write this book. She and her husband have two daughters and four grandchildren. Their son was killed in 1987.

Other books by the author

The Promise of Paradise
Death Comes Dancing
Drunk on the Divine
The Ultimate Risk
Meditation: The Art of Ecstasy (editor)
The Psychology of the Esoteric (editor)
I Am the Gate (editor)
— and others

AUTO ACCIDENT SURVIVOR'S GUIDE FOR BRITISH COLUMBIA

Navigating the medical–legal–insurance system

Jill Franklin

A consumer advocacy guide

STONE MOUNTAIN BOOKS
PORT COQUITLAM, BRITISH COLUMBIA
2005

Published by Stone Mountain Books, Port Coquitlam, British Columbia
Cover design by Rayola Graphic Design
Interior design and production services provided by New Star Books
Printed and bound in Canada by Transcontinental Printing

LIBRARY AND ARCHIVES CANADA CATALOGUING IN PUBLICATION DATA

Franklin, Jill, 1942–
Auto accident survivor's guide for British Columbia : navigating the medical–legal–insurance system / Jill Franklin.

Includes index.
ISBN 0-9736611-0-0

1. Traffic accident victims — British Columbia — Handbooks, manuals, etc.
2. Traffic accident victims — Legal status, laws, etc. — British Columbia.
3. Personal injuries — British Columbia. 4. Automobile insurance claims — British Columbia. I. Title.
HE5614.5.C2F72 2005 346.71103'23 C2004-906151-8

Author's Note

While much of the material in this book will be helpful to people injured in auto accidents anywhere in Canada or the United States, the book is based on the medical-legal-insurance system in British Columbia. To simplify the text, the Insurance Corporation of British Columbia is referred to as "an insurance company" (even though it's a provincial-government Crown corporation), and all motor-vehicle accidents are referred to as "auto accidents" regardless of the type of vehicle involved.

I've tried to make the book as accurate as possible. However, legal statutes and regulations change all the time as do government benefit programs. You need to check with a lawyer or your insurer, or the appropriate government agency, to make sure the information provided is still correct.

This book isn't intended to be a substitute for professional advice. It should be used solely as a consumer advocacy guide.

Disclaimer

This publication is designed to provide accurate and authoritative information in regard to the subject matter covered. It is sold with the understanding that neither the author nor the publisher is engaged in rendering health care, insurance, legal, financial or other professional services.

The author and publisher specifically disclaim all and any liability, loss, or risk, personal or otherwise, which is incurred as a consequence, directly or indirectly, of the use and application of the contents of this book. Before acting on any suggestion presented in this book, legal or other professional assistance from a competent and qualified person should be sought.

The analysis contained in this book represents the experiences and opinions of the author. The author and publisher make no claim as to the accuracy of the information in this book nor for the occurrence of any errors or omissions.

Business, organization and product names used in this book are for identification purposes only, and may be registered trademarks, trademarks or trade names of their respective owners. The author and publisher disclaim any and all rights in those marks.

For Juliette and Billiam

— and, as always, in memory of Billy —

Contents

Acknowledgements

In researching the material for this book, I've been helped immeasurably by lawyers, health care providers, insurance and government agency employees, advocacy support group staff people, financial professionals and others. In addition to the interviews these people gave me, many reviewed the relevant material in their fields, making crucially important suggestions. Any errors that exist are solely my responsibility and the opinions expressed are solely my own. I'd like to thank the following people: Yousef Ali, Joe Battista, Janelle Breese Biagioni, Steven Bovencamp, Geoffrey Cowper, Louise Gaudry, Joyce Grant, Linc Johnson, Hugh Legg, Robyn Littlefield, Mike Long, Cindy Marshall, Bill Morley, Paris Simons, Lynn Turberfield, Brian Webster, Ursula Wild - and especially, Ed Good and Joe Murphy. While ICBC officially declined to review my material, many of their staff people were open and forthcoming in interviews, providing me with internal documents to which I wouldn't have otherwise had access. If I've neglected to mention these people by name, it's out of respect for their privacy, not because their help isn't deeply appreciated. I'd also like to thank Jane Franklin for typing interview transcripts and helping to structure the book. Lastly, I want to express my deep gratitude to psychologist Paul Peel and my husband Nick Franklin for their continued encouragement. Their recognition of how vital it is for people to have the information presented in the book kept me going over the many years it took to complete this.

Introduction

This isn't the kind of book I normally write, but it's the book I wish I'd had after I was hit by a car while crossing the street in Vancouver. I trusted B.C.'s medical-legal-insurance system to work for me without realizing that it was up to me to make sure it did.

While my personal experiences aren't discussed in this book, they made me realize how much a book like this is needed. My injuries required extensive surgery, and I spent two weeks in the hospital, six months in a wheelchair, and several years in rehab. ICBC admitted full liability early on and initially paid my medical and rehab expenses, but they didn't want to compensate me for my lost income. (The publication of a book I'd finished writing prior to my accident had to be postponed for two years.) Instead, I was sent to a series of medical experts as ICBC tried to find someone who would deny that my injuries had left me with on-going disabilities. My case went to trial, then ICBC appealed the court Judgment. Seven years after my accident, I finally received the money I was awarded, and my lawyers' accounts were settled.

The problems I encountered are similar to those faced by many auto accident survivors. Doctors may not detect conditions that require treatment. Insurers often assume that claimants exaggerate their problems. The experts they hire tend to downplay people's disabilities. Accident-related income losses can be hard to prove to an insurer's satisfaction, and lawyers' billing practices aren't always fair. If you're injured in an auto accident, you need to know how to get good medical care, necessary financial help, and competent legal advice. You also need to know what your legal rights are, when to pursue legal action, and how to safeguard your interests.

Every year, over 60,000 people in B.C. are injured or killed in auto accidents.[1] The vast majority of these people (or their families) file claims with ICBC, WCB and other insurers for benefits or compensation. Thousands of these claims go to trial, mediation, arbitration or appeal each year.

I'm not a lawyer, nor have I ever worked for the government or an insurer. While my personal experiences motivated me to write this book, I have no point of view to support other than my belief in the public's right to be informed about the issues that affect their lives.

A year after my insurance claim settled, I began my research by interviewing personal injury lawyers, doctors, rehab therapists, insurance and government agency employees, disability-group staff people, financial advisers and auto accident survivors. I read widely in many fields and analyzed insurance documents and statistics, legal statutes and regulations, and current case law. I also had access to ICBC internal claims procedure manuals that outline their policies and practices. Knowedgeable professionals reviewed what I wrote and offered advice when needed.

I've tried to de-mystify the medical-legal-insurance system in British Columbia and "level the playing field" for people who are injured in auto accidents by writing a balanced, objective guide that explains difficult concepts in simple, everyday language. Readers are given specific, detailed information about the actions they may have to take and what they need to be aware of. While the book focusses on the help that's available to B.C. residents through public and private sources, much of the material will be useful to people who live outside the province as well.

PART I

Getting the Help You Need

CHAPTER 1

When an Accident Happens

Knowing what to do after an auto accident can reduce the possibility of future problems occurring and ensure that you get the help you need, and when appropriate, fair compensation for your injuries. While the Insurance Corporation of British Columbia (ICBC) is usually the primary insurer when an accident occurs in the province, other public and private insurers may be involved as well.

Immediate Action to Take

Unless it's clear that no one was hurt in an accident, your first priority is to send for medical help or to ask someone else to do this. The emergency response number in the area (or 911) will connect you to a dispatcher who will want to know what happened, where it happened and what kind of help is needed: police, fire, ambulance or all three. You may also be asked if anyone was badly hurt. If anyone is unconscious, bleeding heavily, having trouble breathing or in shock, the dispatcher may suggest emergency first aid to do until help arrives.

Flares should to be set up to safeguard the accident scene, protect injured people from traffic, and warn cars coming from either direction that an accident lies ahead. Unless the road needs to be cleared for safety reasons, the cars should remain where they are until the police arrive. (The police are always notified when someone phones for an ambulance.)

Getting Prompt Medical Attention

Unless you were injured yourself, it's your civic duty to provide reasonable assistance to anyone who needs it. This doesn't mean performing emergency first aid that you're not qualified to do. An injured person shouldn't be moved unless he's in danger where he is: improper handling can cause life-threatening complications. Assuring someone who is injured or in shock that help is on its way may be the best (and only) thing you can do for him.

CAUTION! **An un-inflated airbag can inflate suddenly during a rescue attempt, causing serious injuries. Never try to de-activate an airbag yourself: emergency workers are trained to do this safely. (While the smoky powder an inflated airbag sometimes releases isn't dangerous, it can be irritating to the eyes and skin.)**

After the ambulance paramedics have evaluated the situation, if more than one person was injured they'll decide the order in which to treat them. Once they've provided emergency treatment to anyone whose life is in danger, they'll try to stabilize people's injuries. While you shouldn't get in their way while they're working, they may want to ask you some questions, which you should try to answer clearly and simply.

Anyone who was injured will normally be taken by ambulance to the hospital. If someone has life-threatening injuries, the ambulance will usually go to the nearest hospital. If you're taken to a hospital that doesn't have the staff or equipment to deal with your injuries, you'll be transferred to another facility.

If you were involved in the accident but decide not to take an ambulance to the hospital, the paramedics will usually ask you to sign a form stating that you were offered this opportunity but refused it. You'll be advised to see a doctor if you experience dizziness, stiffness or other accident-related symptoms.

The ambulance paramedics document everything they do from the time they arrive at an accident scene until they leave everyone who was injured in the care of an emergency room doctor. If you were injured or treated for shock, an ambulance report will be made out for you noting the nature of your accident ("head-on collision", "rear-ender", "pedestrian hit"), details of your injuries and mental state, the changes that were observed in you, and the treatment you were given. You should be able to get a copy of this through BC Ambulance Services. If your accident results in an insurance claim or legal proceedings, an insurer or lawyer may want a copy of this as well. (Ambulance paramedics are sometimes asked to testify in personal injury trials.)

After being in an accident, you should have a comprehensive medical exam done at the hospital or your doctor's office. Serious injuries can occur without being visible or obvious. Moreover, unless you're checked out by a doctor and her observations documented, ICBC (or another auto insurer) may deny that your problems were caused by your accident.

If you don't feel right in the days, weeks or months ahead, you should talk to your doctor about this as soon as possible. A soft tissue injury may not become apparent for several days, while it can take several months or more for post-traumatic stress disorder (PTSD) or symptoms of a mild traumatic brain injury (TBI) to become obvious. Changes in your moods or behaviour should be taken as seriously as your physical symptoms. The sooner you receive treatment, the better your overall recovery usually is.

TBI ALERT! Regardless of the nature of your accident, you may want to monitor yourself for brain injury symptoms for several months. Even a minor accident can cause damage to your brain with on-going consequences. You don't have to lose consciousness for this to happen. (See Chapter 7.)

Who Will Notify Your Family?

Unless you're too badly injured to do this, you should be able to phone a relative or friend from the hospital to tell her what happened and where you are. The hospital staff may also do this for you. If you have significant injuries, the police will normally try to contact your family (or a close friend), so you have someone with you in the hospital.

When anyone is seriously injured (or killed) in an accident — or a minor is injured — the police make every effort possible to notify the family in person.

Exchanging Information

Before leaving the accident scene, the involved drivers will need to exchange basic information with one another and with anyone injured. If you were driving, you'll have to give the other driver (and anyone injured) your name and address; home phone number; driver's licence number; and the name and address of the car owner, if this isn't you. If you have auto insurance through a company other than ICBC, you should also provide your insurer's name, your policy number, and the name, address and phone number of your insurance agent. Besides getting this same information from the other driver, you may want to make a note of the year, make, model and licence plate number of her car and the province (or state) it's licenced in. You'll also want the names, addresses and phone numbers of witnesses and anyone injured. If someone is charged with a traffic violation or criminal offence, your insurer will want to know who this is and what charges he faces.

Since the police may not speak to every witness, you should make sure that anyone who saw what happened and doesn't feel you were at fault — or solely at fault — can be located later to give a statement to ICBC or another insurer. (After a hit-and-run accident, an insurance claim may be denied unless uninvolved witnesses can be found.) If someone is reluctant to give you her name or phone number, you can ask her to give this to an attending police officer. You may also want to give her your phone number so she can contact you later if she changes her mind about making a statement.

If you hit an unoccupied car, it's your responsibility to locate the owner or to leave identifying information about yourself in a visible place — usually the car windshield.

The Role of the Police

The police will want to speak to everyone involved in the accident as well as to witnesses. While you need to co-operate fully with them, when you're emotionally upset isn't the time to assess whether (or to what degree) you were at fault. You may not remember what happened clearly because your mind clicked off in some way, or you may have focused on something minor and missed what was significant. You may also be in shock or denial and not able to accept the reality of what happened. When giving a statement to the police, it's better to admit that you don't remember something than to provide inaccurate information. Stick to the facts you're sure of, being as brief as possible.

How thoroughly the police investigate your accident will depend on how serious it is, how much time a particular police officer has, and how much effort he tends to put into these situations. While the police are expected to report the facts objectively, not decide who was at fault, insurers rely on police reports to a large extent in determining liability.

You (or another driver) may be charged with a traffic violation or criminal offence in connection to your accident. Speeding, driving without due care and attention, failing to yield to a pedestrian or other car, and failing to obey a traffic light or road sign are traffic violations. Driving while impaired, dangerous driving, and failing to remain at an accident scene are criminal offences. An initial charge of dangerous driving may be changed to a lesser offence like failing to yield when the police don't feel they have enough evidence to prove a criminal charge. (When anyone is killed in an accident, criminal charges are routinely made.)

Refusing to give the police a breath or blood sample upon request subjects you to the same criminal charges as driving while impaired. If a police officer feels your ability to drive was affected by alcohol or drugs, you may be charged with impaired driving even though your blood-alcohol level is within legal limits.

Reporting Your Accident to the Police

If anyone was injured in your accident, the accident should be reported to the police within 24 hours in an urban area and within 48 hours in a rural area. The police should also be notified after a hit-and-run accident and when property damage exceeds $1,000 (or $600 in a motorcycle accident.) If you can't report your accident to the police yourself, someone can do this for you. When a driver isn't able to report an accident but a passenger can, it's her responsibility to do this.

Whenever the police are present at an accident scene, a police report is automatically filed. Besides identifying the people involved and some witnesses, the police report will note whether anyone was injured or any charges made. A rough diagram may be drawn that shows where the cars were when the police arrived and what direction they were facing. The police officer's observations may be briefly described as well.

As the driver (or owner) of a car involved in an accident, you can get a free copy of the police report later, upon request. If your insurance adjuster asks to see this, you'll have to mail him a copy within 24 hours. ICBC (or another auto insurer) can purchase a copy of the police report for their own use. They only thing they'll have to share with you is the names of the involved drivers, car owners, and witnesses.

A police report is only admissible as evidence in legal proceedings following an auto accident when someone is accused of making false statements to the police, which is a criminal offence. If an insurance claim ends up in court, a police officer who testifies at the trial can review his report to refresh his memory, but the report itself won't become part of the trial evidence.

Reporting Your Accident to the Insurance Company

NOTE: Basic Autoplan insurance is compulsory in B.C. and is presently provided solely by ICBC. While additional coverage can be purchased from other auto insurers, the assumption in the book is that ICBC is the sole insurer involved unless otherwise mentioned.

As a B.C. resident, if you're in an auto accident in the province, elsewhere in Canada, or in the United States, your accident should be reported to the ICBC Dial-A-Claim centre — if possible, within 24 hours. An out-of-province accident should first be reported to the police in the area where it happened. If you live outside B.C., you weren't in a B.C.-licenced car, no other cars were involved, and no B.C. residents were injured, your accident only has to be reported to your auto insurer, not ICBC.

If your injuries prevent you from contacting the Dial-A-Claim centre, someone can do this for you but it should still be done promptly. While the police will notify ICBC if you were seriously injured, a close relative or friend should contact them on your behalf as well.

If you were a passenger, pedestrian or cyclist, the Dial-A-Claim staff will want to know whether you or anyone in your household has Autoplan insurance and, if so, what the policy number is. You may be entitled to both accident benefits and compensation.

CAUTION! Before phoning the Dial-A-Claim centre, give yourself time to calm down and review what you're going to say. Reporting your accident to Dial-A-Claim isn't the same as filing a claim for accident benefits or compensation. (See Chapter 8 for information on how to do this.)

Supporting an Insurance Claim

It's important to watch what you say at the accident scene — as well as later on when discussing your accident. Apologizing when you weren't at fault, or trying to rationalize what happened (both of which are common), could jeopardize your insurance claim or place you at risk if someone files a claim against you.

If it's possible to do this, you may want to write down the comments people make about what caused the accident. When a driver won't accept responsibility for what he did, the statements made by the passengers in his car can help prove liability (or fault). People are often willing to restate on record what they said immediately after an accident when they're reminded of this. (Without this reminder, they may later try to protect a relative or friend who was driving.) Since the people directly involved in an accident often have different opinions about what happened (and why), independent witnesses who know you weren't at fault can be crucial in supporting a claim you make for compensation (or damages).

The police will usually document relevant evidence that's brought to their attention. An expired inspection sticker on a car may indicate mechanical problems that contributed to your accident, while bald tires may have caused another car to skid. A driver may seem intoxicated, or he may not have been wearing glasses as his driver's licence indicates he should.

There are a few things you should jot down about your accident while you're at the accident scene, including the location of the accident, what time of day it was, and what the weather or road conditions were. From a fixed point in the area, where did the collision occur and where did the cars end up? If a pedestrian or cyclist was hit, where was she on impact and where did she land? You should also make a note of any damage done to the cars involved and earlier dents or scratches. (See the section on working with your adjuster in Chapter 9 for other information you may want later.)

It may also be helpful to make a quick sketch of what happened, showing where any cars (or pedestrians) were, what direction they were going in, the length and direction of any skid marks, and other details that occur to you. Street names should be included in this as well as the location of traffic lights, road signs, and anything that might have limited a driver's visibility.

CAUTION! If anyone you don't know asks you about your accident, have him identify himself before responding. (You won't want to talk to an insurer, lawyer or investigator about your accident without knowing that you're doing this.) Since even relatives and friends may misinterpret what you say, don't discuss your accident with anyone unless you have to.

Over the next day or two, you may want to write down your recollections of what happened. Your memories are bound to fade over time, and there may be things you need to know later for legal-insurance purposes. If you have to pursue legal action to get accident benefits, or your claim for damages (if any) goes to trial, it may be many years before your case is heard. A description in your own words of what happened, what injuries you had, and your emotional reactions, will help refresh your memory later.

If you were driving and had prior warning of the accident, what did you do to avoid it or minimize its consequences? How fast were you and the other cars going? Where were you going to (and coming from) and who was with you? (You can also ask the passengers in your car to write down their recollections and share this with you.)

What parts of your body did you injure? Did you have any cuts, bruises, abrasions or lacerations; or any tenderness, swelling, stiffness, numbness, or loss of sensation? Would you describe your pain as sharp, dull, shooting, throbbing or aching? How has this changed, if at all? Have you been examined by a doctor? What injuries did she say you have and how did she treat these?

You may also want to take some photos of the accident scene even if the cars are no longer there. The sooner these are taken the better: skid marks disappear quickly and could prove you weren't at fault. If your car was damaged, take photos of it before it's repaired. You should also take photos of your visible injuries, if any.

If you're served with legal papers in connection to your accident, you may want to show these to a personal injury lawyer. He can advise you on what to do and tell you whether the papers need to be given to your insurer.

It's a good idea to keep file copies of all material relating to your accident, injuries and insurance claim, including letters, medical records, insurance forms, and legal documents. You may also want to keep a written record of your conversations with insurers, lawyers and health-care providers.

You won't get reimbursed for accident-related out-of-pocket expenses without dated receipts that clearly show what they're for. You'll also have to be able to document any work time that you (and your spouse or partner) lose as a result of your accident to get your lost wages reimbursed. If your child was injured, keep a record of how much time you take off work as a result of this, including sick days or vacation time. You may be reimbursed for this later.

When to Consult a Lawyer Immediately

If you may have been at fault in an accident in which anyone was seriously injured or killed, you'll want to hire a lawyer right away to represent you in all legal actions and hearings (including a Coroner's Inquest, if relevant). If you're charged with a criminal offence in connection to your accident, you should also hire a lawyer as soon as possible.

If more than one person was injured in your accident or you have serious injuries, you may have to file an Underinsured Motorist Protection (UMP) claim. Hiring a lawyer early on in these situations is your best hope of being fairly compensated. After a hit-and-run accident, hiring a lawyer quickly is often essential as well. (Other situations where you'll need a lawyer are discussed in Chapter 12.)

CHAPTER 2

Initial Medical Treatment

NOTE: Neither the material in this chapter nor in later chapters is intended to be taken as medical advice. Your medical (and psychological) concerns should be discussed with your doctor.

Unless you only have minor injuries, you'll normally be taken by ambulance to the hospital. During the ride there, you'll be monitored by the ambulance crew, given necessary treatment, and an effort will be made to stabilize your condition. Once you reach the hospital, the triage nurse will decide the order in which you and the other patients are to be treated. The more urgently you need medical attention, the sooner you'll be seen by a doctor. An ambulance paramedic will usually remain with you while you wait.

After the admissions staff has gotten some basic information from you (assuming you're in a condition to give this), an emergency room nurse will ask you what's bothering you; whether you've had other problems in this area of your body; what other medical conditions you have; what medication you take regularly; and whether you're allergic to any drugs.

> **CAUTION! If anyone from ICBC approaches you in the waiting room, you're not required to speak to him — and probably shouldn't. While you're upset and confused, or in shock or denial, isn't the time to talk about your accident or injuries with an insurer.**

❖

Initial Assessment and Treatment

It's important to tell the emergency room doctor about every ache, pain, or unusual feeling you've had since the accident first happened. Something that seems insignificant may indicate a serious problem. Don't be afraid to question the doctor about your injuries, the nature of any recommended tests or treatment, and why you need these. While you can refuse to have a suggested procedure done, unless the doctor thoroughly investigates what's going on, she won't know the best way to treat you. Before any diagnostic tests are done, you'll usually be asked to sign a consent form agreeing to this.

Once a preliminary diagnosis has been made, you'll either be treated and released, admitted to the hospital, or transferred to another facility. If you're released, you'll want to find out whether you should restrict your activities in any way and, if so, for how long. Is it all right to drive, go to work or school, or participate in sports? Try to get a written description of how to take care of your injuries and what you need to be aware of. If you may have a concussion (or you've bumped or jarred your head), be sure to ask for a Head Sheet that lists common brain injury symptoms. (Trauma Sheets and Head Sheets should be available in most emergency rooms.)

If you're given medication to take home, find out what it's for, what potential side effects it has, and what you should do if you have a negative reaction. If you take other medication as well or drink even in moderation, ask what effect this might have on you while you're taking the hospital medicine. Don't assume that the doctor knows about other medications you take (or drugs you're allergic to) just because you told the nurse. This information can easily be overlooked.

As good as most emergency care is in the province, errors can (and do) occur. Your obvious injuries may be treated and less apparent ones ignored; your trauma levels may not be monitored properly, causing serious complications; and your emergency room records may not document all your symptoms and complaints or all medical findings, preventing you from getting the care you need and, when relevant, fair compensation for your injuries. (You may want to look over your emergency room records while you're with the doctor. If she's forgotten something, you can ask her to add it.)

Common Medical Problems After an Auto Accident

Over two-thirds of the injuries suffered in auto accidents are soft tissue injuries,[2] most of which are temporary in nature. An injury that you're expected to recover from within six months is considered minor even when you're left with some residual pain. A moderate injury is one that requires extensive on-going treatment and creates significant lifestyle changes for up to two years. An injury is only severe when it continues to cause problems for over two years and permanent lifestyle (or career) changes are necessary.

Shock reactions are common after auto accidents and can sometimes be fatal. You can go into shock even if you're not injured. Shock may be caused by pain, anxiety and fear as well as by excessive blood loss and other conditions. If you're in shock, you may seem dazed, confused or anxious and feel nauseous or thirsty. Your skin may be cold or clammy, your breathing irregular, and your pulse weak and rapid. In some cases, you may eventually lose consciousness. Regardless of why you're in shock, it's a sign that your cardiovascular system is too depressed to support normal bodily functions. Prompt medical attention is essential.

> **CAUTION! Never give anyone who is in shock anything to eat or drink. If he's lying down, his legs should be slightly elevated. Make sure his clothes are loose and he's warm but not overheated. Talk to him reassuringly until medical help arrives.**

Bruises, abrasions, lacerations and excessive bleeding: Skin wounds are the most visible injuries that occur in auto accidents. When the skin is bruised but not bleeding, the underlying tissue may be damaged but there's little risk of infection. Bruises are normally treated with cold compresses to relieve pain and swelling.

With an abrasion, the skin surface is scraped, leaving it raw and bleeding. While the bleeding is usually fairly limited, the area can get infected as the underlying tissue is exposed. Laceration wounds tear the skin and can be bloody and gory. If there's any dirt, the wound can easily get infected. While some laceration wounds leave scars, most heal without complication when properly treated. Since all open wounds are contaminated to some degree, both abrasions and lacerations should be thoroughly cleaned and covered with a sterile dressing, which may have to be changed frequently to prevent infection.

Due to the large number of blood vessels in the palm of a hand, a simple hand wound can cause excessive bleeding. Bleeding on the scalp can be profuse as well and may accompany a skull fracture. Mouth wounds tend to bleed a lot but are rarely serious. They're usually caused by a loose tooth, damage to the tongue or cheek, or a fracture to the face or jaw. (Broken glass from a shattered windshield can cause profuse facial bleeding. Shards of glass can also get embedded in the eye and other exposed areas. A doctor should remove these.)

If you've broken any bones or your body was badly crushed or mangled, you could have internal bleeding. Severe swelling near a fractured limb is one sign of this. If extreme pressure was placed on your torso in the impact of a collision, you may have life-threatening bleeding from internal organs. Coughing up red, frothy blood usually indicates damage to the lungs, while vomiting up blood may indicate stomach bleeding. Red or smoky-brown urine is a sign of bladder or kidney bleeding, while blood in your stools (or tarry black stools) usually indicates bleeding in the bowels. (Abdominal pain and shock after an auto accident may be a sign of a ruptured spleen.)

Severe blood loss is always cause for concern as it can result in a sudden drop in blood pressure, leading to shock or death. The symptoms to watch for include cold, clammy skin; rapid, weakening pulse; shallow breathing; yawning or gasping for air; faintness or dizziness; nausea or thirst; anxiety; restlessness; and eventually loss of consciousness. Emergency treatment should be directed towards stopping the blood loss, preventing infection, and investigating possible complications. If the ambulance crew feel you're losing too much blood, they'll try to prevent you from going into shock, then rush you to the nearest hospital for immediate medical attention.

Muscle, ligament and tendon injuries aren't always immediately apparent. Hours (or days) may go by before you realize you were injured. It's not unusual after an auto accident to feel fine when you go to bed at night, only to wake up the next morning barely able to move.

When you move the wrong way or tense up to protect your body from an accident, you can overstretch one or more muscles, causing them to tear, bruise or strain. While most muscle strain disappears in a few days, severe muscle bruising can take a long time to heal. Torn muscle fibres may take several weeks or more to heal. The more muscle fibres you've torn, the more pain you'll normally have.

A muscle spasm isn't an injury. It's your body's attempt to limit your movements in an area you've injured. Cold compresses can relax the spasm and reduce the swelling caused by muscle damage.

Ligaments are the connective tissues holding your bones together at the joint. When too much stress is placed on them, they can stretch or tear, making the joint unstable and painful to move. You may not feel much discomfort initially, then have increasing pain as the days pass. Ligament injuries often take a long time to heal and can sometimes cause chronic pain and permanent disability. Cold compresses can help reduce the pain and swelling, while massage therapy can help prevent adhesions and scar tissue from developing. (Damaged spinal ligaments may cause persistent lower back pain after an accident. All ligament injuries should be treated like fractures until x-rays rule out this possibility.)

Tendons are the tough tissues connecting your muscles to your bones. A tendon injury can be very painful and take months (or years) to heal even with proper treatment. The more tendon fibres damaged, the more pain there usually is and the longer the healing process. A tendon you injured in the past can easily be injured again as you'll have a structural weakness in this part of your body. Since tendons are very vulnerable to re-injury while they're healing, make sure your doctor tells you what activities or movements to avoid doing — and for how long.

A compressed spinal disc or pinched nerve can look like a tendon or ligament injury and cause severe pain. It may take several office visits to a doctor, chiropractor or physiotherapist to determine what's happening so you can get appropriate treatment.

Whiplash injuries can occur in low-velocity collisions and rear-enders as well as in more serious accidents. How badly you're injured will depend in part on whether you tensed up for your accident or were relaxed; what kind of car you were in; where (and how) you were sitting; the position of your head and neck; whether your seatbelt and headrest were properly adjusted; and the angle and speed of the impact. The length of your neck and the weight of your head — as well as your age and whether you've had a similar injury in the past or have structural problems in your neck — can also affect whether you get a whiplash injury and, if so, how severe it is.

When your head and neck are violently jerked, the muscles and ligaments that support your head and spine can overstretch or tear; the nerve roots in your neck can stretch and become irritated; your spinal discs can bulge, tear or rupture; and your vertebrae can move out of normal position. These conditions are what's known as whiplash. If your muscles or ligaments were torn, your injury will be more severe than if they were just stretched.

After a whiplash injury, your neck and shoulders may be stiff, and you may have painful muscle spasms, lower back pain, face or jaw pain, and headaches. This may be accompanied by numbness, tingling or pain in your limbs, difficulty swallowing, dizziness, nausea, blurred vision, or ringing in your ears. If you experience these symptoms after an auto accident, you should be examined by a doctor as soon as possible. Unless you get early treatment for a whiplash injury, prolonged inflammation can produce scar tissue, leading to chronic pain, on-going symptoms, and in some case, permanent disability. You may be told to avoid certain activities, prescribed muscle relaxants, and given exercises to do. You may also be referred to a physiotherapist or chiropractor.

While some whiplash injuries are apparent right way, it can also take several months for symptoms to be diagnosed as whiplash.

Insurers tend to be suspicious of soft tissue injuries. Unless objective evidence of your injury is documented in your medical records — including decreased range of motion, muscle spasms, or swelling — you may have to take legal action to get accident benefits or compensation. While physiotherapists and massage therapists are usually better than family doctors at recognizing soft tissue injuries, for legal-insurance purposes you should initially be assessed by a medical doctor or chiropractor. Both insurers and the courts place greater weight on doctors' opinions.

Burns: How serious a burn is will depend on where it is, how deep it goes, and how large an area it covers. Muscles, bones, nerves and blood vessels can be burnt as well as skin. With a first-degree burn your skin may be red, painful and slightly swollen but you're unlikely to be left with permanent scarring. A second-degree burn damages deeper layers of the skin, causing it to blister and become red and shiny. With a third-degree burn your skin may be destroyed down to the fatty tissue, leaving the area charred and white or greyish in colour. While bones and muscles may be damaged, you won't have much pain initially if your nerve endings were destroyed.

Not only can a third-degree burn be fatal, so can a second-degree burn that covers a large area of your body. While you're waiting for an ambulance to arrive, your burns should be lightly covered with a clean, lint-free cloth to prevent further injury or contamination.

Extensive reconstructive surgery may be needed after a serious burn. While plastic surgeons are highly skilled in repairing and replacing burnt skin, burn survivors often have a hard time emotionally due to extreme pain and trauma, multiple surgeries, long hospital stays, prolonged rehab, and in some cases, the need to adjust to an altered appearance. Early psychological counselling is essential.

Fractures: With a closed fracture, the skin surrounding the broken bone remains intact. With an open fracture, the underlying skin tissue is exposed and the end of the bone may protrude. A comminuted fracture means a bone is broken in more than one place, while a hairline fracture is a narrow crack in the bone surface.

A bone may be so badly bruised that it feels broken. X-rays may be needed to determine what's happened. If you think you may have a fracture, you should be examined by a doctor and have x-rays taken. When fractures aren't promptly treated they can heal incorrectly, causing future problems.

Unexplained swelling or discolouration, pain or tenderness that's aggravated by movement, and feeling a grating sensation when you move are all signs of a fracture. In some cases, you may have felt your bone break. A limb or joint that looks deformed or unnatural may be fractured or dislocated. (A steering wheel can fracture a driver's ribs, while a seatbelt can cause rib, sternum or collarbone fractures as well as other injuries.)

Any bone you may have broken should be supported and stabilized before you're moved. The sharp edges on a broken bone can damage surrounding blood vessels, nerves, muscles, and skin. When a broken bone punctures an artery, there can be severe internal bleeding.

A cast or brace may be needed to hold a broken bone in place as it heals. A severely-comminuted or splintered bone may require a bone graft or internal fixation. (Surgically-implanted hardware can usually be removed after a year or two.) Your chest may have to be bandaged to prevent a fractured rib from damaging internal organs.

Depending on your age, what bone(s) you've broken, and the type of fracture(s) you have, it can take a few months to a year to recover. A fractured bone or joint will never be as strong as it once was, especially when muscles, tendons or ligaments were torn as well. When a fracture extends into your hip (or knee) joint, you may eventually require hip (or knee) replacement.

❖

CAUTION! **A fracture can be overlooked or a cast put on the wrong limb. You may not realize at first that an error was made. If you have pain, swelling or discolouration near a bone or joint, you may have a fracture the doctors missed.**

Multiple injuries frequently occur in auto accidents. In these situations, there's always a danger that less obvious injuries won't be noticed. You can lessen the possibility of an oversight occurring by making sure you're thoroughly examined by a doctor and all necessary diagnostic tests are done. The doctor who examines you should be told about any discomfort you're having, including slight twinges of pain or odd sensations, as these may be signs of a serious underlying problem. If you're bewildered and confused, or you feel distant and removed from what's happening, you need to let the examining doctor know this as well. You may have an undiagnosed brain injury or other trauma-related condition.

Spinal Cord Injuries

Auto accidents cause over 40% of all spinal cord injuries.[3] When you have a spinal cord injury (SCI), the nerves above the level of your injury continue to work the way they always have, while the nerves below this level lose their ability to send (and receive) messages to (and from) your brain. Your spinal cord doesn't have to be severed for this loss to occur, nor do your back or neck have to be broken. You can break your back or neck, in fact, and not have a spinal cord injury if only your vertebrae were damaged. Direct damage to your spinal cord can cause complete (or partial) paralysis and loss of sensation. Breathing and bowel or bladder control may be affected and some sexual dysfunction occur.

If you've fractured (or dislocated) your spine, special precautions will have to be taken at the accident scene to prevent further injury and life-threatening complications. Incorrect movement or handling could damage your spinal cord, causing permanent paralysis. Since you may have fractured your neck if you have a head injury, your neck should be supported and stabilized before you're moved.

The first thing most people notice after a spinal cord injury is a loss of sensation in the extremities, particularly the lower limbs. If you can't feel your legs after an auto accident, the ambulance paramedics need to be told this. To prevent neurogenic shock from occurring, they'll strap you to a spinal board and raise your legs to encourage blood to flow to your heart. (Neurogenic shock is caused by damage to the nerves that control the size of the blood vessels. It only occurs with spinal cord injuries.) Once your body has been stabilized and artificial respiration given if needed, you'll be taken by ambulance to the hospital.

While all spinal cord injuries result in some sensory or motor impairment, the level of your injury — and whether it's a complete or incomplete injury — will affect how permanently disabled you are. All other things being equal, the higher the injury is on your spine, the more disability you'll have. An injury in the cervical spine (or neck) can cause quadriplegia, with loss of movement and sensation in both the upper and lower body. An injury in the thoracic (or lung) region can cause paraplegia. You'll have little movement or sensation in your lower body, but your upper body and arms won't be affected. Damage to your spinal cord in the lumbar region or sacrum usually causes some functional loss in the hips and legs, without total paralysis. Since an injury can occur at any point along the spine, you may have more (or less) movement or sensation than noted.

If you have a complete spinal cord injury, both sides of your body will be equally affected and you'll have no sensation, function or voluntary movement below the level of your injury. Incomplete SCIs vary a great deal: only one side of your body may be affected; you may have some sensation or functioning below the level of your injury; both sides of your body may be affected with one side weaker and less functional than the other; you may have no functional abilities on either side of your body but some sensation on one side; and you may eventually get back some movement or feelings. Recent improvements in acute trauma care have resulted in more than half of all new SCIs being incomplete injuries.[4]

In the first few hours after a spinal cord injury, certain conditions can arise that cause greater damage than the original trauma. Swelling, excessive blood loss, low blood pressure, ischemia (inadequate blood flow), tissue hypoxia (insufficient oxygen to the tissue), high fever and low blood sugar can cause secondary damage to the nerve cells and spinal cord, while misalignment of the spine can place continued pressure on the spinal cord. Surgery and drugs[5] may be needed to prevent permanent paralysis.

Once you're diagnosed with a spinal cord injury, a neurologist will come to the emergency room to evaluate you and see whether immediate treatment is needed to relieve the pressure on your spinal cord. (If emergency respiratory assistance is needed, an anaesthesiologist will be called in as well.) An MRI may be done to determine how much damage was done to your spinal nerves. The neurologist will make sure your spinal column is properly aligned and stabilized. Traction, weights and a special bed frame may be used to stop you from moving.

After the neurologist knows the location of your spinal cord injury and how severe it is, he should have some idea of how much mobility and sensation you'll have as time goes on. If your spinal cord is only bruised or swollen, the nerves may begin to work once the swelling goes down. It's generally believed that the sooner you regain some functioning or sensation, the greater your overall improvement will be. This being said, persistent efforts on your part may lead to far better recovery than your doctors initially predict.

You'll probably be in the hospital for two or three weeks after a spinal cord injury. While you may struggle with feelings of self-pity and depression at first, wondering whether life is worth living, if you're like most people with SCI, you'll soon become absorbed in learning the new skills you'll need to get on with your life. Once acute hospital care is no longer necessary, you'll generally be transferred to a residential rehab centre. (The psychological issues you may face are discussed in Chapter 5 and living with SCI is in Chapter 7.)

Eighty-five percent of the people who survive a spinal cord injury for 24 hours are still alive ten years later (and much longer).[6] However, your life expectancy may be reduced. You may also have neurological problems that continue to require specialized care and treatment.

Traumatic Brain Injuries

If you've fractured your skull, there's usually physical evidence of this: an obvious skull depression; a swollen, bruised or lacerated scalp; blood (or straw-coloured fluid) coming from your nose or ears; or discolouration of the skin below your eyes or behind your ears. If you're unconscious, emergency treatment will be directed towards making sure you don't choke on your vomitus.

Traumatic brain injuries range from a mild concussion to severe brain trauma. A concussion isn't always obvious. Loss of consciousness may be brief or not occur at all. While shallow breathing, nausea or vomiting, cold clammy skin, and a rapid weak pulse may be signs of a concussion, these symptoms can be caused by other conditions as well. If you're unconscious, twitching, or having convulsions — or the pupils of your eyes are unequal in size, abnormally large, or unresponsive to light — you may have severe brain trauma, and too much pressure may be building up in your brain. (How excessive intra-cranial pressure is treated is discussed below.)

Both the ambulance paramedics and the emergency room staff will normally use the Glasgow Coma Scale to check your level of consciousness. (The GCS assesses brain impairment according to the ability to move on command, open your eyes, and respond to simple questions.) The more impaired your brain functioning, the lower the GCS score. While insurers generally only consider a brain injury catastrophic with a GCS score of 9 or less, you can have the highest score possible (15) and still have a brain injury.

While traumatic brain injury (TBI) is the number one disabler and killer of Canadians under 40, and 50% of all brain injuries are caused by auto accidents,[7] TBI continues to be under-diagnosed and ignored in emergency rooms and hospitals. Even in a relatively minor accident, the "acceleration-deceleration effect" can cause a concussion that leads to permanent impairment. (When the impact of a collision forces your head to abruptly accelerate or decelerate, your brain may bounce around inside your skull, bruising and swelling. While the brain damage that occurs in these situations is usually temporary, if surrounding brain cells degenerate, you could have on-going deficits.)

The fact that you can damage your brain without losing consciousness may be the reason why so many brain injuries are overlooked. Even if you briefly lost consciousness, neither you nor anyone else may be aware of this. When loss of consciousness is obvious, it may be blamed on more apparent injuries, or on shock, surgery or medication. You may be able to answer questions, carry on conversations, and appear alert and aware, and still have a brain injury with lifelong consequences. (How long post-traumatic amnesia lasts is a sign of how severe a brain injury is. See the section on getting good care in the hospital in Chapter 3.) Even severe brain injuries don't always show up on early CAT scans and MRIs.

You may not be admitted to the hospital with a concussion unless you have other injuries as well. Even if you're not aware of having a concussion, if your head may have been bumped, jarred or shaken in your accident, you should be carefully monitored for at least 24 hours to make sure no pressure is building up in your brain. If your breathing becomes irregular or noisy, your pulse slow, and your face flushed — or you start vomiting or have headaches, dizziness, convulsions or a high fever — you need to be rushed to the nearest hospital.

While more people now survive traumatic brain injuries than they used to, survivors often require care and treatment throughout their lives. If you're unconscious for several days, you may be left with on-going deficits. Even a mild brain injury can cause lifelong problems. If you (or others) feel that you're exhibiting the TBI symptoms in Chapter 7, you need to be assessed by a neuropsychologist as soon as possible. Early treatment offers the best hope for a full recovery.

If you're unconscious and can't be aroused, a neurosurgeon will be called to the emergency room to co-ordinate your treatment and determine whether surgery is needed to prevent further damage to your brain. The doctor's focus will be on minimizing the pressure in your brain and making sure your brain gets enough oxygen. He'll also try to lessen the possibility of a brain infection occurring.

A newly-damaged brain often increases in size, leading to a spiraling of complications. Since your skull can't expand to accommodate the swelling, excessive intra-cranial pressure (ICP) may be created. This decreases the flow of blood and oxygen to your brain, causing further swelling. Intra-cranial pressure increases even more and the cycle continues. Unless this cycle can be controlled through surgery or drugs, severe brain damage (or death) may occur.

Your ICP levels can be monitored through a device implanted in your skull. If your intra-cranial pressure becomes dangerously high despite the drugs you're given, a shunt may be used to drain excess fluid. Surgery may be done to remove blood clots pressing on your brain and repair damaged blood vessels in the brain so they don't continue to bleed. By relieving the pressure on your brain, oxygen and blood can flow more freely, hopefully breaking the swelling-compression cycle. Severely damaged brain cells may have to be surgically removed to give healthy cells in the area a better chance to survive.

You'll usually be placed in the neurology intensive care unit where your progress can be monitored with special attention paid to your ICP levels. Your body may have to be tied down so you don't hurt yourself through involuntary movements. You may also be placed on a life-support system.

While your doctors may not know how long you'll be unconscious, they should be able to give your family some general information about your situation, how they intend to treat you, what the risks are in doing this, and what other treatment options exist, if any. Once your survival is no longer in doubt, they may be able to predict how fully you'll recover and what long-term problems you may have.

Special Concerns When a Child Is Injured

Nearly 5,000 children in B.C. are injured in auto accidents each year.[8] Since a young child may not realize he was injured or be able to describe what hurts him, he should be checked out thoroughly in the emergency room to make sure he's all right and to treat any problems he has. You'll normally be allowed to stay with your child while he's being assessed. The more comforting and reassuring you are, the less traumatic the experience is apt to be for him. (If you were injured as well, you'll usually be treated in the same hospital.)

If your child is nauseous, dizzy, or acts strangely after an accident, he may have a concussion. Even when this seems unlikely, you should take home a copy of the hospital Head Sheet. While the information on this probably won't be child-specific, it will tell you what symptoms to watch for over the next 24 hours. (See the section above on traumatic brain injuries.) You may want to monitor your child's moods and behaviour for several weeks.

At your child's follow-up visit to your family doctor, she'll want to know the details of his accident; what the emergency room doctor said; what treatment he was given; and what changes you've noticed in him, if any. It's important not to downplay your concerns: the doctor needs a clear picture of what's going on. If you don't feel your child has been acting normally since his accident, you may want to ask for a referral to a neuropsychologist who specializes in assessing and treating children with brain injuries.

When an infant or young child has a brain injury, the healthy parts of his brain often take over the role of the damaged parts. When this doesn't happen, the child may have on-going functional and behavioural problems.

Keeping a Diary of Your Recovery Process

If you intend to file an insurance claim, it may be useful to keep a written record of your recovery process. You may initially want to make daily entries in a notebook or diary about what's bothering you and how you're dealing with it. To make sure you include every problem you're having, start from the top of your head and work your way down your body to your feet, noting what hurts you, when the pain is most severe, and what lessens your discomfort. If you've been getting headaches since your accident, document where they are, how strong they are, how long they last, when they usually occur, and what seems to cause, aggravate or relieve them.

You may also want to describe in your recovery diary how your daily routine differs now from what it was like before your accident. Does it take you longer to perform tasks than it used to, and are there activities you can no longer do? How much time do you spend on medical and rehab treatment or rehab exercises? Are you having emotional (or psychological) problems or trouble sleeping? Is pain or stress making it hard for you to enjoy life or be with others? (If your insurance claim ends up in court, the anecdotes and descriptions in your diary will remind you of your post-accident experiences and how these affected you.)

Reviewing your recovery diary before office visits to your doctors and other health-care providers will refresh your memory about what's happened since your last visit. Any new problems you're having can then be added to your medical records. You may also want to keep a record of what you discuss with your doctors and rehab therapists during office visits, what treatment they give you, and what exercises or suggestions they make. If you're taking prescription drugs, make a note in your recovery diary of what they're for and any negative side effects you have.

CHAPTER 3

If You're Admitted to the Hospital

After you're taken to your hospital room, a nursing assessment will usually be done. The nurse will ask you about your injuries and medical history, whether you've ever been hospitalized before, and whether you've had previous problems in the areas of your body that you've now injured. You may also be asked if you smoke or drink, how often you exercise, and what kind of work you do. Any dietary restrictions you have should be mentioned at this time.

If you're anxious or confused and you give the nurse the wrong information, she may not realize this if your responses make sense to her. Since your initial nursing assessment will be referred to throughout your hospital stay, and later assessments and reports may be based on this, you (or a relative or friend) should review what the nurse has recorded and make sure any errors are corrected. Unless your hospital records are accurate, you may not get the care you need, and ICBC (or another insurer) may blame your accident-related problems on pre-existing medical conditions.

How long you'll be in the hospital will depend on the nature and extent of your injuries. It may be a while before the doctors can predict how fully you'll recover and how much time this might take. As you become more impatient with the hospital routine, take this as a positive sign: it probably means you're recovering.

Getting Good Care in the Hospital

Hospital closures in B.C. have made patient advocacy more essential now than ever. You (or a relative or friend) may need to be persistent in making sure you get good care. Your doctors should be questioned about your treatment and you should insist on getting clear answers. If you don't understand what you're told, another staff doctor may be able to clarify the situation for you. Your family doctor can also be phoned for information or advice.

Before a diagnostic test is done, ask your treating doctor what she thinks it will show (or rule out) and how necessary it is. What will be done to you; how painful is it; and what are the risks involved? Could an alternate procedure be done instead? (To minimize your exposure to radiation, ask your doctor to mark on your hospital records: "Limit all x-rays!")

If surgery is recommended, you may want to ask what the consequences would be if you decided against this. If you agree to have the operation done, how long will it take and how much pain can you expect to have afterwards? If you may have a brain injury, how will you be monitored during surgery so you don't get secondary brain damage? Will the surgical and recovery room staffs be informed both verbally and in writing that you have (or may have) a brain injury? How much of the operation will be done by a surgical resident (a doctor still in training)? How often has he performed this procedure in the past? When will you and your family learn what the outcome is?

You'll also want to find out what any medication you're given is for, what side effects it can have, and how long you'll have to take it. If you took other medication prior to your hospital admission, will a floor nurse give this to you now or should you take it on your own? (This needs to be clarified up front so you don't take double doses of a drug or neglect to take what you should.)

A serious injury may be overlooked during your hospital stay. A fracture may not be noticed on a neurological ward, nor a brain injury detected on an orthopaedic ward. If you have multiple injuries, treatment for one may aggravate another. Unless your hospital records note every injury or medical condition you have, even those not being actively treated, someone who is taking care of you may accidentally do something that harms you. (A nurse who doesn't realize you've fractured your pelvis, for example, may upset the alignment needed for proper healing when you're bedridden with other injuries.)

If anything a hospital staff person does causes you extreme pain, you need to let both her and your supervising doctor know this. If you're concerned that a diagnostic test, medical procedure, rehab exercise or other activity might do you more harm than good, discuss this with your treating doctors. Your reluctance to start walking or practice a particular exercise, for example, may stem from an underlying condition the nurse or rehab therapist is unaware of.

The possibility of an undiagnosed brain injury should be kept in mind after any auto accident, especially one serious enough to hospitalize you. To prevent secondary brain damage from occurring, blood loss, fever, hypoxia, low blood pressure and abnormal carbon dioxide levels need to be aggressively treated after even a mild brain injury. If your breathing is shallow or you're short of breath, your blood oxygen levels should be monitored. If you're anemic, a blood transfusion may be warranted. (The risks associated with transfusions should be discussed with your treating doctors.)

If you don't remember your accident, or you only have scattered memories of what's happened to you since then, you need to let your doctors know this. Until your memories become continuous, you're in a state of post-traumatic amnesia (PTA) even when your level of consciousness seems normal to others. How long PTA lasts is a more accurate indication of how severe a brain injury is than how long you're unconscious, if at all. When PTA continues for more than 24 hours, you may be left with permanent brain injury deficits even if you never lost consciousness. (With a mild brain injury, post-traumatic amnesia usually lasts less than an hour. Longer-term PTA generally indicates a more severe brain injury.)

Despite the importance of documenting the presence and duration of post-traumatic amnesia, this rarely happens outside neurology wards. Unless the hospital staff questions you about what you do (and don't) remember, they may not realize there are gaps in your memory that can't be accounted for. You may not realize this yourself, assuming that you were unconscious, asleep or heavily medicated during times and events you don't recall. To determine whether you've had post-traumatic amnesia — and, if so, for how long — you may want to review what's happened to you since your accident with a nurse, relative or friend. How much do you remember of the accident itself; the ambulance ride to the hospital; being evaluated in the emergency room; being brought to your room; or being taken to and from surgery? Who has visited you and how often have they come? Do you recall your conversations with visitors, doctors, nurses, and other patients? If there are significant gaps in your memory, or you're still having headaches, dizziness or blurred vision several days after your accident (or after undergoing surgery), you may need to be assessed by a neurologist who specializes in trauma or by a physiatrist who specializes in brain injury rehab.

If You're Put into the Intensive Care Unit (ICU)

After a serious injury, you may be put into the intensive care unit until your condition stabilizes. While you're in the ICU, you'll be constantly monitored. Besides being hooked up to an I.V., you may be put on a respirator to help you breathe. You may also be connected to equipment that monitors your pulse, blood pressure, heartbeat, temperature, brain functioning, and where applicable, intra-cranial pressure. Tubes may be inserted into your nose, mouth, chest or other body areas.

How long you'll be in the ICU will depend on many factors, including how long you need to be on a life-support system, if at all. If you're in a coma, it may be a while before you regain consciousness. In the meantime, your family may be advised to go home and resume their normal activities as much as possible so they'll be able to offer you the support you need when you emerge from your coma. Until it's clear that you're out of danger and no complications are likely to arise, though, a relative or friend should try to be with you at all times. Not even the most dedicated ICU nurse will watch for signs of danger — or improvement — as closely as someone intimately connected to you.

If you're in the ICU for more than 24 hours, someone should act as your patient-advocate. This can be a relative, friend, or professional case manager. When no one has the legal authority to make medical decisions for you, the Public Guardian and Trustee will make sure you're properly cared for.

How Family and Friends Can Help

Few things are more devastating than learning that someone you love was in an auto accident and is in the hospital. If you're like most people, you'll think the worst and pray for the best as you rush to the hospital where your spouse, partner, child, parent or friend may be seriously hurt with the outcome uncertain. It may be up to you to make difficult decisions about his care and treatment.

Once you've identified yourself to the hospital staff as a close relative or friend of the injured person, you should be told what injuries he has; what treatment he needs; what the risks are in doing this; what alternative approaches there are; and what the probable outcome is, if known. A single family member or friend should handle all communications with the staff so they're not constantly interrupted with the same questions. If you're the family spokesperson, you should be introduced to the doctors who are involved in the injured person's care. If he was in a major-impact accident, you may want to ask them how they intend to monitor him in case he has a brain injury, even if he wasn't diagnosed with this. (The repercussions of secondary brain damage are too serious to risk having this issue ignored.)

No matter how upsetting the situation is for you, you should try not to let the condition of your relative or friend devastate you. While even minor injuries can look gruesome initially, most people who are injured in auto accidents fully recover. Despite the budgetary cutbacks in the province, B.C. hospitals still provide excellent acute care.

Visiting someone regularly in the hospital may be the most helpful thing you can do for him. Even if he has serious injuries, you should try to remain positive when you're with him. This doesn't mean diminishing what's happened to him, though. Telling him that he'll soon be fine may feel like you're belittling his experiences and denying his reality. Even if his injuries are relatively minor, he may be emotionally traumatized.

Never try to pressure an injured person into talking about what happened or what he's feeling. If he brings up his accident himself, it's important for him to feel that you're accepting what he says, not judging him. If he seems irrational or excessively distressed, you can try to arrange for a hospital psychologist or trauma counsellor to see him. It's not your role to set him straight about what happened or to offer him false hopes. It's to reassure him that you're there for him and will help him get the best care possible.

If the emotional responses or behaviour of the injured person seem abnormal to you, talk to his doctors about this, not him. They may understand why he's behaving this way and can give you an idea of how long this is apt to continue. When altered behaviour or extreme anxiety persists for far longer than expected, this could be a sign of an undiagnosed problem. You may have to convince the doctors to explore what's happening as they may not realize how unusual the injured person's behaviour is for him personally. (A relaxed easy-going person, for example, may now be tense, angry and demanding.)

You may also want to review the hospital records that are normally kept at the foot of a patient's bed. If the medical history your relative or friend provided seems inaccurate, or all his injuries and altered behaviour aren't documented, you can ask a floor nurse to correct this.

CAUTION! **Don't try to convince an injured person to snap out of it or try harder to recover. He'll have to do this at his own pace — with the help of his treating doctors and therapists.**

How badly injured your relative or friend is will affect what you can do to help him when he's in the hospital. While he'll probably appreciate having outside food brought in, check with his nurse first to make sure he's not on a restricted diet. (He won't be allowed to eat for several hours before or after surgery, and he may need to be on a liquid or bland diet.) If you're able to take over some of his household responsibilities, this is bound to be appreciated as well.

A family member or friend who is spending all her time at the hospital will probably be grateful for outside food, quarters for the phone and home help as well. She's also likely to appreciate clean clothes, visits from others, and an offer to stay with the injured person so she can take a break. If you're at the hospital most of the time yourself, you shouldn't hesitate to ask other relatives or friends of the injured person for help. Most people are glad to help out in these situations when they can.

You may need to let the injured person's employer know what's happened and contact ICBC or other insurers on his behalf. (You may also want to speak to a personal injury lawyer.) If your relative or friend will be in the hospital for a while, and a lot of people want to be kept updated on how he's doing, you can set up a communications network that will allow you to phone the same few people each day, who can then pass on your information to others.

Keeping a journal of what's happening to the injured person may be helpful to him later if questions arise about the cause, nature or extent of his injuries. The journal can include your own observations, as well as what the doctors, nurses and rehab therapists tell you.

When a relative or friend is catastrophically injured, it's important to remain optimistic and reassuring when you're with him. Even a person in a coma can sense what's going on around him and it can influence his recovery. Expressing your confidence in his ability to recover may give him something encouraging to hold on to. As understandable as your confusion and despair are, you need to put these aside when you're with him. Hold his hand. Stroke his forehead. Tell him about what's going on in your life and in the lives of other people he's close to. Let him know who has asked about him or visited him, and read him the get-well cards he's gotten. If you're able to take over part of his personal care, this may be as helpful to you as it is to him. There are few things worse than feeling helpless in the face of a loved one's suffering.

While your relative or friend is in the acute stages of a catastrophic injury and most medical decisions are being made by his doctors, it may be a good time to learn as much as you can about his injuries and what lies ahead. You may want to speak to various medical and rehab specialists, as well as to the hospital social worker, who should be able to help you locate an appropriate support group.

Despite your concerns about the injured person, you'll have your own emotional and psychological issues to deal with. New responsibilities may fall on your shoulders just when you feel least capable of handling them. It may feel like your whole world is falling apart as your life changes in ways you'd never have imagined. A hospital psychologist or trauma counsellor can help you understand how your loved one's injuries may affect you both in the future.

It's important to take good care of yourself in this difficult, trying time. If you burn out from being constantly at the injured person's bedside, or you fall apart emotionally or physically, you won't be much help to anyone. You'll need strength and courage in the weeks (and months) ahead, so make sure you eat properly, get plenty of rest, and take time to deal with your own reactions to what's happened. Other family members may need comfort and support as well. Accepting the help that other people offer you will make it easier to deal with the situation and cope with the on-going stresses in your life.

Power of Attorney, Committeeship and Related Topics

If your injured relative or friend expects to be in the hospital for a while, he may want you to have power of attorney for him. A general power of attorney will allow you to handle his legal and financial affairs, while a specific power of attorney will only let you take specific action on his behalf (such as selling his car). In order to give you power of attorney, your relative or friend must be 19 or older and of sound mind.

A pre-existing power of attorney for someone who is *incompis mentis* (not of sound mind) is only valid when it contains an "enduring" clause. When no enduring power of attorney exists, you can apply to the court to be appointed Committee of the injured person's estate. This will allow you to make financial and legal decisions for him; collect his wages and disability benefits; pay his bills; and initiate (or defend) a legal suit on his behalf. You may also have to prepare his tax returns and run his business.

A lawyer can help you file your application to the court. You'll need written opinions from two doctors stating that your relative or friend is incapable of looking after his own affairs. (When no one can take on the responsibility of being Committee of an injured person's estate, or there's a dispute about who should do this, the Public Guardian and Trustee or a trust company can serve in this capacity.)

As Committee of someone's estate, you'll have six months to provide the Public Guardian and Trustee with an inventory of his income, expenses, assets and debts. A detailed statement of accounts will be expected every two years for as long as your Committeeship continues. While you're not allowed to pay yourself for the work you do as Committee, the Public Guardian and Trustee will review the services you provide and set an appropriate fee for this, which will come out of the injured person's estate.

Before anyone is made Committee of an injured person's estate, the family should jointly decide who the best person is to do this. They should also decide how much feedback they'll want on any legal or financial actions taken. These decisions can be reviewed every few months and altered as needed. Whenever possible, all large expenditures should be authorized by more than one person. Having a disinterested third party (such as the injured person's accountant) periodically review all financial records and decisions should reduce the possibility of funds being misused.

An enduring power of attorney won't give you the right to make medical or personal decisions for your injured relative or friend. You can only do this by becoming his legal guardian or personal Committee. This is different from being Committee of his estate and again requires a court order. As the injured person's legal guardian or personal Committee, you'll be authorized to make decisions about his physical well-being, including what medical treatment he receives and where he lives when he's discharged from the hospital.

When no one has an enduring power of attorney for an *incompis mentis* relative or friend, you can volunteer to become a Trustee of Government Pension Income for him. This will allow you to collect and manage the money paid to him through various federal programs such as the Canada Pension Plan, Old Age Security and Veterans

Affairs, Canada. You'll need a certificate from a doctor verifying that the injured person is incapable of managing his financial affairs.

> **TBI ALERT! Unless a declaration of incompetency is filed with the court, a person is assumed to be able to manage his own affairs even after a serious brain injury. You're not giving up hope that an injured relative or friend will recover by applying for guardianship (or Committeeship) of him. It's better to have someone who is close to him assume this role than for the Public Guardian and Trustee to do it. Once he becomes mentally competent again, your guardianship (or Committeeship) can be dissolved by court order.**

Medical-Legal-Insurance Considerations

Most personal injury lawyers recommend that people don't talk to insurers while they're in the hospital. If you were catastrophically injured, though, an ICBC rehab co-ordinator may be assigned to you early on. You need to remember when you're with her that what you (or others) say in her presence could be passed on to your claims adjuster. When relevant, this may be used to reduce the compensation you're entitled to.

If you'll be hospitalized for a while and weren't at fault in your accident, you may want to hire a lawyer before you're discharged. When warranted, he can then arrange for a professional case manager to oversee your care. Or, he may be able to personally ensure that a good medical-rehab team is assembled to treat you. Your lawyer (or case manager) can also make sure you're sent to a good rehab centre when you leave the hospital. He should assess your financial situation as well and arrange for you to get the benefits you're entitled to from public or private sources.

If You're Transferred to a Rehab Centre or Extended-Care Facility

Once you no longer need acute hospital care after a serious injury, you may be sent to a rehab centre or extended-care facility. Doctors usually only send patients directly to extended (or long-term) care when they don't feel they'll benefit from a comprehensive rehab program. People (18 or older) with spinal cord injuries and brain injuries often go to the G.F. Strong Rehabilitation Centre in Vancouver for in-patient rehab. (Other rehab facilities in the province also offer in-patient rehab to people with SCI and TBI. Children with these injuries may be sent to Children's Hospital or Sunny Hill. There are other provincial rehab facilities for amputees and people with serious orthopaedic injuries). Burn survivors may be admitted to G.F. Strong as well.

While you're waiting to get into an extended-care facility (or group home), or for renovations to be made to your home to accommodate your injuries, you may be able to stay at G.F. Strong even though you're not undergoing rehab there. (If you have high level quadriplegia and will need more hands-on care than you can get at home, you may be sent to an extended-care facility when you leave residential rehab.)

If the B.C. Ministry of Health Services agrees that you need extended (or long-term) care, the Medical Services Plan of British Columbia (MSP) will pay their basic allowable rate for this. ICBC or another insurer will be expected to pick up the additional costs. To be eligible for provincially-funded extended (or long-term) care, you must be 19 or older, a Canadian citizen or legal resident, and have lived in B.C. for at least three months for extended care (and twelve months for chronic long-term care). A Ministry of Health caseworker will assess your level of functioning to determine your needs.

While the provincial government plans to open more extended-care facilities, there presently aren't enough beds available for everyone who needs them. (As a result of this shortage, people in long-term comas often remain in the ICU, while people with severe brain injuries sometimes end up in psychiatric wards.) Moreover, few public facilities offer much more than a bed to sleep in. While a patient in a private extended-care facility may receive several hours of rehab a day, no public funding is available for this. Neither MSP nor ICBC will cover your rehab costs in an extended-care facility; they only pay for basic care.

The hospital social services department or your case manager, if any, will normally try to find funding to cover your stay in a rehab centre or extended-care facility. (A personal injury lawyer may also be able to help with this. Some advocacy support groups have access to funding sources as well.) Since private extended care can cost $1,000 or more a day, ICBC won't cover this cost as an accident benefit without a court order, even when no publicly-funded facilities are available or appropriate. If you weren't at fault in your accident, you may be given an advance against your claim for damages so you can stay in the facility your doctors recommend. (ICBC maintains that they can't pay for private extended care as an accident benefit as this would quickly deplete a claimant's accident benefits fund, shifting a burden that they're legally obligated to bear to other government agencies.[9] In fact, the burden of caring for injured people after an auto accident is continually being shifted to various government agencies.)

Arrangements to Make Before Leaving the Hospital

Before you're discharged from the hospital, you may be given an opportunity to meet with a staff social worker to discuss the ongoing treatment you'll need and where you can get this. The social worker should be able to refer you to a rehab agency near your home. Unless ICBC (or another insurer) will pay for your follow-up care up front, or you can afford to cover this cost yourself, you may want to ask the social worker to fax a referral for you to the B.C. Ministry of Health Services' "Home and Community Care" branch. A Ministry caseworker can then come to your home to assess you and arrange for necessary care and treatment. (You may be able to set up an assessment on your own as well.)

If you'll need someone to take care of you at home, the hospital social worker should make sure you have this help. When there's another adult living in your home, she may assume that he'll be available to handle your needs. If you expect to be alone most of the day, the social worker should be told this so she can arrange for home help, as needed.

If you don't have anywhere suitable to go when you leave the hospital, you can ask the social worker about residential possibilities in your community. She may be able to arrange for you to stay in a group home if you're not ready to live on your own. Or, you may be able to move into an ICBC-funded transition unit or an independent-living apartment. (See Chapter 7.)

Unless you've already seen a hospital psychologist or trauma counsellor, you may want to ask the social worker if she can recommend someone in your community. She may also be able to suggest an appropriate support group for you and give you some basic information about ICBC (and WCB) benefits and various government benefit programs.

The Emotional Reality of Going Home

Coming home from the hospital will probably be your first time in a car since your accident. Many people find this initial experience disturbing. Even when the person who is taking you home drives very slowly and is extremely cautious, every car on the road may feel like a threat to you. You'll be less inclined to distract the driver and upset yourself if you sit in the back with your eyes closed. While you'll eventually get used to being in a car again, it may take a while before this happens.

Your first few weeks at home may be very stressful as well, especially if you were in the hospital or a residential rehab centre for a long time. Since you're unlikely to have around-the-clock attendant care at home, your family will have to handle your needs as best as they can. (You may be able to get some help at home. See the next section.) Being limited in what you can do on your own isn't the same when you're in a hospital or rehab centre as it when you're dependent on others at home. Your family may be as troubled as you are by how much on-going help you still need.

As delighted as your children may be to have you back home, they may also find it very difficult. You may be too preoccupied with your own situation to give them the attention they want, increasing the tension in the family. (Suggestions on dealing with the challenges that you and your family may face are discussed in Chapter 5, while caregiver issues are in Chapter 7.)

Who Will Take Care of Your Needs Now?

Unless a relative or friend can take care of your on-going needs, you may require outside help for some time. ICBC will often pay for at-home care even when they won't pay for other necessary services. Home-care agencies typically offer help with personal care and hygiene, housekeeping and other daily needs, including shopping and meal preparation. They may also provide some physiotherapy and occupational therapy.

Depending on what a home-care agency's nursing assessor feels you need, a support worker may be assigned to you for a specific number of hours a day (or week). In addition to providing you with the help noted above, she may take you for walks and accompany you to medical and rehab appointments and elsewhere. She should also make sure you take any prescribed medications.

The insurer that pays for your at-home care is entitled to see the internal reports written by the agency staff. While you can ask to see this yourself, some home-care agencies say that insurers don't allow them to share this information with their clients. To deal with this situation, they may let their staff write up reports in a client's presence. You may want to find out what a home-care agency's policy is before allowing them in your home. Your privacy is more likely to be protected by an agency that will let you see the reports your insurer gets.

CAUTION! You need to be discreet in what you say and do in your support worker's presence. Some home-care agencies in B.C. have allegedly informed insurers of what clients do in the privacy of their homes.[10]

An occupational therapist (or OT) can help you modify your home to accommodate your injuries. It may be difficult to arrange for this on your own, though. OTs in the province often won't take on a client who is injured in an auto accident unless ICBC pre-authorizes this. You'll first have to file a claim for accident benefits — which you may not want to do until you've hired a lawyer.

CHAPTER 4

On-Going Care

Unless you're hospitalized after your accident, you should get yourself checked out by your family doctor as soon as possible. It's good to do this even if you've been examined by an emergency room doctor.

If you were hospitalized, once you're discharged you should continue to see your family doctor on a regular basis until you either recover fully or no further improvement is likely. You need to tell any health-care providers who treat that you were in an auto accident. They may be contacted by one or more insurers.

Follow Up Visits to Your Doctor

Your family doctor will normally oversee your recovery process. Even when an ICBC rehab co-ordinator (or professional case manager) co-ordinates your care, your doctor should be in contact with the various health-care providers who assess or treat you. It's her responsibility to address your health concerns and see that you get necessary treatment. Before you undergo treatment or participate in a return-to-work program recommended by an ICBC (or WCB) medical or vocational adviser, you may want to discuss this with your doctor. If she feels the recommendations are too aggressive, she may suggest a safer alternative.

It's important not to downplay your injuries or symptoms when speaking to your doctor. She needs to know about everything that's bothering you, no matter how minor or insignificant it seems. For legal-insurance purposes, you'll want her records to include every accident-related problem you have, whether it's physical, psychological, emotional, functional, behavioural, or cognitive.

Your doctor can advise you on what to expect in the days (or weeks) ahead as a result of your injuries. She should be able to estimate how long you'll be out of work or school, if at all, and how long it will be before you can resume your normal activities. She may refer you to other doctors and to various rehab therapists. A soft tissue injury may eventually require you seeing an orthopaedic surgeon; you may have damaged internal organs; the stress you're under may upset your gastro-intestinal system; medicine for one condition may create other health problems — the list of potential complications is long and varied.

Your family doctor may not have the training or experience (or spend enough time with you) to recognize brain injury symptoms, post-traumatic stress disorder, chronic pain disorder, or other trauma-related problems. If close friends or relatives notice changes in your functioning level, moods or behaviour, they should discuss this with your doctor. They may have more insight than you do into how well (or poorly) you're doing. If you're not functioning as well as you should be as time goes on, you may need to be assessed by a physiatrist (a rehab doctor), neurologist, neuropsychologist, clinical psychologist or chiropractor. Once your problems are identified, appropriate treatment can begin. The sooner this happens, the less likely it is that you'll be left with permanent disabilities.

TBI ALERT! While most people fully recover from a mild brain injury within two years or less, this isn't always the case. Unless your doctor is familiar with common brain injury symptoms, she may not know what to look for.

Unless you only see your doctor once or twice after your accident, she may be asked to write a progress report for ICBC. If you're unable to return to work or school within two weeks, she may have to update your adjuster periodically on how you're doing. If you file a claim for damages against an at-fault driver, your doctor may be asked for detailed information about what she's observed in examining you, how long she thinks you'll be out of work or school, and whether you may have on-going disabilities or restrictions in your daily activities. She may also be asked for a medical-legal report.

Doctor-patient confidentiality: When you file an insurance claim after an auto accident in B.C. you give up your right to doctor-patient confidentiality. Not only can your doctor's treatment notes and clinical records be subpoenaed, ICBC can question her privately about any matter they feel might be relevant to your claim. While you should be informed beforehand that they intend to do this, only a court order — or your doctor's refusal to speak to them — can prevent this from happening. The courts usually support ICBC on this issue.

Since problems stemming from your accident may be blamed on earlier conditions or health concerns you've had, if ICBC requests a copy of your doctor's clinical records, you can ask her to send these to your lawyer (if any) instead. He can then black out what doesn't relate to your accident or injuries before sending over the records to ICBC. If they feel the blacked out portions may be pertinent to your insurance claim, they can ask a judge in chambers to rule on whether the deleted information should be released.

Common Rehab Treatment

If you're entitled to accident benefits from ICBC (see Chapter 10), they should provide you with the medical and rehab treatment you'll need to return you to your previous (or optimal) functioning level, taking into account the permanent effects of your injuries. There's currently a $150,000 cap on these benefits. While this may seem like a lot of money, it won't last long if you have catastrophic injuries. Even with less serious injuries, if you'll continue to need treatment for a long time, you'll have to be careful how you use these funds — especially if you won't be getting money through a claim for damages.

Your rehab program may be set up by your doctor or case manager, if any, or by ICBC or another insurer. (The treatment that WCB covers is discussed in Chapter 6.)

Physiotherapy is the most frequently recommended treatment after an auto accident. It can reduce pain, mobilize soft tissues and joints, improve range of motion, and increase strength and flexibility. Your physiotherapist can also help you overcome muscle weakness, lack of muscle tone, and de-conditioning. Some of the methods that may be used are manual manipulation, electrotherapy, ultra-sound, heat, cold compresses, and exercise.

After an orthopaedic injury, spinal cord injury, brain injury, amputation or serious burn, you may have to learn new ways of moving and performing daily activities. Your physiotherapist's emphasis will be on preventing new problems from arising and helping you maximize your independence and mobility. When relevant, you may be taught pain control and skin care, or how to strengthen residual limbs and use prosthetic devises. In-home care may be provided when needed. A physiotherapist may also come to your home or workplace to analyze your activities and movements, so she can help you function more efficiently with less pain. (Your doctor will be expected to monitor your treatment.)

Massage therapy is recommended for soft tissue injuries, fractures and the relief of body tension. It can loosen tight muscles, reduce swelling and tissue scarring, increase joint mobility, and ease chronic pain. By increasing blood circulation in an injured area, strained muscles, tendons and ligaments can heal better. Your body may try to compensate for pain or dysfunction in one area by tensing up in another area or using the wrong muscles, causing muscular tension in non-injured areas of your body. Massage therapy can relieve this tension and prevent further pain and dysfunction. (Your doctor will have to monitor your treatment.)

Chiropractic treatment can help with back, neck and spinal injuries, joint problems, and other musculoskeletal conditions. In addition to doing spinal manipulations, chiropractors use many of the same techniques as physiotherapists and massage therapists. (They may also do acupuncture.) Your chiropractor will look for orthopaedic and neurological problems, and she may take x-rays to see whether you have spinal abnormalities. ICBC may ask her for a summary of your condition, her diagnosis and treatment plan, and what outcome she expects. A detailed report may be requested later, describing your response to treatment. Your chiropractor may also be questioned about aggravating factors that could be contributing to your condition and about future complications that might arise.

Occupational therapy can help you become more independent, regardless of the nature or extent of your injuries. Your OT may have to teach you new ways of performing daily life skills, including dressing, grooming, bathing and eating. Once you've mastered these skills — or immediately when these issues don't have to be addressed — a rehab program can be built around the skills you'll need to carry out your responsibilities at home, work, or school.

An OT can help modify your home, workplace or school environment to accommodate your injuries. She can also set up a work-hardening program for you and advise your family, employer or teachers about strategies to help you compensate for your deficits. (If you're unable to return to full-time work within the time frame ICBC feels is appropriate, you may be required to participate in a work-hardening program to continue receiving accident benefits. Your doctor should be consulted to make sure there are no medical reasons why you shouldn't do this.)

Acupuncture is a method of encouraging your body to heal itself. Sterile needles are used to stimulate points along the energy lines (or meridians) beneath the skin surface. Heat or electrical stimulation may be applied where the needles are inserted. Acupuncture often reduces the need for painkillers and muscle relaxants. It's high success rate in getting people back to work makes it the only alternative therapy that ICBC routinely supports.

Psychological counselling can prevent you from developing emotional or psychological problems after an auto accident. A few sessions with a clinical psychologist or trauma counsellor may help you deal with your reactions to what's happened and any guilt feelings you have. If you're constantly thinking about your accident, or you develop physical symptoms of psychological distress, you may need longer-term treatment. Psychological counselling is essential after any catastrophic injury.

Neuropsychological counselling deals with brain dysfunction. If you have a brain injury — or your known injuries have healed and you're still not functioning the way you should — a neuropsychological assessment may be warranted. (ICBC or a personal injury lawyer may recommend this even if your doctor doesn't.) To determine whether you have on-going effects from a known (or unknown) brain injury, you'll usually be given a battery of tests, interviewed at length, and your behaviour carefully observed. Once the neuropsychologist scores your tests, reviews your medical reports, and interviews one or more people about the changes they've noticed in you, she'll compare your present functioning level with your pre-accident work (or school) history. If she feels you have a brain injury with on-going consequences, she'll recommend appropriate treatment. This may include psychological counselling and stress reduction as well as cognitive retraining. You may be taught compensatory techniques to help you overcome deficits in your thinking processes and behaviour. Unless brain injury deficits are promptly treated, you could end up with serious lifelong problems. (See Chapters 5 and 7.)

CAUTION! Before you're assessed by an ICBC-hired neuropsychologist or one recommended by your doctor, you may want to consult a personal injury lawyer. Some neuropsychologists in B.C. are believed to do biased assessments to benefit insurers. (See the section on independent medical examiners in Chapter 11.)

Speech-language therapy deals with all language skills, including reading and writing. This treatment option may be appropriate if you're having trouble communicating or understanding what you read or hear.

Pain management programs are generally run by a team of health-care providers, including a psychologist, physiotherapist, OT and physiatrist. If you're still in a lot of pain six months after your accident, despite having undergone various types of rehab therapies, once the presence of a serious underlying problem has been ruled out, your doctor (or ICBC) may recommend that you participate in one of these programs. You'll be taught to identify movements that cause you pain; learn exercises to increase your strength and flexibility; and practice new ways of moving. You may also be taught to use adaptive devices to perform daily tasks with minimum discomfort. Some psychological counselling may be provided, and you may be taught relaxation techniques to help reduce the tension that comes from living with chronic pain. An effort may also be made to reduce your reliance on painkillers.

Fitness and exercise programs may be recommended by your doctor. She may also suggest that you get exercise equipment for your home or recommend one-on-one fitness training.

Alternative therapies — treatment options that aren't supported by recognized scientific research — can be helpful when traditional therapies fail to eliminate physical or psychological problems. Your doctor may suggest that you try yoga, applied kinesiology, Pilates, Feldenkreis, the Alexander technique or prolotherapy[11] to relieve your pain and raise your functioning level. Hypnosis, meditation, biofeedback and *qi-gong* may be recommended for anything from pain to emotional distress. You may have to research the benefits and availability of alternative therapies on your own rather than relying on your doctor for this.

Rehab Treatment After a Catastrophic Injury

By the time you leave the hospital or rehab centre after a catastrophic injury, you'll probably have had several weeks (or more) of intensive rehab. You may continue to need on-going treatment for many years.

Your recovery process should be co-ordinated by someone who knows what rehab options are both necessary and available. This can be a professional case manager, ICBC (or WCB) rehab co-ordinator, doctor, relative or friend. (Occasionally, a personal injury lawyer will do this.) An advocacy support group such as the BC Paraplegic Association can sometimes provide case management services as well. Your medical-rehab team may include a neurosurgeon, neurologist, physiatrist, clinical psychologist (or psychiatrist), speech-language therapist, physiotherapist, occupational therapist, and your family doctor.

If you're exhibiting the brain injury symptoms noted in Chapter 7, neuropsychological treatment should be started as soon as possible. Once you develop poor coping strategies, it can be hard to learn effective compensatory techniques. Rehab agencies that work with brain injury survivors typically offer one-on-one rehab through an interdisciplinary team that may include a vocational counsellor and recreational therapist as well as various types of health-care providers and support workers. Among the services that may be provided are cognitive and life-skills training; vocational assessment and job coaching; help re-entering the community and returning to work or school; and family support.

Should You Hire a Professional Case Manager?

If your injuries may lead to permanent disability, or you'll need extensive on-going rehab treatment, you may want to hire a case manager while you're in the hospital. She can then arrange for a team assessment to be done by the doctors and rehab therapists who are looking after you. She'll also oversee your care and monitor what's happening. Once you're discharged from the hospital, she'll co-ordinate the efforts of your medical-rehab team. While hiring a case manager is expensive, if you weren't at fault in your accident you should eventually get this money back as part of a claim for damages. In some situations, a personal injury lawyer may hire a case manager for you and wait to be reimbursed for this when your insurance claim settles.

A case manager usually has a degree in social work. In addition to researching and evaluating rehab options for you, she can act as your advocate with government agencies and insurers; explore housing options; and get you financial aid, if needed. (After a severe brain injury, a case manager can be instrumental in getting you help once you no longer need acute hospital care.)

While your family doctor is unlikely to have the time, training or experience to effectively co-ordinate your rehab treatment after a catastrophic injury, it may not be cost-effective to hire a case manager if you were solely at fault in your accident. Case management services can often be provided by a rehab centre social worker or by a physiatrist or occupational therapist on your medical-rehab team. When ICBC or another insurer provides case management services, the treatment recommended is usually oriented towards getting you back to work or school as quickly as possible at the lowest cost possible. You'll normally get better care when the person who co-ordinates your medical-rehab team is sensitive to the issues involved in supporting an insurance claim. This obviously can't be someone who is employed by the insurer responsible for paying out the claim.

If a relative or friend oversees your care, she'll have to be persistent in her advocacy efforts; able to analyze your needs objectively; know what questions to ask the professionals who treat or assess you; and know what information to pass on to others. She'll also have to educate herself about traditional and alternative therapies so your doctors can be asked for referrals. Besides learning about the help that's available through various sources, she'll have to be able to navigate her way through complex legal, financial and bureaucratic issues. While it can be hard for non-professionals to obtain (and interpret) the information needed to make intelligent decisions, advocacy support groups can sometimes help with this.

Who Will Pay for Your Rehab?

The Medical Services Plan of British Columbia (MSP) presently only pays for rehab treatment when you're entitled to Premium Assistance (or supplementary benefits). People who are getting income assistance from the B.C. government, First Nations people, some residents of long-term care facilities, and some low-income working families are eligible for this. (You can apply for Premium Assistance through MSP. Your tax returns will determine whether you qualify.)

If you can't afford to pay for necessary treatment after you're discharged from the hospital, and this cost isn't being covered by an insurer, the B.C. Ministry of Health Services' "Home and Community Care" branch may provide these services free of charge. If the B.C. Ministry of Human Resources feels that you have "persistent multiple barriers to employment", or they designate you a "person with disabilities", you may be given enhanced medical coverage and financial support so you can get necessary rehab treatment. (See Chapter 6.)

If you're entitled to accident benefits from ICBC, they should cover most of your rehab costs. If they don't, you may have to initiate legal action. While it's often hard to get your rehab treatment paid when you have a large claim for damages, these costs should eventually be reimbursed to you. Rather than going without the treatment you need because you can't afford it, you can ask your adjuster for an advance against your claim. (While some personal injury lawyers used to cover rehab costs up front, this is rarely done now.)

Even if ICBC agrees to pay for your rehab, you may need pre-approval for certain treatment to be covered. Anything that might help you return to work has a good chance of being supported. (After a serious injury, funding for your rehab may go through ICBC's rehab department.)

If another insurer pays for accident-related rehab and you'll have to reimburse them when your claim for damages (if any) settles, you should receive money for this as part of your damages.

NOTE: The information below relates solely to accident benefits from ICBC. User fees are currently paid, but this may change. The treatment WCB covers is in Chapter 6.

Unless your rehab therapists bill ICBC directly, you'll have to pay for your treatment up front and submit your receipts to your adjuster. You should be reimbursed within 60 days. If you were solely at fault in your accident, you won't be reimbursed for therapy charges in excess of ICBC's established payment schedule. If you weren't at fault, this additional money should be paid to you as part of your damages.

You'll need a doctor's referral for ICBC to pay for your physiotherapy. They may pay a higher-than-standard rate when more than one body area is treated or you have catastrophic injuries. A doctor's referral is also necessary for massage therapy to be covered. If your adjuster doesn't agree with your doctor on the number of sessions you need, you may be sent to an ICBC medical adviser, whose opinion will usually be followed.

ICBC should cover the cost of chiropractic treatment, including emergency, night, holiday and home visits, when needed. If your adjuster has any concerns about the treatment you're getting, he may discuss this with your chiropractor, and you may be sent to another chiropractor for an evaluation.

If ICBC feels you need occupational therapy, they'll either send you to someone or send an OT to your home. If your adjuster doesn't feel you need the level of help recommended, this may have to be resolved in court or through arbitration. You should be reimbursed for any out-of-pocket occupational therapy costs you have when you settle your claim.

Since ICBC often sends claimants for acupuncture, they should pay for this if your doctor sends you. They rarely pay for other alternative therapies as an accident benefit, though. You may have to go through arbitration to get an alternative therapy paid. Or, you may have to cover the cost yourself and try to get the money back later as part of a claim for damages.

ICBC should pay for psychological and neuropsychological counselling when this is part of an established rehab program. While short-term therapy that might help you return to work or school is often covered, ICBC may resist paying for long-term treatment. A psychologist or neuropsychologist may be willing to treat you without getting paid until your insurance claim settles. (If ICBC sends you to a psychologist or neuropsychologist for an assessment or treatment, they'll pay for this up front.)

If you need speech-language therapy, the ICBC rehab department is probably involved in your care. Your rehab co-ordinator should be able to arrange for you to get this treatment as an accident benefit. After a mild-to-moderate brain injury, you may have to pay for speech-language therapy up front and let the court (or arbitration proceedings) resolve whether ICBC should cover this cost.

ICBC may pay for you to participate in a pain management program if they feel this will reduce their overall costs by getting you back to work or school quickly — or helping you function more effectively when you're there. If they won't pay for this up front, the court may award you money for it as part of a claim for damages. (If you're not entitled to damages but your doctor recommended the program, the cost may be reimbursed when you settle your claim.)

When a fitness or exercise program is recommended by your doctor, ICBC should cover the cost as an accident benefit. If you belonged to a gym prior to your accident, you'll be expected to continue paying for this yourself; otherwise, reasonable membership fees should be covered. If there's a community gym near your home, you'll have to join this, not a private health club. You may have to cover the cost of one-on-one fitness training up front and wait to be reimbursed in settling your claim.

ICBC may buy exercise equipment for you if your doctor recommends this for a specific purpose and the cost is reasonable. If the equipment you need is available in a local gym, it may be rented for you while you're home-bound, but you'll be expected to go to the gym once you can get around.

If you weren't at fault in your accident, your insurance settlement should be large enough to cover the cost of getting rehab treatment for as long as needed. If you were at fault, you may be able to negotiate a cash buy-out of your accident benefits in settling your claim. Unless you have catastrophic injuries, this should provide you with enough money to pay for on-going rehab treatment. (Buy-outs are discussed in Chapter 18.)

ICBC Rehab Programs

The ICBC rehab department deals exclusively with accident benefits and is independent to the claims division. You may be referred here when it's apparent that your recovery will take years, not months. After a serious injury, a rehab co-ordinator may be assigned to you while you're in the hospital.

Your rehab co-ordinator will normally set up a rehab program for you that can be paid for without exceeding the $150,000 cap on your medical-rehab benefits. The goal of the program will be to help you gain the independence and skills you'll need to return to work or school. If you're unlikely to be able to resume your pre-accident (or similar) work, vocational retraining may be provided.

A rehab co-ordinator may be able to authorize items and services that aren't always covered as an accident benefit. This may include anything from modifications to your home or car to sex or art therapy. (See Chapter 10.) To qualify for these benefits, you'll have to undergo the treatment recommended. Rehab co-ordinators have a lot of discretion in the services they can provide, and ICBC may pay for treatment for you that they won't fund for someone else. The department's payment policy seems to differ from one injured person to another and from one rehab co-ordinator to another.

If you have concerns about your rehab co-ordinator's recommendations, you should discuss these with her as soon as possible. Ignoring her suggestions will place you at risk of losing your accident benefits. In some situations, you may have to file a complaint with ICBC's Fair Practices Review department. (See Chapter 9). You may also want to consult a personal injury lawyer.

While a good rehab co-ordinator should act as your advocate with ICBC, she'll also try to keep their costs to a minimum. No matter how sincerely she wants to help you, her primary loyalty will be to her employer: ICBC.

> **CAUTION! If you file a claim for damages, your rehab co-ordinator may pass on remarks you make in her presence to the ICBC legal-defence team. Keep your conversations with her brief, and don't volunteer unnecessary information. If possible, have someone act as an intermediary between you.**

If you only have soft tissue injuries, your adjuster may refer you to ICBC's Soft Tissue Injury Program. An ICBC-hired physiotherapist or occupational therapist will then set up a rehab program for you in consultation with your doctor and treating therapists. The most cost-effective community-based services will normally be used and a return-to-work plan developed. If your claims adjuster doesn't support the recommended treatment plan, the ICBC rehab department may be asked to decide what's appropriate.

Fairly aggressive treatment options are usually suggested, and anything that won't help you return to work or school may not be supported. If you're put into a pain-management program and can't return to work or school after completing this, ICBC may refuse to fund further treatment for you.

ICBC's Head Injury Unit handles all mild brain injury claims when this is the only injury suffered. Many personal injury lawyers feel that the sole purpose of this program is to deny accident benefits and compensation to people with mild brain injuries. In most cases, little treatment is recommended and few benefits provided. If you're referred to the Head Injury Unit, you may want to consult a lawyer who specializes in brain injury claims before being assessed.

CHAPTER 5

Psychological Issues and Interpersonal Relationships

It's not unusual to have emotional or psychological problems after an auto accident. You may find yourself constantly thinking about what happened and worrying about future accidents. Anything that reminds you of your accident — whether it's being near the accident scene, witnessing other accidents, or talking to doctors, lawyers or insurers — may upset you. You may develop psychosomatic problems; previous medical (or psychological) conditions may worsen; and memories of earlier traumas may be awakened.

Your understanding of the world can be shattered after an accident. You may blame yourself for what happened even if you weren't at fault and feel enraged at others even when they weren't involved. As time passes, you may continue to have disturbing thoughts and feelings, making you constantly nervous and on edge. Stressful situations may be harder to handle, and you may slip into emotional overload when things don't go your way.

Accepting even temporary lifestyles changes is never easy. Your injuries may make you dependent on others, and you may need help from the medical-legal-insurance system that you can't always get, increasing your feelings of helplessness and vulnerability. If you become clinically depressed or develop another psychological (or psychiatric) disorder, you may need long-term psychological counselling.

Children's emotional and psychological reactions to an auto accident tend to be similar to those of adults but may be exaggerated. A young child may feel bewildered and confused by what's happened and frightened by a visit to the emergency room or a hospital stay. Your calm presence in the face of your child's fears will help reassure her that everything will be all right.

The likelihood of your child having psychological problems after an accident may have little connection to how severe the accident was or how badly she (or anyone else) was injured. (Symptoms of distress to look for in children are noted in the next section.)

Post-Traumatic Stress Disorder (PTSD)

Acute distress coming from a real (or perceived) threat of serious injury or death can create permanent changes in your brain that cause you to have persistent flashbacks (or nightmares) of the traumatic event. When the following symptoms continue for over a month, you may have post-traumatic stress disorder: insomnia, recurring dreams or nightmares; intrusive memories of your accident; avoidance of (and emotional distress in) situations that remind you of what happened; increased agitation, irritability and rage; an exaggerated startle reflex; emotional detachment; and an apathy towards things that used to interest you. Your symptoms may be apparent immediately or not for several months. You don't need to be injured to develop PTSD.

Nearly 40% of the people who seek medical treatment after an auto accident show signs of PTSD within a few months. (Within five years, this percentage increases to 68%.)[12] While half these cases resolve spontaneously without treatment, symptoms can also worsen over time, especially when accident-related stress continues. While women are more likely to get PTSD than men, pre-existing psychological problems don't affect whether someone develops this condition.[13]

In the early stages of post-traumatic stress disorder, you may be obsessively preoccupied with your accident, continually re-living it in your mind, and dwelling on how easily you (or others) could have been seriously injured or killed. This may be accompanied by overwhelming feelings of helplessness and a sense of not being in control. Once this acute stage subsides, your attention may shift from your accident to somatic symptoms such as headaches, dizziness, chest pains, and stomach problems. You may become anxious and despondent or develop chronic pain disorder, anxiety (or panic) disorder, an adjustment disorder, or clinical depression. Meanwhile, your relationships with others may deteriorate. Since chronic PTSD can be hard to treat, it may lead to permanent disability. EMDR[14] and cognitive-behavioural therapy are sometimes helpful. Anti-anxiety drugs may also be prescribed.

Twenty-five percent of the children and adolescents who are injured in auto accidents develop PTSD.[15] Older children and those with parents who have this condition are most likely to develop it. A child with PTSD may worry about dying and develop psychosomatic ailments. Her emotional reactions may be extreme, and she may get enraged frequently for no apparent reason. She may have sleep problems, persistent fears, refuse to go to school, and revert to immature behaviour or continually misbehave. She may also withdraw from family and friends, lose interest in her normal activities, and become apathetic and irritable. Since PTSD is largely unrecognized in children, it can become chronic with on-going consequences.

Secondary Wounding

Secondary wounding refers to the psychological damage that can occur when your health concerns are belittled or dismissed, you're denied necessary treatment, or you feel unsupported by the people and institutions you turn to for help, including relatives, friends, health-care providers, insurers, government agencies, and the courts. Secondary wounding can cause (or intensify) PTSD, creating more long-term problems than the original trauma.

Ignorance and insensitivity are major causes of secondary wounding. Your health-care providers may have limited experience treating trauma survivors, while your relatives, friends and co-workers may not understand what you're going through. Since insurers have a vested interest in minimizing accident-related problems, you may have trouble getting the help you need and are entitled to. When you're blamed for an accident you didn't cause, or treated as if you're exaggerating your problems, some secondary wounding is probably inevitable. The stress of taking your case to court can also cause secondary wounding. (See Aphrodite Matzakis' book on PTSD, "I Can't Get Over It".)

Survivor's Guilt

People often blame themselves for an accident even when they weren't at fault. You may feel guilty for having escaped with minor injuries when other people were badly hurt. Even when you're not personally involved in an accident, if someone close to you was injured you may feel responsible for this on some level. If anyone was seriously injured (or killed) in an accident in which you were at fault, deep-rooted guilt feelings may be unavoidable.

Regardless of whether your guilt feelings are rational or not, you shouldn't ignore them. A psychologist who works with trauma survivors can help you resolve your guilt in a healthy way so you can rid yourself of destructive self-judgments. Looking at what happened from an objective viewpoint, and remembering your past strengths and accomplishments, may make it easier for you to accept your role, if any, in your accident.

Challenges for Family Members and Friends

When a close relative or friend is injured in an accident, your own life may be affected as well. There may be new responsibilities for you to take on and new roles to play. If the injured person is admitted to the hospital, you may have to make difficult medical decisions for him. Once he's discharged, you may become his primary caregiver or be responsible for finding people to do this. You may need to update his health-care providers periodically on changes or setbacks that occur; research treatment options; arrange for him to get necessary treatment; co-ordinate his care; and deal with lawyers, insurers and government agencies on his behalf. You may also have to find a local support group for people with similar injuries and go with him to support group gatherings.

Your opinion about who caused his accident is something you should keep to yourself. He'll have to deal with this in his own way to recover emotionally. By letting him express his thoughts and feelings without commenting on it or judging it, you can help him move beyond the issues of blame and responsibility so he can begin to accept what happened.

Whether the injured person's functional or lifestyle changes are temporary or permanent, it will be easier for him to cope with them if you encourage him to pursue activities that aren't beyond his reach. By helping him establish a daily routine that takes his current capabilities into account, he should eventually be able to achieve his optimal functioning level.

It may be harder for you to accept that a close relative or friend has a catastrophic injury than it is for him. While there's no way he can escape his situation, you may long to get away from it sometimes, no matter how devoted you are to him. If you're his primary caregiver, unless you get outside help on a regular basis it may be hard to remain totally supportive as time goes on. You need to take daily breaks from your caregiving tasks so you don't burn out and start resenting the injured person or your responsibilities.

You'll also have to make sure that the needs of the other people in your family (particularly your children) are being met. The toll that the injured person's problems are taking on family members should be discussed with his doctors. If anyone in the family becomes clinically depressed or develops PTSD — both of which are common after a catastrophic injury — psychological counselling will be needed.

TBI ALERT! If a close relative's or friend's behaviour after a brain injury is disturbing to you or others, make sure he gets appropriate treatment, even if this means personally taking him to therapy sessions.

Changes in Family Dynamics

Family dynamics are often affected when someone is injured in an auto accident. Even if you expect to fully recover, if you were the primary wage earner, disciplinarian, homemaker or decision maker in your family, someone else may have to assume these roles until you're back on your feet again.

The more flexible your family is about sharing responsibilities, the easier it will probably be to re-define family roles in a way that's acceptable to everyone. If you're all comfortable expressing and sharing your feelings, you should be able to deal with most problems that arise before undue tension is created. Nonetheless, even an emotionally supportive family that communicates well with one another may need family therapy to ensure that everyone adjusts well to necessary life changes. This is especially important after a serious injury when one family member may suddenly have multiple unfamiliar roles to play: patient-advocate, caregiver, sole wage earner, confidant, and for all practical purposes, single parent.

The emotional strength of the individuals in your family will affect how well they deal with your injuries. A child with pre-existing psychological problems may have a particularly hard time adjusting to necessary changes and need professional guidance.

The Effects of Serious Injury (or Death) on Children and Adolescents

The worse someone's injuries are, the more his family shares the consequences. When a parent is seriously injured, the children in the family may feel as if they've lost both parents. Not only may the injured parent seem very different now, the other parent may be so involved in taking care of him that she has little time or energy for anyone else. When a child is seriously injured, both parents may be so focused on her needs that her siblings feel neglected and unloved.

A serious injury is always threatening to the children in the family. They may feel that there's nothing they can hold on to or trust anymore, not even their parents. Nothing can protect them from the catastrophic and unexpected occurring at any moment, drastically changing their lives; they've seen this first-hand in what's already happened. While they're feeling vulnerable and insecure, they'll need more love and attention than ever. If you're too preoccupied with your own (or another family member's) injuries to give your children the nurturing and support they need, make sure they get this from someone else before they resort to negative, destructive behaviour to gain your attention.

It's not uncommon for children to resent a parent or sibling whose injuries have altered their lives. They may be angry at his need for continual care, embarrassed by his limitations, and enraged by life changes they don't understand. Saddened and depressed, they may withdraw from others rather than seeking the comfort they need. You may have to continually reassure your children that what they're feeling is natural under the circumstances. Encourage them to express their thoughts and feelings in a way that won't be hurtful to the injured person. A family (or child) psychologist can help with this process, providing a safe environment where negative feelings can be explored and expressed.

If your child is seriously injured, downplaying what's happened and giving her unrealistic expectations is short-sighted at best and a denial of her reality. Unfounded optimism, however well-intended, may make it harder for her to trust you. This can hamper her recovery and increase tension in the family. There's nothing wrong with honestly acknowledging your concerns as long as you do this in a non-threatening way. An injured child should be given age-appropriate information to help her understand what's going on. She needs to be assured that she's in safe hands and is getting the best care possible. Let her know that you have faith in her ability to cope with what lies ahead. She may surprise you with the depth of her understanding and acceptance. Whatever grieving you need to do should be done behind closed doors, away from *all* the children in the family.

Children with serious injuries often blame themselves for this, feeling that they're being punished for something they did (or thought). You need to make it clear to your injured child right from the beginning — and continue to remind her — that she's not responsible for what happened. As hard as it is to accept that life is unfair sometimes, this may be the healthiest outlook possible.

As time goes on, your injured child may become increasingly angry with you and her doctors for not making her better than she is. Impatient with the care and attention she still needs, she may become bitter and withdrawn, blaming everyone around her for her situation. No matter how much you feel her pain, you can't allow her to terrorize the rest of the family and make them miserable. Psychological counselling may give her the emotional support she needs to cope with her feelings.

Catastrophic injuries that occur during adolescence can be particularly devastating. Not only will the injured adolescent have to alter her expectations of herself at least to some degree, she'll have lost her independence just as she's struggling to achieve it. The more negative her self-image becomes, the harder it will be for her to develop realistic new goals. Her relationships with others may suffer as well, intensifying her loneliness and rage. With all the obstacles she's facing, she may become rebellious or suicidal. Should this happen, she needs to get prompt treatment from a psychologist who specializes in working with adolescents with disabilities.

As a concerned parent, you should make sure that your injured adolescent isn't isolated or over-protected, and that she maintains as normal a routine as possible. An advocacy support group should be able to put her in contact with other people her age who have dealt with similar injuries and can be good role models for her.

You need to respond to your teenager's strengths, not just her problems. She should be encouraged to build on the talents she has and explore new interests. Learning about her disabilities will empower her and help her feel more in control of her life. If legal action is taken on her behalf, letting her play an active role in this process will increase her self-confidence and self-assurance.

When a family member or close friend is killed: Pre-school children usually view death as temporary: the cartoon figure on TV is back again the next day having new adventures. Between the ages of five and nine, children begin to think more like adults with respect to death, without expecting it to happen to anyone they know. At whatever age your children are when they're forced to confront death up close, you can help them accept this by being truthful with them. The sooner they realize that the deceased person won't magically re-appear one day, the sooner they'll pass through their grieving process.

A grieving child needs to have her fears addressed and be reassured that she's not to blame for what happened. It's important to validate her feelings and help her deal with emotions and thoughts that are beyond her control. She may feel abandoned and rejected, and hostile towards the deceased person, or blame her parents or siblings for his death even if they weren't involved in his accident. Her rage may be expressed externally through explosive or destructive behaviour, or it may be internalized, making her moody and despondent. She may revert to infantile (or immature) behaviour, constantly demanding attention. These reactions are only cause for concern when they continue for several weeks.

A grieving child may try to live in the past, idealizing the deceased person, even taking on his characteristics. She may quickly transfer her affection to someone new to make up for the love she's lost. While she may be reluctant to attend school, she should be encouraged to continue her normal activities. She needs to learn that life goes on, despite the death of someone she loves.

A grieving adolescent may be overwhelmed with guilt, or be numb and in shock for months, unable to believe what's happened. She may try to dull her pain with alcohol or drugs; become sexually promiscuous to distract herself from despair; or be depressed and suicidal. Other signs of distress to look for include insomnia, exhaustion, lose of appetite (or over-eating), lowered self-esteem, academic failure, dangerous or unusual behaviour, and lost friendships. An adolescent who acts overly strong or brave in the face of death (or catastrophic injury) may be in denial. Until she confronts what's happened, she won't be able to mourn her loss and move on.

You may have to remind your teenager that it's natural to feel emotionally distraught when someone she cares about dies. As independent as she wants to be, she needs to know that she's not alone in her grief: you're there to support her if and when she wants this. If she's willing to share her thoughts with you, listen to her with compassion, but don't try to minimize her pain or cure her of it. Help her understand that her grief is healthy and that the pain she feels won't continue forever. Encourage her to talk about the deceased person as much as she wants, sharing her memories and dreams with you. Don't be worried if she feels that she's still in contact with him and hears him talking to her. This may be a comfort to her and is unlikely to go on for very long. Writing a farewell letter to the deceased person may lessen her pain and help her let go of him so she can begin to heal.

While you may be able to ease your adolescent's grief by being there for her, you won't be able to eliminate it. She'll have to work through this in her own way. An adolescent-oriented psychologist or bereavement counsellor can help her gain insight into her feelings and resolve any underlying conflicts she has.

If You Have a Brain Injury

People with traumatic brain injuries are often misdiagnosed as having psychiatric problems. TBI symptoms can mimic those of clinical depression, chronic pain disorder, and other conditions. A neuropsychological assessment may be needed to determine whether your symptoms are caused by organic damage to your brain or are psychological (or psychiatric) in nature.

Since people with TBI often lack insight into themselves, you may not realize how disturbing your behaviour is to others. You may over-react to situations, becoming angry and aggressive one minute and anxious or depressed the next. Despite finding it hard to keep up in social situations or cope with your responsibilities, you may resent other people's attempts to help you, feeling they're intruding. While other people may find you unresponsive and insensitive, you may think they don't like you and distance yourself from your family and friends. What makes this particularly unfortunate is that the quality of your support system can have a large effect on how well you recover from the consequences of a brain injury.

The more mind-oriented you are, the more devastated you're apt to be by decreases in your cognitive abilities (or thinking processes). Frustrated at not being able to function the way you used to, you may continually feel that you've failed even when you haven't. As problem-solving difficulties cause a spiraling of complications in your life, you may develop a stress-related disorder. Pre-existing psychological problems may also become exaggerated. (See Chapter 7 for more on TBI symptoms.)

Failing to recognize brain injury symptoms for what they are can lead to unnecessary emotional turmoil. While there's no cure for

TBI, compensatory techniques can help you live a normal life. Psychological counselling can help you accept (and cope with) changes in your personality and behaviour; cognitive therapy can teach you concrete strategies to deal with specific problems; and behaviour-modification therapy can help you learn to recognize and change negative behaviour patterns. Biofeedback, meditation, and stress reduction techniques may be helpful as well, and medication may be prescribed.

To prevent emotional problems from breaking up the family unit, other family members may need counselling as well. Too many couples separate after one of them has a brain injury. (Couples with young children are more likely to stay together.)

Psychological Counselling

In an ideal world, family doctors would be trained to recognize the emotional after-effects of an auto accident so they could refer their patients for treatment. While your doctor may prescribe antidepressants for you if she's aware that you're having problems, what you may really need is a referral to a clinical psychologist or trauma counsellor. Discussing your accident and its impact on your life with a trained professional can help prevent long-term psychological problems.

After a serious or catastrophic injury, psychological counselling can help you adapt to your disabilities and lifestyle changes; recognize old strengths and discover new ones; and develop a positive new self-image. Family therapy can help family members adjust to the changes in your life (and their lives) and teach them effective ways to communicate and resolve conflicts. Individual therapy can provide a troubled family member with the emotional support he needs to deal with his personal issues surrounding your accident and injuries. In the privacy and safety of a psychologist's office, he can vent his rage and release it. He can also learn non-destructive ways to express his negative feelings in the future.

You may have to specifically request that your doctor refer you to a psychologist (or psychiatrist) for counselling. You should be aware, though, that if the issues you're struggling with stem from a brain injury, this may not be picked up by either your family doctor or treating therapist. If you don't respond to treatment within a reasonable period of time, a neuropsychological assessment may be warranted.

Finding the Right Therapist

Some psychologists have a general broad-based background, while others have specialized training in areas such as family therapy, child (or adolescent-oriented) therapy, neuropsychology, cognitive-behavioural therapy, bereavement counselling, or trauma counselling. You may want to meet with more than one psychologist (or psychiatrist) prior to beginning treatment. Before your initial consultation with a therapist, check with your personal injury lawyer, if any, to make sure he has no objection to you seeing her.

You may want to ask a prospective therapist some preliminary questions over the phone. Is she registered with the College of Psychologists of BC or another professional organization? (If she's a psychiatrist, where did she train, what are her areas of specialty, and what board certification does she have?) How long has she been in practice and has she treated other auto accident survivors? Depending on which circumstances apply to you, has she had special training in trauma counselling or in working with people who have permanent disabilities, brain injuries, chronic pain or fatigue, or fibromyalgia? Does she do family therapy or work closely with someone who does? What does she charge and does she have a sliding scale based on need? Will you be charged for your initial consultation with her? If so, what will this cost?

It may be helpful to bring a summary sheet with you to your first meeting with a therapist. This should note the changes that you (or others) have noticed in you since your accident and the issues you'd like to work on in therapy. If anyone helps you prepare your notes, or the symptoms (and changes) you mention were pointed out to you by others, you need to let the therapist know this: it may be significant.

You may want to ask a psychologist (or psychiatrist) how much of her practice comes from ICBC (or WCB) referrals. Have they ever paid her to treat someone whom they haven't directly referred? If she bills them for your sessions, what kind of feedback will she have to give them? Will she show you any reports she writes for them before she submits these, and/or inform you beforehand of what she intends to tell your adjuster? What steps is she prepared to take to protect your privacy? If your work with her awakens memories of earlier traumas — or these have already resurfaced since your accident — does she feel that therapy time devoted to this is a cost that ICBC (or WCB) should cover?

You can also ask a psychologist whether she'll wait until your insurance claim settles before getting paid, if necessary. (ICBC may refuse to pay her, or they may stop paying her midway through your treatment.) How available will she be to you while you're undergoing therapy with her? If you need to speak to her outside regularly-scheduled sessions, will you be able to do this? How will phone conversations with her be billed?

At the end of your initial meeting, the psychologist (or psychiatrist) should tell you what she thinks your basic problems are, what treatment approach she thinks would be most effective, how long you may need to be in therapy, and what outcome you can expect.

If You're Put on Medication

If your treating psychologist feels you might benefit from a psychotropic (or other) drug, she'll refer you to a psychiatrist, who will decide what medication is right for you and monitor your use of it. (Psychotropic drugs alter your brain chemistry, affecting how you think and feel.)

> **TBI ALERT!** **While people with TBI are often given antidepressants and other mood-altering drugs, this is no longer considered good clinical practice. Careful monitoring by a psychiatrist who has experience in treating people with brain injuries is imperative.**

You'll want to find out as much as you can about any psychotropic drug you're prescribed. What are the benefits and side effects, and how will the drug affect your behaviour? Will it start to work immediately? Is it addictive, and will you have to increase your dosage over time? How will you be monitored while you're on the drug? What might happen if you suddenly stopped taking it or you accidentally took more than prescribed? If you forget to take a dose, what should you do? How does the drug interact with alcohol and other medications?

While psychotropic drugs are useful in treating a wide variety of symptoms, they can have disturbing side effects. You may get muscle tremors, dizzy spells, headaches, nausea, constipation, difficulty urinating, a dry mouth or a skin rash — even seizures. Your libido (or sex drive) may be reduced; you may be tired all the time; and you may have trouble concentrating. No two people react to these drugs in the same way and what works for someone else may be ineffective or harmful for you. Any negative side effects you have should be discussed with your prescribing doctor as soon as possible. You may on the wrong drug or the wrong dosage.

CAUTION! If you feel suicidal or out of control while you're on a psychotropic drug, or you're hallucinating or delusional, you need to contact your psychiatrist immediately! If she doesn't phone you back within an hour, or return less urgent calls within 24 hours, find someone more responsive to treat you.

Who Will Pay for Your Counselling?

While MSP won't cover your care when you're treated by a clinical psychologist, treatment from a psychiatrist should be covered, since a psychiatrist is a medical doctor. Unless ICBC, WCB, an extended health-care insurer or your employer will pay for a psychologist to treat you, you'll have to cover this cost yourself and try to get reimbursed later.

Psychological counselling isn't specifically mentioned as an accident benefit in the Insurance (Motor Vehicle) Act. However, ICBC should pay for this when it's part of a structured rehab program.

Before you begin treatment, try to get pre-approval from your adjuster (or rehab co-ordinator, if any) so ICBC can be billed directly. Counselling that may help you return to work or school has a good chance of being covered. While ICBC sometimes covers the cost of short-term therapy for depression, PTSD, and other trauma-related neuroses, whether they'll do this for you personally will depend on how your claim is being handled.

ICBC rarely pays for psychological counselling for people with mild brain injuries. Since early treatment of TBI is crucial, some neuropsychologists in the province will treat people on account, waiting until their insurance claims settle to bill them.

If ICBC won't pay for counselling that your doctor recommends, you may have to initiate legal action. You'll have to prove that you have a right to accident benefits; that you need the recommended treatment; and that your need for this stems from your accident. If you weren't at fault in your accident, you should receive money to cover the cost of accident-related psychological counselling as part of a claim for damages.

ICBC should also pay for counselling for members of your immediate family as part of your damages when this is needed as a direct result of your accident. Money for this purpose can be requested as part of an "in-trust claim". (See the section on other money you may be awarded in Chapter 15.)

ICBC will sometimes pay for grief counselling and treatment of depression for family members as an accident benefit when someone has catastrophic injuries or is killed in an accident.

Psychological Issues and the Legal-Insurance System

The adversarial attitude that insurers frequently take with claimants can create (or intensify) post-traumatic stress disorder. Since people with PTSD typically try to avoid situations that remind them of their accidents, they often accept inadequate compensation rather than pursuing legal action that would force them to repeatedly confront what happened. Legal action may be necessary, though, if you want your medical and rehab treatment paid, and where relevant, fair compensation for your injuries. If your case goes to trial, your lawyer can request that you be excused from testifying if your treating psychologist (or psychiatrist) feels this would be psychologically damaging. If the defence lawyer insists that you testify, he'll at least have been warned in the judge's presence to be sensitive in questioning you.

Since it's easier to prove that an auto accident has caused post-traumatic stress disorder than to prove that it's caused other psychological (or psychiatric) conditions, symptoms of other disorders are often blamed on PTSD. Only a thorough assessment by a psychologist or neuropsychologist, and a careful review of how (and when) your symptoms developed, can determine whether you have PTSD, chronic pain disorder, clinical depression, another psychological (or psychiatric) condition, or a brain injury.

Once a psychological condition becomes chronic, it may be resistant to treatment, leading to permanent disability. This can have a major effect on a claim for damages. If your case goes to court, to minimize the money ICBC has to pay you, they may try to prove that your problems don't exist, or that "even if" they do, they weren't caused by your accident — and "even if" they were, you only need short-term therapy. ICBC may argue at trial that the psychological problems you've had since your accident are the result of pre-existing issues or earlier traumas.

You'll need to make it clear to your treating psychologist (or psychiatrist) how your accident has affected earlier issues you've had. If she feels your psychological problems were caused (or aggravated) by your accident, her opinion should have more weight in court than that of an ICBC-hired expert who has had limited contact with you.

CHAPTER 6

Obtaining Financial Help

Being injured in an auto accident can place a financial burden on you and your family. While help is available through a variety of public and private sources, neither insurers nor government agencies make it easy to find out about income assistance or other benefits you may be entitled to. Legal statutes frequently change, particularly on the provincial level where there's been a steady reduction in benefits and services. By knowing what help is out there and how to get it, you should be able to manage financially even if you're out of work for a while. If you're unable to look after your own affairs, the court can appoint someone to act on your behalf or the Public Guardian and Trustee can do this.

Benefits and Compensation Through ICBC

Regardless of whether you were at fault in your accident, you may be entitled to accident benefits from ICBC. (See Chapter 10.) Among the benefits provided are medical and rehab treatment, wage-loss benefits, and death benefits. If you don't have medical insurance, your hospital bills may be paid. Ambulance services and medical supplies or equipment should be covered as well.

If you weren't at fault, you may also be entitled to compensation (or damages) from the at-fault driver, who will normally be insured by ICBC when an accident occurs in the province. (He may have other auto insurance as well.) You may be able to get an advance against your claim if you're having financial problems. Advances are usually made in relatively small amounts that won't exceed in total what your adjuster is authorized to offer you as a settlement.

Workers' Compensation Board Benefits

NOTE: Since WCB regulations constantly change, check with your union "rep", a WCB workers' adviser, or a personal injury lawyer to make sure the information in this section is current.

The Workers Compensation Act doesn't allow one worker to sue another for bodily injury. If both you and the other driver were working, you can file a WCB claim, but not a claim for damages. If only you were working and not the other driver, you can file a claim with either WCB, ICBC or both. WCB's wage replacement policy is more generous than ICBC's and you'll get better health care benefits. (ICBC won't provide you with benefits you can get from another source.) The Workers' Compensation Board has the sole right to decide whether your accident was work-related. (See Chapter 8.)

If you elect to get WCB benefits while still filing a claim for damages from an at-fault driver, the Board may place a lien on your claim to make sure they're reimbursed for the benefits they provide. The Board will only let you file a claim for damages if you do this within three months of your accident, or they grant you an extension. If you receive less money in damages than you'd have gotten in WCB benefits, the Board should make up the difference to you; you shouldn't be penalized for taking legal action against an at-fault driver. If you elect to get WCB benefits without filing a claim for damages that you're entitled to, the Board may do this on your behalf.

Most employed people in the province have WCB coverage whether they work full-time, part-time, on contract, as casual labour, or in their own business. If you're self-employed or your business isn't incorporated, you'll only be covered if you've purchased a Personal Optional Protection plan.

Before you can get benefits from WCB, you'll have to fill out an application for compensation. The application form will ask you to describe what happened and what injuries you have. If your employer wasn't notified of your accident right away, you'll have to explain why. You'll also have to provide salary and employment information, as well as the names and addresses of the doctors who have treated you, witnesses to the accident, and anyone whom you feel was at fault. If a pre-existing condition was affected by your accident, or you've made previous WCB claims, this should be noted on your form as well.

Once you've submitted an application for compensation, if you're unable to work, you'll be given a personal access number so you can check on your benefit payments. Since the Board processes around 180,000 claims a year, you may need patience and persistence in getting benefits. You should keep copies of all paperwork related to your claim, including receipts for prescriptions and other health-care benefits. You may also want to keep a record of your phone conversations and meetings with WCB staff people and health-care providers.

Unless you only have a short-term claim (three weeks or less), you may have to deal with numerous WCB staff people. If you have serious injuries, a claims adjudicator or case manager will oversee your medical-rehab team, which may include Board medical advisers and a vocational rehab consultant.

You can ask to see your WCB claims file at any time. The Board may disclose information from this to various government agencies without informing you.

Wage-loss benefits begin the first day you're unable to work after an injury. Before you can receive these benefits, the Board will have to agree that your accident was work-related and that your injuries reduce your ability to work, limiting your potential to earn income. Your doctor (or a Board medical adviser) will be asked to estimate how long it's likely to be before you recover or your condition stabilizes. She may also be asked whether a pre-existing medical condition might affect your injury, recovery process, or ability to work in the future.

WCB wage-loss benefits are based on your current average net earnings, how long you're expected to be unable to work, and how disabled you are from full-time employment. While scheduled overtime is factored into this, money deducted from your earnings for taxes, Employment Insurance (EI) and Canada Pension Plan

(CPP) contributions is excluded. (EI benefits are considered part of your earnings when you work in an occupation or industry that's seasonal or temporary.) Contributions your employer made to EI, CPP, an employee pension plan, extended health-care plan, disability plan, or life insurance plan are also excluded from your net earnings. If you're still unable to do full-time work after ten weeks, your wage-loss benefits will be adjusted to reflect your average net earnings during the 12 months prior to your accident.

WCB will pay you up to 90% of your average net earnings in wage-loss benefits. (The maximum annual earnings allowed in 2004 is $60,700.) Four types of benefits are currently available: temporary total and partial disability benefits and permanent total and partial disability awards. (Any condition that prevents you from working or limits your ability to work is considered a disability.)

Unless you have catastrophic injuries, you'll initially get temporary disability benefits. These will continue as long as you have the disability but are likely to improve. Once your condition stabilizes to the point where only minimal improvement is expected over the next year, your temporary disability benefits should be replaced by a permanent disability award.

If you're able to work but only in a reduced capacity at lower wages, you should be paid temporary partial disability benefits that are equal to 90% of the difference between your average net earnings at the time of your accident and your present average net earnings — or, a permanent partial disability award equal to 90% of the earnings that the Board estimates you'll lose according to their loss-of-function schedule. (Critics call this "the meat chart approach".) Based on where your injuries are, how severe they are, and how they affect your ability to work, a disability percentage will be assigned to you. This will then be applied to your average net pre-injury earnings to determine the size of your benefit payments. (If you're 50% disabled according to WCB's loss-of-function schedule, and your average pre-accident earnings were $900 a week, you should receive $405 a week in wage-loss benefits. Fifty percent of $900 is $450 and 90% of this is $405.)

The disability percentages in WCB's loss-of-function schedule are low: amputation of an arm is presumed to leave you 50-75%

disabled; amputation of a leg, 25-65% disabled; immobility of a lower extremity, 5-30% disabled; a compression fracture of the cervical spine, 0-4% disabled; nerve damage, 8-40% disabled; and psychological, emotional or behavioural disturbances, 0-100% disabled.[16] (The Board uses disability percentages from other jurisdictions for injuries that aren't on their loss-of-function schedule.)

Before you can receive disability benefits for a psychological condition, a Board medical adviser will have to assess you. Subjective complaints or having trouble adjusting to a new disability don't make psychological problems disabling according to the Board's standards. There has to be objective evidence that your problems are interfering with your ability to work.

A disability awards officer will use his judgment in arriving at a disability percentage he thinks is appropriate. He'll consider how impaired you are; your age; the nature of your pre-accident work; and the opinions of your doctors and Board medical advisers. Other disabilities or medical problems you have will be taken into account as well. If you were getting partial disability benefits at the time of your accident, you may be entitled to increased payments.

If the combination of your disabilities and pre-accident occupation is so unique that the Board doesn't feel their loss-of-function method will fairly compensate you, a loss-of-earnings award may be paid instead. Your wage-loss benefits should then be 90% of the difference between your average net earnings prior to your injury and your projected average net earnings in an occupation that the Board feels would be suitable for you.

You may be able to get an advance against your future benefits to pay off your debts, start a new business, or make a down payment on a home. You'll have to present the Board with a debt-repayment schedule, sound business plan, or evidence of the income you'll use for your mortgage payments. You may be given an advance to cover school costs if the Board feels that attending school would increase your job options or is therapeutically warranted. (Your advance will be discounted to a present-dollar value.)

While you'll stop getting a permanent disability award when you reach retirement age, you should receive money for your retirement. (WCB is required to put an additional 5% of each permanent disability payment they give you into a retirement account. You can also put 1 – 5% of your periodic payments in this account.) If you die before retirement age, the money that you'd have received for your retirement will be given to your heirs.

Determining the degree to which you're disabled from working, what you might have earned in the future "but for your accident", what alternative work is suitable for you, and what you might earn doing this, is open to widely varying interpretations. The Board may grossly underestimate what you should be paid. You may not agree with the disability awards officer on what your average net earnings were, nor how long you should continue to receive wage-loss benefits. It can also be hard to prove that you're totally incapable of working or that your disabilities are permanent. A personal injury lawyer can help you with these issues and advise you on whether your wage-loss benefits are fair.

Many lawyers find WCB even tougher to deal with than ICBC. Their medical advisers may make light of your injuries, encouraging you to return to work sooner than you should. You may also be accused of malingering to avoid full-time work. If you refuse treatment recommended by a Board medical adviser (or vocational retraining recommended by a Board vocational rehab consultant), your benefits will stop. They may also be suspended if you refuse to participate in a return-to-work program or you do anything that could delay your recovery. If the Board doesn't think your disabilities are as bad as you say — or they suspect that you started working without reporting this — you may be investigated for fraud.

If you're getting CPP disability benefits for the same injury that you're getting wage-loss benefits from WCB, your WCB payments will be reduced by half your CPP benefit amount. You'll have to reimburse any EI benefits that cover the same period as your WCB wage-loss benefits. Before you can get hardship assistance from the B.C. Ministry of Human Resources, you'll have to authorize WCB to pay the Ministry back, deducting this from your wage-loss benefits. If ICBC (or another auto insurer) pays you damages that cover your lost wages, WCB will be reimbursed for the wage-loss benefits they've given you before you recover any money yourself.

Health-care and related benefits: Even if you don't stop working after your accident, once WCB accepts your claim they should provide you with the health-care benefits you'll need to cure or relieve the effects of your injuries. In addition to medical, surgical, hospital and nursing care, they should pay for your rehab treatment, medical supplies, prescription drugs, home-care needs, transportation costs, and vocational retraining, as-needed. You'll normally have to reimburse them for the benefits they provide if an at-fault driver (or his insurer) pays you damages.

WCB pays health-care costs based on their contracts with professional associations. The amount they'll pay and the number of sessions they'll cover changes constantly. You'll have to pay any fees in excess of their established rates as well as user fees. If you require treatment from more than one health-care provider at a time, you'll have to get pre-approval for this.

WCB's approach to rehab is fairly aggressive and is oriented towards getting you back to work as quickly as possible. You'll need a doctor's referral for both physiotherapy and massage therapy to be covered. Only areas of your body that are part of your current claim will be treated. You don't presently need pre-approval for up to 22 office visits a week to a physiotherapist during the first six weeks after an injury, or for up to five weeks of massage therapy.[17] Pre-approval is needed for more than the established number of sessions.

If you have a soft tissue injury, healed fracture, or you're recovering from surgery, your physiotherapist is supposed to set up a work-conditioning program for you after three weeks — unless you're already undergoing active therapy with her in a pre-approved treatment plan; there's a medical reason why you can't do activities to improve your strength, endurance and mobility; or there's a valid reason why you won't be able to return to work. (WCB may directly arrange for a therapist to set up a work-conditioning program for you.)

When a work-conditioning program isn't appropriate, you may be sent for occupational therapy. Your OT will set up a return-to-work program for you and monitor your return to work.

After four weeks of chiropractic treatment, your chiropractor will have to submit a treatment plan (and return-to-work plan) to your case manager for approval. If she thinks you'll need more than eight weeks of treatment, she'll have to be able to justify this to a Board medical adviser.

You need pre-approval for up to five sessions of acupuncture over a two week period. (Additional sessions may be authorized as well.)

For psychological counselling to be paid, you'll need a referral from a WCB psychologist or clinical treatment co-ordinator. Neuropsychological counselling has to be arranged through WCB's head injury unit. If you have debilitating pain that isn't responding to traditional medical treatment, you may be sent to a chronic pain (or early pain) program at a WCB-approved clinic.

Unless you have catastrophic injuries, you'll usually be sent for vocational rehab fairly quickly if you're unlikely to be able to continue doing the same work you did prior to your accident, or your injuries place you at a long-term disadvantage to other people doing this. If you have psychological or emotional problems that prevent you from working, or you're under severe financial stress, you may also be referred to WCB's vocational rehab unit.

If you need to take time off work for medical or rehab appointments that can only be scheduled during work hours, most of the wages you lose as a result of this should be paid to you as a health-care benefit. While less than two hours of missed work at a time isn't reimbursable, once your lost hours begin to accumulate significantly you should be paid back for this. WCB will normally cover your transportation costs to medical and rehab appointments.

If you're unable to drive or use public transportation, a taxi account may be set up for you. If it isn't, you'll need prior permission for your taxi costs to be covered. Only valid dated receipts will be reimbursed. If you have to travel anywhere for an assessment or treatment, WCB should pay your travel expenses, meals, and accommodations, up to a pre-defined amount. (Your case manager can tell you what this currently is.)

If you have serious injuries, WCB may give you a personal-care (or home-maintenance) allowance so you can hire someone to help you at home, and you don't have to be hospitalized. Modifications may also be made to your home, car, or workplace to accommodate your injuries.

Funeral expenses and survivor's benefits: When someone dies in a work-related accident, his employer is expected to pay for his body to be taken to the nearest funeral home. WCB will then pay up to about $1,200 for his body to be transported elsewhere, and up to about $7,200 for funeral expenses.[18]

The Workers Compensation Act states that where two workers are married to each other, and both contribute to the support of a common household, each is deemed to be a dependant of the other. Thus, even a surviving spouse or partner who paid most of the household expenses should receive survivor's benefits. The Board will pay a dependent spouse or partner a little over $2,000 upon the deceased's death. Monthly compensation is paid as well. The amount paid is based on what the deceased's total disability award would have been if he'd lived; what his dependants receive in CPP benefits; and how many dependants he had. (This includes any child to whom he acted as a parent, including a stepchild or grandchild.) A dependent child must be under 19; under 25 and still in school; or disabled from working. When there's no surviving spouse or partner, the deceased's dependent children will receive monthly compensation.

The minimum amount that WCB currently pays to a surviving spouse or partner without dependent children is a little over $900 a month. A surviving spouse or partner with dependent children may be paid several thousand dollars a month.[19] Payments to a surviving spouse or partner continue throughout her life. The Board may provide a dependent spouse or partner with vocational counselling and job placement services.

When a deceased worker has no surviving spouse, partner or

children, a dependent parent or sibling may be eligible for survivor's benefits. In some situations, a non-dependent spouse, partner, child or parent who would have benefited financially from the deceased's life may receive survivor's benefits.

Help with legal issues: When you file a WCB claim after an auto accident in which you weren't at fault, if the Board feels that a claim for damages is worth pursuing, they'll provide you with a lawyer — or they'll piggyback on your claim if you hire your own lawyer. (You'll need their permission to do this.) If they don't feel your lawyer will protect their interests, they'll assign their own lawyer to your case. The Board will control the case and pay most of the costs involved.

If you decide not to file a claim for damages that you're entitled to, WCB may do this on your behalf. Their lawyers will handle your claim, and the Board will decide whether to accept a settlement offer or proceed to trial. Once your claim is paid out, WCB will deduct their litigation and administrative costs, as well as the cost of any benefits they've provided, and give you the remainder of the money recovered.

If you're reluctant to return to work because your wages may be garnisheed by someone to whom you owe money, you may be given free legal advice about this. If you buy a new home to accommodate your injuries, the Board may pay your legal fees, conveyance fees, and related expenses. If you can't manage your own affairs, your family may be given free legal advice about this.

Disputing a WCB decision: All Board decisions are communicated by letter and can be appealed. If you receive a letter with factual errors in it, or you don't understand why a decision was made (or you disagree with the reasons given), you can ask the person who signed the letter or his supervisor for an explanation. You can also request a formal review or appeal. While most claims disputes are initially heard by the Board's Review Division, a dispute about reopening your claim will go directly to a Workers' Compensation Appeal Tribunal, which is independent to WCB.

You'll have 90 days from the date of the disputed decision letter to send a review request to the Board's Review Division. (Extensions are sometimes granted.) A copy of the decision letter should be attached to your request form. You'll have to explain why you disagree with the decision in question and what outcome you want. If you'd prefer an oral hearing, you'll have to explain why this should be allowed. When complex medical issues are involved, this should be noted as well.

Unless you plan to represent yourself in the review process, you'll have to provide the name of the person who will represent you. (This may be a lawyer, union "rep", or other advocate.) Without a lawyer's help, it may be hard to prove that your accident was work-related, what injuries you've had, how serious they are, and what treatment you need. You'll probably want legal representation as well in a dispute about whether you're totally or permanently disabled; what kind of work is suitable for you; what disability percentage should be used in calculating your benefits; what your average pre-injury earnings were; and how long you should continue to receive benefits.

In addition to the documents and records you submit to support your position, the Review Officer may want other information. Various experts may be asked for their opinions as well. Most decisions are reached within 150 days of a review request. If your dispute is about vocational rehab benefits, the Board's refusal to pay out your pension in a lump sum, or the size of your partial disability percentage (where the allowable range is under 5%), the Review Officer's decision will be final. Other issues can be appealed to an independent Workers' Compensation Appeal Tribunal (WCAT).

You'll have 30 days from the Review Officer's decision to appeal this. You'll need to submit evidence to support your position and additional information may be gathered. If a medical issue is involved, the Appeal Tribunal may want independent medical advice, so you may be examined by a WCAT-selected health-care provider. (This won't be anyone who has treated you, nor will it be a Board medical adviser.) You'll have a chance to comment on the medical examiner's report before the Appeal Tribunal makes its decision. Most decisions are made within 180 days. At WCAT's discretion, some of your appeal expenses may be reimbursed.

Once you request a review or appeal, you should be given a copy of your claims file. Information the Board considers privileged will be deleted from this. If you want to see your claims file before deciding whether to appeal a decision, contact WCB's disclosures department.

Canada Pension Plan Benefits

If you're 18 or older (but under 65) and you've contributed to the Canada Pension Plan for four of the last six years, you'll be eligible for a CPP disability pension if you meet their disability criteria. (Your disability must be severe enough to prevent you from working regularly at any job and either be long term in nature or potentially fatal.) Your contribution years may be adjusted if you were at home raising young children under the age of seven; you have CPP credits from a former spouse or partner; or you've contributed to another country's pension plan. If you delayed applying for disability benefits and no longer meet the time requirement, you may still qualify.

On your disability application form you'll be asked to describe your work history and disabilities. CPP will want to get a medical report from your doctor, and they may ask for permission to collect information about you from various sources.

Your disability payments will be based on the size of the contributions you have made to CPP and how long you made them. (Some cost-of-living increases may apply.) Payments should begin within four months of the date that CPP agrees you qualify for benefits. Up to 12 months of back payments may be made. You may be assessed from time to time to see whether you've regained the ability to work, and vocational rehab services may be provided. (See Chapter 7.)

Once you return to work or become capable of working, CPP should be notified of this immediately. You won't lose your disability benefits if you attend school or do volunteer work as long as you let CPP know beforehand what you're doing. Your disability benefits will stop once you no longer fit CPP's disability criteria, or you reach age 65 and start getting a retirement pension.

If you're 60-65 when you first become disabled from working, you can choose to get a retirement pension or a disability pension.

While disability pensions are larger, the application process takes longer. People often apply for both pensions at the same time. If their disability pension is approved, they're reimbursed retroactively for the difference between the two pension amounts.

If you're eligible for CPP benefits, you'll have to apply for them before you can get income assistance from the B.C. Ministry of Human Resources (MHR). Since there's no limit on the assets you can have with a CPP disability pension — and you won't be disqualified from getting this if you have income from other sources, or your spouse or partner can support you — CPP benefits are preferable to those available through the provincial government. If MHR helps you out while you're waiting for your CPP benefits to begin, they'll be reimbursed directly from your benefit payments.

Survivor's benefits include death benefits, a survivor's pension, and children's benefits. To qualify for these, the deceased must have contributed to CPP for at least one-third of his contributory period, which is defined as the number of years during his lifespan in which he could have made contributions. (At least three years of contributions are required.)

CPP will pay a one-time death benefit to a qualified contributor's estate, the person responsible for his funeral expenses, his surviving spouse or partner, or his next of kin. The amount paid is the lesser of $2,500 or six months of the CPP retirement pension the deceased would have received if he'd lived.[20] A monthly pension will also be paid to a surviving spouse or partner even if they were legally separated. This is paid for life, regardless of remarriage.

While monthly pension payments to a surviving spouse or partner begin a month after the deceased's death, the first payment may not be received for a while. The size of each monthly payment will be based on how much (and for how long) the deceased contributed to CPP; how old his spouse or partner was at the time of his death; whether children's benefits are being paid; and whether his surviving spouse or partner is also getting a CPP disability or retirement pension. (When a surviving spouse or partner is under 35, not disabled, and not raising dependent children, she won't receive a survivor's pension until she turns 65 or becomes disabled.

If she's 65 or older, she'll be paid a percentage of the deceased's retirement pension amount.)

Children's benefits to a dependent child are the same whether her parent died or is disabled from working. To be eligible for this, a child has to be 18 or under, or 18-25 and a full-time student. If you're getting a CPP disability pension, your child's benefits will stop when yours do; when she's no longer in your custody or care; or when she no longer qualifies for benefits because of her age or school status.

Children's benefits aren't based on the CPP contributions her parents made. A flat rate is paid, currently $192.68 a month.[21] When both parents contributed to CPP for the required amount of time and are either deceased or disabled, a child is entitled to a monthly benefit payment for each parent.

Children's benefits for someone under 18 are paid to her parent or the person who has custody or care of her. Once she's 18, her benefit payments will go directly to her. She'll have to give CPP a signed "declaration of attendance at school or university" form to prove she's pursuing full-time studies.

Employment Insurance

If you were employed at the time of your accident and can't work as a result of your injuries, you should apply for EI sickness benefits immediately. If you were already on EI, you'll need to change your benefit classification to correspond to your new situation. This may extend the amount of time you can be on EI. If you're unable to apply for sickness benefits right away, EI may agree to backdate your claim to the date you first became incapable of working. (Waiting more than four weeks to file an EI claim may result in some loss of benefits.)

While you're on EI, any income you have (or work you do) has to be reported to them. Income that affects an EI claim includes wages and commissions, wage-loss benefits from an insurer (*except* when EI benefits were deducted from this), and retirement or pension income. CPP disability benefits, payments from a private disability insurer, retroactive salary raises, a lump-sum settlement from WCB, the reimbursement of medical and rehab expenses, *most* damages from an at-fault driver, investment income, alimony, and an inheritance aren't considered earnings for EI purposes. (Money you get for lost income as part of a claim for damages is considered earnings for EI purposes *unless* EI was taken into account in calculating the award amount. If you were unemployed when your accident happened, your damages for lost income won't be earnings for EI purposes.)

When you file a claim for accident benefits from ICBC, money you're entitled to get from EI is deducted from your total disability (wage-loss) benefits *even if you don't apply for EI*. If you start to get wage-loss benefits from WCB while you're on EI, you'll have to reimburse EI.

Application forms for EI sickness benefits are available at local Human Resources Centres of Canada (HRCC) offices throughout the province and on-line. You'll have to provide details of your latest employment earnings and submit a medical certificate from your doctor stating how long she thinks you'll be unable to work. (While there's usually a two-week waiting period before sickness benefits are paid, this is sometimes waived.)

You'll only be eligible for sickness benefits if you worked at least 600 hours during the last year (or since the start of your last EI claim) and your weekly earnings have decreased by 40% or more. Sickness benefits may be paid for up to 15 weeks, while combined sickness, maternity and parental benefits may be paid for up to 50 weeks — or in some cases, up to 65 weeks. Once you recover, if you can't find a job you may be able to get regular EI without a waiting period. How long you can be on regular EI will depend on how many hours you worked during the last year and the unemployment rate in your area.

EI's basic benefit rate is 55% of your average insured earnings over the last 26 weeks. The current weekly maximum is $413.[22] A Family Supplement will be added to your EI payments if you get a Child Tax Benefit from CCRA. (EI sickness benefits don't have to be repaid.)

You have the right to question any EI decision you feel is unfair. Meeting with an EI caseworker may clarify why the decision was made. Any new information you have can be presented at this time.

If you're not satisfied with the results of your meeting, you can file a formal appeal by writing to your local EI office to tell them what decision you disagree with and why. This must be done within 30 days of the disputed decision. Your appeal letter should mention whether you want to attend the appeal hearing. You'll also have to provide the name of the lawyer (if any) who will represent you in this action.

Four levels of appeal are presently available. These range from a review by the Board of Referees to an appeal before the Supreme Court of Canada. Since these are complicated legal processes, you'll want to consult a lawyer before proceeding. EI and HRCC offices can provide you with more information on EI appeals and benefits.

Help Through the B.C. Ministry of Human Resources

The B.C. Ministry of Human Resources (MHR) is the "payer of last resort" when all other sources of funding have been exhausted or are insufficient to meet your needs. You'll only be eligible for help from the Ministry if you've already tried to get support money from all available sources, including ICBC, WCB, CPP and EI. If the money you receive from these sources is less than the financial assistance you'd get from MHR, they may make up the difference. While you're waiting for benefits from another source to begin, you may be able to get hardship assistance from the Ministry. (This may also be available on a month-to-month basis if you're already getting income assistance and you have unexpected expenses.)

The mandate of BC Employment and Assistance (BCEA) is to get people back to work quickly so they don't need financial help. To be eligible for BCEA, you have to be a Canadian citizen or legal resident and live in the province. If you're outside B.C. for more than 30 days in a calendar year, you can only get income assistance from MHR if you got permission from them to participate in an educational program or get medical treatment outside the province. Cases of extreme hardship may also be considered. (If you're 19-24 and not disabled, you'll only be eligible for income assistance if you've lived away from your parents for two or more years.)

In exchange for receiving financial assistance from MHR, an adult under 65 without disabilities is required to actively participate in an employment plan. (A single parent with a child under 3 or one with disabilities is exempt from this requirement.) If the Ministry feels you're capable of working, you can only get income assistance for two out of five years.

If you're unable to work and you've been getting income assistance from MHR for 12 of the last 15 months, you may be eligible for a higher-than-standard support allowance — and in some cases, enhanced medical coverage — if you're considered a "person with persistent multiple barriers" to employment (PPMB). You'll have to prove that there are compelling reasons why you can't work and won't be able to in the foreseeable future, and that you've had a medical condition for at least a year that's likely to continue for two or more years. While there's no limit on how long you can get financial assistance as a PPMB, you may be assessed every two years to determine whether you still qualify.

If you're 18 or older and have a severe mental or physical impairment, you can apply for designation as a "person with disabilities" (PWD). You don't have to be on income assistance to apply for this. You'll get a more generous support allowance as a PWD than as a PPMB. You'll also be entitled to enhanced medical coverage and subsidized transportation costs. While there's no time limit on how long you can get income assistance as a PWD, whether you still qualify will be reviewed every five years. Both PWDs and PPMBs are encouraged to take advantage of MHR's employment strategies. (See Chapter 7.)

BC Employment and Assistance is based on financial need. The assets and income of everyone in your household is taken into account in determining whether you're eligible for financial help. Besides your home and a car worth under $5,000 or modified to accommodate your disabilities, you'll have to sell any assets you have in excess of the amounts below and use this to support yourself before you can get financial assistance. (Locked-in pensions and employer-sponsored RRSPs are exempt from this requirement.)

If you're single and employable, you can't have more than $1,500 in assets (or more than $150 in cash) and get income assistance. A couple with dependent children is allowed to have up to $2,500 in assets (and up to $250 in cash), while a PWD can have up to $3,000 in assets without dependent children and up to $5,000 with them. A person with disabilities can also have up to $100,000 in a trust fund that's used exclusively for disability-related expenses. (Larger amounts may be allowed with Ministry approval.)[23] As a PWD, you can also have funds to renovate your home to accommodate your disabilities without disqualifying for benefits.

Regardless of the type of financial assistance you get from MHR, you'll have to tell them when there are changes in your life — including your marital or work status, health, rent, income, assets or number of dependents — that affect the level of help you need. You'll also have to pay the Ministry back for any money they give you to tide you over while you're waiting for benefits from other sources. (WCB and CPP will reimburse MHR directly, deducting this money from their payments to you. If you file an ICBC claim, you shouldn't have to pay back money that would place you in financial hardship. If you're asked to reimburse funds you can't afford to pay back, talk to a lawyer about this.)

Before you can apply for BC Employment and Assistance, you'll have to attend an orientation session and prove that you've spent three weeks looking for work. (If you're unable to work, you'll need a letter from your doctor to be exempt from the mandatory job search requirement. You may not have to look for work if this would cause undue hardship to you and your family.) You'll be told what documents to bring to your application interview. The Ministry may confirm the information you provide before deciding whether you meet their criteria for income assistance.

A different application process is used when you apply for designation as a person with disabilities. You, your doctor, and another qualified assessor (usually a health-care provider or social worker) will have to fill out a 23-page form for the Ministry. Before filling in your section, you may want to look at the help sheet put out by the BC Coalition of People with Disabilities (BCCPD). Their checklist outlines over 100 activities of daily living to consider. Whether you can perform these activities at all, how long they take you, and whether you need to use adaptive devices or get help from someone (or a seeing eye dog), will determine whether you're designated a person with disabilities.

While you are not required to describe your disabilities on your application form, BCCPD strongly suggests that you list and explain *every disability you have, no matter how minor*. Every activity you need help with should be mentioned, even when you're not currently getting this help. If it takes you longer to recover from doing something than it would take most people, this should be noted as well.

You may want to show your doctor and the other assessor how you've filled in your section of the form before they fill in their sections. You can also photocopy their sections and fill these out the way you feel is appropriate. They can use this as a guide in understanding how your disabilities affect you on a daily basis. (BCCPD may be able to supply you with sample letters to doctors and assessors, clarifying the information needed from them.)

Most MHR decisions can be reconsidered or appealed. If you feel that a decision to deny, reduce or stop your benefits is wrong, or your PWD application is rejected, you'll have 20 business days to ask for this to be reconsidered. Reconsideration request forms are available in BCEA and MHR offices. Support letters should be included with your request. If you have new medical information about your disability, you can re-apply for PWD designation.

If you're not satisfied with the answer to your reconsideration request, you'll have seven business days to file a Notice to Proceed to Tribunal. You may want a community advocate or lawyer to represent you in this. The Tribunal panel (whose members are selected by the B.C. government) won't consider new evidence, nor will they consider whether a Ministry decision was based on an error in law. If you don't feel the Tribunal's ruling is fair, the B.C. Supreme Court can be asked to rule on this.

If you're already getting financial assistance from MHR when you appeal a Ministry decision, you should continue to receive this while waiting for the dispute to be resolved. You'll have to agree in writing to pay back any money that the court (or Tribunal) decides you're not entitled to.

Financial Help From Other Sources

You may be able to get financial help from your employer, union or professional association, a private disability insurer, a disability or fraternal group, or Veterans' Affairs, Canada. If you were injured in an accident involving an out-of-province car, the at-fault driver's insurer may offer you an advance against your claim for damages, pending the final settlement of your claim.

Wage-replacement benefits from a private disability insurer will be based on the policy terms. Money you get from CPP is normally deducted from this. (Private disability and extended health-care benefits will reduce the accident benefits you get from ICBC.)

An insurer may "subrogate" (or place a lien on) your claim for damages so they're reimbursed directly out of your award or settlement money. (When your employer paid the insurance premiums, you usually have to pay back the insurer. You may not have to do this if you paid the premiums.) As part of your damages from an at-fault driver, you should receive money to reimburse an insurer that covered your treatment and care costs or paid you wage-replacement benefits. (A person whose negligence or wrong-doing caused you harm is responsible for the economic losses you have as a result of this.)

Benefits from a private disability insurer frequently change after one year. Instead of being eligible for benefits because you can no longer work at your pre-accident job, you may only continue to receive benefits if you're totally incapable of working. How far an insurer can go in insisting that you accept a lower-paying job may have to be determined in court.

Before you apply for interim benefits from any source, you may want to discuss the potential consequences of this with a personal injury lawyer.

Help Through the Public Guardian and Trustee

The Public Guardian and Trustee of B.C. is a provincial government appointee who is accountable to the attorney general, the courts, the public, and the people he helps. His mandate is to protect the legal rights and financial interests of people who are unable to manage their own affairs. If your doctors don't think you're capable of handling your affairs and no one has an enduring power of attorney for you, the Public Guardian and Trustee will review applications to the court from anyone who wants to be appointed Committee of your estate and make a recommendation. The Public Guardian and Trustee's office or a trust company can also provide the necessary services. (See Chapter 3.)

The Public Guardian and Trustee is always involved in a personal injury case when a minor is injured in an accident. Before a settlement offer is accepted, he'll review it to make sure it's in the minor's best interests. He may also petition the court to reduce the legal fees charged by the minor's lawyer.

An insurance settlement paid to a minor in B.C. is held in trust for her by the Public Guardian and Trustee until she's 19. Funds may be released from time to time for her medical-rehab treatment, schooling or other purposes. The Public Guardian and Trustee will work with her parents or legal guardian to make sure her needs are met. (The fee charged for these services is based on the size of the minor's trust fund and the income it earns.)

CHAPTER 7

Dealing With On-going Issues

Coping with Permanent Lifestyle Changes

While a serious injury can totally change your life from one moment to the next, it can take a long time to accept what's happened. You may have to go through a grieving period to come to terms with what you've lost before you can reconcile yourself to necessary life changes.

As hard as it for most people to accept being dependent on others, if you feel guilty about needing help and resent the people who give it to you, you'll make things more difficult for everyone. Graciously accepting the help you need is something you owe to yourself and the people you care about. As time goes on, you should become increasingly more independent.

If your pre-accident career goals are no longer realistic, a vocational counsellor can help you explore and evaluate achievable new goals. Since returning to work or school can be a crucial step in regaining your self-confidence and self-esteem, you'll probably want to start moving in this direction once your recovery process no longer consumes all your time and energy.

The G.F. Strong Rehabilitation Centre in Vancouver offers in-patient and out-patient rehab treatment (and provincial-wide out-reach programs) for people with on-going disabilities. Their Adolescent and Young Adult Services program (AYA) focuses on the physical, social and emotional needs of young people (aged 12-19) with spinal cord injuries, brain injuries and congenital disabilities. An adolescent will only be enrolled in the program if she's physically capable of participating and is likely to benefit. She'll need the cognitive ability to set realistic goals for herself and the potential to develop skills to increase her independence. While some in-patient beds are available for adolescents who need daily medical management and nursing care while undergoing rehab, most AYA services are provided on an out-patient basis.

To help adolescents with disabilities move into adulthood and become independent, AYA holds workshops on topics that range from relationships and self-esteem to self-advocacy, housing, recreation, transportation, and career planning. A monthly group, Teen Scene, provides adolescents 19 and under with a chance to socialize with their peers while they learn about issues that relate to growing into adulthood with a disability.

Teen Scene for Parents offers support to the parents of adolescents with disabilities. Besides learning about available community resources, parents are offered advice on how to guide their teenagers towards a secure adult life. AYA also sponsors a Teen Independence Camp where adolescents with disabilities can learn independent living skills as they deal with special life challenges.

Living with a Spinal Cord Injury

No matter how burdensome your injury seems initially, most people with spinal cord injuries go on to lead happy, productive lives. They work as doctors, lawyers and teachers; in private businesses and government agencies. They also drive, ski, sail and climb mountains; fall in love and have children. One need only look at some prominent people with SCI to be encouraged: B.C.'s man-in-motion, Rick Hansen; cartoonist John Callagan; and "wheelchair war journalist" John Hockenberry.

This doesn't mean life will be easy for you, especially in the first few months after your accident. You may need to re-learn basic life skills, such as how to feed, dress and groom yourself. You and one or more of your relatives or friends may have to be trained in all aspects of your care from routine self-care tasks to bowel- and bladder-management, mobility issues, and wheelchair transfers. As you're mastering these complex skills, your social and cognitive abilities will be addressed as well.

If you're 18 or older, once your medical problems are stable enough to be manageable in a rehab centre, you may be admitted to G.F. Strong's Spinal Cord Injury Program — unless the specialized services you need are available closer to your home. A doctor's referral is needed for this. You'll have to be capable of actively participating in the program and be likely to benefit from it. You won't be admitted if you have acute psychiatric problems or significant cognitive deficits. (Past disruptive behaviour won't disqualify you from the program, but you'll have to agree to follow a pre-arranged behavioural management plan.) Funding for the program has to be pre-arranged. While your basic daily costs may be covered by MSP, your on-going expenses for equipment and supplies will have to come from elsewhere, possibly ICBC (or WCB). Before you start the program, you'll have to know where you're going when you're discharged. (People can also participate on an out-patient basis.)

G.F. Strong sponsors workshops for people with SCI who are no longer in residential rehab and for their relatives and friends. Workshops cover everything from physical issues and the latest medical research to housing options, community resources, coping skills, and managing attendant-care employees. There are also peer group social gatherings for people with SCI and support groups for family members.

The BC Paraplegic Association's peer support program links people who have spinal cord injuries with role models and mentors during the early stages of an injury and later on. BCPA also hosts social gatherings and offers support to adolescents with SCI and their families.

After months in the hospital and residential rehab, the thought of leaving may be very threatening. Not only have your surroundings become familiar by now, you've had a chance to bond with other people with similar injuries. The staff has been there to guide and support you, making sure your needs are met. Your value as a human being has never been in question: you and the other patients have been the focus of everyone's attention and concerns. To be thrust out into the world-at-large again takes tremendous courage.

In most cases, you'll be with an attendant the first time you leave the confines of the rehab centre. As you gradually begin to function in the outside world by participating in social and recreational activities, you'll have a new set of realities to face. You may find many able-bodied people cruel and insensitive, even when they don't mean to be.

Once you're discharged from residential rehab, you may live with your family or go into an independent living situation. While you're struggling with your ability to perform everyday tasks on your own, you may have to deal with financial worries, family and sexual issues, bladder and bowel problems, and chronic pain. This is bound to take an emotional toll on you no matter how well-adjusted you were in the rehab centre. The consequences of never being able to walk again (if this is your situation) may make you angry with yourself, your doctors and the people close to you, and negative to the world around you. It may feel as if your current problems will never end, and you'll always be a burden to others.

You can reduce your stress and minimize the pressure you place on yourself and others by concentrating on what's important to you and letting other people handle the rest. Having someone help you bathe or dress in the morning will give you more time to spend on your education, career or family. You're not giving up control of your life by getting help from others; you're gaining the freedom and flexibility to pursue your own interests and become more independent. While ICBC (or WCB) may cover the cost of a personal-care attendant for a while, if you start working you'll be able to pay for this yourself. Once you decide what your priorities are you should focus on these — even if it means that you'll need more help from others than you would by leading a more restricted life.

Social isolation can become a problem after you leave residential rehab. The need for special transportation may limit where you can go and when, and you may find many supposedly accessible places (including public bathrooms) too poorly designed to use. If you need to use adaptive devices for eating or drinking, you may be embarrassed to do this in public at first and avoid these situations. You may continually think that people are staring at you even when they're not, and find it equally as disturbing when able-bodied people seem to look right past you as if you're not there. As overwhelming as these obstacles may seem, you'll gradually become more comfortable in your interactions with the world as you start getting around more on your own.

Being in a wheelchair shouldn't interfere with your relationships with the people you're close to. If you have young children at home, though, you may need to help them understand that your wheelchair isn't you; you're still the same loving parent you always were. The more you accept your own situation, the less anxious they're apt to be. You should be honest and up front with your children, discussing what's happening in terms they can understand. They may need frequent reassurances from you that things will get better and easier over time. By acknowledging and accepting the problems they're having adjusting to your disabilities, you can help them learn to accept the changes in their lives, and the changes in you.

A catastrophic injury affects everyone in the family. Like it or not, you're all in this together. As hard as your own daily struggles are, you need to make sure your children's emotional and practical needs are met. Encourage them to maintain as normal a routine as possible, while teaching them to perform tasks for themselves that you can no longer do. Try not to absent yourself from their lives: talk to them, laugh and play with them, read to them, help them with their homework, watch TV together. If they're angry at you, let them express this without judging them for it even if you feel hurt by it. If their hostility continues, individual or family counselling may be warranted.

While most SCI survivors now live near-normal lifespans, they tend to have more health problems than other people and get age-related conditions earlier. The most common health problems are pneumonia, hypertension, osteoporosis, arthritis, high cholesterol, diabetes and thyroid disorders. Being dependent on a wheelchair can cause muscle weakness and atrophy, as well as serious skin conditions. Age-related vision and hearing losses can be particularly devastating when your ability to interact with the world is already compromised.

Many alternative therapies have been helpful to people with SCI: Cranio-sacral therapy improves motor functions, bowel and bladder control, spasticity, and overall well-being. Therapeutic touch decreases anxiety and pain, and releases blocked energy, promoting healing. Rolfing releases restrictions in the connective tissues around the muscles, reducing body tension and muscular pain. *Qi-gong* exercises stimulate the *qi* ("chee") or life energy flowing through the body, improving health and restoring balance and harmony in the body and mind. Homeopathy often reduces the need for harmful medications.

More traditional therapies may be helpful as well. Massage therapy can provide temporary relief of spasticity, increase circulation, and eliminate constipation; while acupuncture can reduce spasticity, improve functional abilities, and help with everything from digestive and respiratory problems to sexual and emotional problems.

Excessive weight gain is often a problem after a spinal cord injury. Much of the muscle tissue below the level of your injury is replaced by fat, your metabolism slows down, and you're less active, burning fewer calories. Besides the normal health hazards that come from being overweight, enormous stress will be placed on your arms and shoulders as you use your arms for mobility and wheelchair transfers. The heavier you are, the more intense shoulder pain you're apt to have. You'll also get more pressure sores, and lifting or transferring you may cause back problems for the people helping you. To control your weight, you'll have to substantially reduce your food intake and exercise regularly.

The importance of daily exercise for anyone who spends a lot of time in a wheelchair can't be emphasized enough. While the level of your injury will determine what you're capable of doing to a large degree, persistence in pursuing an appropriate exercise program should improve your health and give you a sense of well-being and accomplishment. *Qi-gong* exercises, aquatic activities and wheelchair sports can be both helpful and fun to do. At recreational facilities and community centres throughout the province, you can train and participate in team sports. (Many of these facilities have special rates for low income people with disabilities.)

Regardless of how much exercise you get and how diligently you look after your health, you may need more help from others as you grow older. You may have to hire a personal-care attendant for the first time in many years or increase how often you have one. This doesn't mean you'll have to give up your independence. A motorized wheelchair (or a van with an electrically-operated lift) can increase your mobility and give you greater access to the things that interest you. By taking advantage of new adaptive technology that comes along, you'll make life easier for yourself and your caregivers.

If you slip through the cracks in the medical-legal-insurance system and don't get the help you need from MSP, ICBC, WCB or a private disability insurer, the BC Paraplegic Association may be able to loan you a wheelchair, scooter, bath bench or other equipment. They may also be able to co-ordinate your rehab treatment and assist you in returning to the world-at-large and living an independent life. In addition to rehab counselling, vocational and employment services, and peer support for you and your family, BCPA offers scholarships and bursaries to help people with SCI attend post-secondary schools.

Recognizing Brain Injury Symptoms

Not everyone who has a traumatic brain injury realizes it. If you recognize yourself in the TBI symptoms below — or other people are aware of you having these problems — you should be assessed by a neuropsychologist to see whether you require treatment. Check with a personal injury lawyer first to make sure the person who assesses you isn't someone that ICBC, WCB and other insurers rely on for expert opinion. (See Chapter 11.)

Common physical problems after a brain injury include insomnia and excessive fatigue, lack of stamina, muscle weakness, headaches, dizziness, light-headedness, problems with co-ordination and balance, numbness or tingling in the limbs, blurred vision, ringing in the ears, sensitivity to light and sound, and changes in taste or smell. Seizures that occur shortly after an accident are less cause for concern than seizures that start several months later. In either situation, a thorough neurological exam should be done as soon as possible. (After a mild brain injury, you're no more at risk of having seizures than the general public.)

Cognitive changes after a brain injury include short-term memory problems, a short attention span, and difficulty concentrating. You may forget people's names, appointments, where you put things, where you're going, and what you've read, heard or been told. You may also get lost frequently and constantly feel confused, wondering why you're doing something. At the same time, you may be prone to extreme perseverance, remaining fixated on a single thought or idea long past the point where this is reasonable.

While your general intelligence might not change, it may be hard for you to follow directions, conceptualize, understand abstractions and generalizations, retrieve information from your memory, integrate new information, keep track of details, and plan, organize or initiate tasks. You may be easily distracted and incapable of doing one thing while thinking about something else, especially when tired or over-stimulated. It may be hard to complete tasks or follow through on your responsibilities due to an inability to make decisions, work under time pressure, or keep track of multiple demands on your attention. Meanwhile, word-finding problems and a tendency to confuse one word with another may make it hard for you to express yourself or understand what people are saying (or what you read).

Behavioural symptoms after a brain injury may include mood swings, emotional outbursts, irritability, compulsive talking, selfishness, inflexibility, and apathy. Negative behaviour patterns from the past may become exaggerated. You may be impulsive and get angry quickly, getting into frequent fights. You may also react inappropriately to situations, laughing, crying or losing your temper for no apparent reason. Often bewildered or disoriented, you may find it hard to accept change or keep up in social situations. Inadequate coping strategies, poor judgment and a low tolerance for frustration may make you lose confidence in yourself and develop a negative self-image.

Hypersensitive to criticism, your feelings may easily be hurt. At the same time, you may be insensitive to other people's feelings. Despite an increased dependency on others, you may feel emotionally detached, isolating yourself from family and friends. You may also lack initiative, becoming passive and withdrawn, or you may feverishly try to accomplish tasks that are beyond your current capabilities. Unable to achieve goals that are no longer realistic, you may quit your job and refuse to help out at home or participate in social or recreational activities. Your automatic pilot (the brain function that monitors and handles over-learned tasks) may no longer function properly, making it unsafe for you to drive, cook, or do other activities that most people take for granted. An inability to self-monitor your actions can also lead to substance abuse and inappropriate sexual behaviour.

The psychological effects of a brain injury can be pronounced as well. An inability to cope with stress, coupled with problems caused by behavioural and cognitive deficits, may make you clinically depressed even if you're not aware of this. You may develop anxiety (or panic) disorder; feel emotionally vulnerable and unsure of yourself; and in some cases, be misdiagnosed with psychiatric problems or believed to be malingering.

Living with TBI

How a brain injury affects you will depend on how widespread or focused it is, where it is in your brain, and how severe it is. Since lack of insight is common in people with TBI, you may not be aware of changes in your behaviour, emotional responses or thinking processes that are obvious to others. While other people may feel that you've become a different person since your accident, you may not see this yourself, blaming your problems on external causes.

There's nothing demeaning about having damaged your brain. It can be an enormous relief, in fact, to finally recognize brain injury symptoms for what they are. You haven't gone crazy: the problems you've been having since your accident are the result of physical changes to your brain. Once you accept this, you can begin to get treatment to overcome your deficits. While most TBI symptoms disappear within six months — and the majority of people with mild-to-moderate brain injuries fully recover within two years — even a brief disruption in normal brain functioning can leave you with some permanent impairment, especially when your symptoms persist for over a year. This being said, with proper treatment there may be improvements even ten years after an injury.

The sooner you receive treatment, the more likely it is that you'll eventually return to your previous functioning level or something close to it. Psychological counselling, cognitive-behavioural therapy, life-skills training, and speech-language therapy, when relevant, can help you lead an independent life without undue stress or frustration, while S.O.I.[24] skill training can help strengthen the cognitive areas you're weakest in. It may always take longer to accomplish tasks than it used to, but in most cases you can learn compensatory techniques to function effectively.

While you may be most disturbed by your physical and cognitive problems, your family, friends and co-workers are likely to be more upset by your behaviour, losing hope as time goes on that you'll improve. A neuropsychologist can help your family learn to cope with changes in your personality and behaviour, while an occupational therapist can work with your employer and co-workers to help minimize on-the-job stress.

G.F. Strong's Acquired Brain Injury Program provides rehab to people with TBI (and stroke survivors) on an in-patient, out-patient and outreach basis. (You have to be over 18 to eligible for this.) Both assessment and treatment are available, and a doctor's referral is needed. The rehab services you'll receive will be oriented towards your individual needs and goals. If your goals can be achieved at home or in your local community, your caregivers will be given guidance on how to help you. (Educational workshops and support groups for family members and friends are also offered.)

Chronic Pain and Fatigue

If you still have chronic debilitating pain six to eight months after your accident, ICBC (or WCB) may send you to a pain-management program if they feel this might help you return to work or school, or function more effectively when you're there.

Chronic pain, fibromyalgia (a specific type of chronic pain) and chronic fatigue can all lead to permanent disability. While doctors and insurers often consider these conditions psychological, medical websites devoted to them offer compelling evidence that this isn't the case. If your family doctor can't refer you to a physiatrist, rheumatologist or other medical specialist who routinely treats people with these conditions, contact MEFM[25] (an advocacy support group for people with chronic fatigue and fibromyalgia) and see if they can suggest someone.

Psychological interventions such as EMDR, and body-mind approaches such as yoga, meditation, hypnosis and biofeedback, are sometimes effective in treating chronic pain. Massage therapy can relieve the pain caused by musculoskeletal conditions, while other traditional and alternative therapies work directly on reducing the underlying causes of pain. Sleeping well is essential for anyone with fibromyalgia, and sleep medication may be prescribed.

Since chronic fatigue can be hard to treat effectively, you'll have to work closely with your doctors and rehab therapists on this.

Sexual and Reproductive Issues

Adolescents and young adults with catastrophic injuries need to be reassured early on that they can have active rewarding sex lives, and in most cases, have children. The Sexual Health Services unit at G.F. Strong is open to anyone having trouble with sexual issues after an injury, including an injured person's spouse or partner. A doctor's referral is needed.

Your sexual possibilities may be limited more by insecurity and a poor self-image than by your injuries. Psycho-sexual counselling can help you regain your self-esteem and self-confidence. Your body has caused you enough pain; you're entitled to get some pleasure from it as well. Sexual contact with someone you love can help heal your body, mind and spirit. (See Ken Knoll's and Erica Levy Klein's wonderful book, "Enabling Romance: A Guide to Love, Sex and Relationships for the Disabled (and the people who care about them)".)

Spinal cord injuries: Some sexual dysfunction usually occurs with SCI, but sexual desire itself is rarely affected. While sexual frequency may decrease, people with spinal cord injuries not only report having good sex lives, both they and their partners often feel that they've become more sensitive, caring lovers.

Your ability to be sexually satisfied after a spinal cord injury may be related less to the level of your injury than to how knowledgeable you are about sex and how openly you communicate with your partner. How much time has passed since you were injured may also affect how well-adjusted you are to changes in your sexual responses. (Sexual counselling is available in most rehab centres.)

If sex is important to you, you'll want to learn as much as you can about it. Besides being open to experimenting with new techniques, you'll have to be able to communicate your needs and feelings freely to your partner and be sensitive to his (or her) needs and feelings. While it may take longer to have sex after a spinal cord injury and intercourse may not always be involved, this can increase the pleasure of you and your partner. You'll have to be more adventurous in your sexual relations than you might have been otherwise, and more knowledgeable about sex, but this will make you a better lover.

If your sexual partner is your primary caregiver, you may want to keep these roles as separate and distinct as your situation allows. If you can afford to hire a personal-care attendant to take care of your non-sexual bodily needs, your sexual partner won't have to do this. (You can request funds for the lifelong cost of a personal-care attendant for this purpose as part of a claim for damages.)

> **CAUTION! Autonomic dysreflexia (AD) can occur after a spinal cord injury when your body is excessively stimulated below the level of your injury. Intense sexual excitement, severe pain or an overfull bladder can trigger this. Symptoms to watch for include a sudden sharp headache, stuffy nose, flushing or sweating. You need to stop what you're doing immediately. AD can lead to a seizure, stroke, or death.**

While a woman's ability to conceive usually resumes within a few months after a spinal cord injury, certain problems may arise with pregnancy and childbirth. The most serious of these is the possibility of AD occurring during labour. Other common problems for pregnant women with SCI include anemia, recurrent urinary tract infections, and severe pressure sores. Weight gain during pregnancy can make wheelchair transfers very difficult as the baby's due date approaches.

For both psychological and practical reasons, you'll want to use an obstetrician who is familiar with the issues that pregnant women with SCI face. The UBC School of Nursing runs child-bearing and parenting programs for people with disabilities. Similar classes may be available elsewhere as well.

When a man's fertility is affected by SCI, the conception methods used at fertility clinics with able-bodied men can usually be used, with the same expected success rate.

Traumatic brain injuries: A variety of sexual problems can occur after a brain injury. While some people with TBI have increased sex drives, a reduced libido is more common. Your ability to respond sexually may be diminished by your injury, medication, or psychological issues. Your doctor may suggest psycho-sexual counselling or prescribe medication.

The greatest concern after a brain injury is the possibility of irresponsible sexual behaviour occuring, which may include perverse or impulsive acts such as molestation or public masturbation. If your judgment or ability to think clearly is impaired, or you've lost the capacity to self-monitor your actions, you may not pay enough attention to where, when, how and with whom sexual behaviour is appropriate.

WARNING! If you begin to have improper sexual thoughts or feelings, or your sexual behaviour is inappropriate, you need to get professional help immediately. Disturbing sexual behaviour can escalate rapidly after a brain injury, resulting in physical (or psychological) harm to you or others, and your arrest as a sex offender.

❖

Issues for Caregivers

As the primary caregiver of someone with a catastrophic injury, you'll need to make sure you have the information to do this properly, and you're well-trained in all necessary procedures. You'll also need to be realistic about what you can (and can't) do. While your injured relative or friend may need help with legal, financial and insurance issues, as well as with his personal care — and he may need to be continually reminded to keep his medical and rehab appointments and do his exercises — you don't have to be personally responsible for all this; other people can be asked to help. You should also arrange to have someone take over for you for a few hours each day so you can take breaks. (Respite care is available through government and community agencies.)

Unless you take care of yourself and look after your own needs, you won't be able to take care of the injured person. Since full-time caregivers are very susceptible to colds, infections, the flu and other health problems, you need to make sure you get enough rest and eat properly. While you're taking your daily breaks, you should try to pursue activities you enjoy. You need to have something fulfilling in your life that sustains you, and distracts you from your responsibilities.

You may want to speak to a psychologist about the problems you're facing and the strain of being a full-time caregiver. A health-care provider who is working with your injured relative or friend may be open to you talking to her about your own issues. The BC Paraplegic Association or the BC Coalition of People with Disabilities may be able to suggest a caregiver support group in your area. Having a nurturing support system in place can be vital to your emotional well-being.

As the injured person's primary caregiver, you may become the focus of his anger and hostility. It may be hard for you to say "no" to him, even when his demands are selfish, irrational, or beyond your capabilities. No matter how much you do for him, neither you nor he may feel it's enough. This can result in you feeling overwhelmed and unappreciated, and angry at not having enough time for yourself or others, including your children. The younger the injured person is, the more burdened you may feel, wondering whether this is what the rest of your life will be like — and, if so, how you'll manage.

Finding something to laugh about every day with the injured person will lighten both your loads and tighten the bonds between you. Meditating or practicing relaxation techniques, either alone or together, can also relieve tension and stress. As hard as this may be to do, you need to look beyond the injured person's disabilities sometimes and see him as someone you cherish, remembering why you're doing what you're doing: because you care. The person you loved before still exists and needs your love now more than ever, no matter how difficult he is or how hard your life is. Be assured: it *will* get easier over time. Not only do people with catastrophic injuries go on to lead happy lives, so do their caregivers.

As someone's primary caregiver, you may want to draw up a Will to provide for his care if he outlives you. (See Chapter 20.)

Returning to Work

Unless you have serious injuries, you may be able to do selective light work at your place of employment while you're recovering. If your company doesn't have a return-to-work program, it may be possible to modify your normal work tasks to accommodate your injuries. If necessary, you may be assigned new duties for a while or given shorter working hours. Your doctor will have to verify that it's safe to do the work you're given in your present condition. If you don't feel you can do assigned tasks safely, discuss this with your doctor and employer. ICBC or WCB may arrange for an occupational therapist (or OT) to assist your employer in creating a suitable work situation for you.

After a serious injury, once you're able to perform daily life skills with ease, an OT can teach you how to carry out your responsibilities at work in a simulated work situation. You may also be given on-the-job supervision and training. While your OT's emphasis will be on raising your performance level, she may address the psychosocial aspects of your return to work as well. If accident-related psychological problems are interfering with your ability to work, either ICBC, WCB or your employer may pay for short-term counselling.

While many people with disabilities hold responsible, high-paying jobs, your physical limitations and other problems may prevent you from doing the same work you did prior to your accident. Your career options may have to be re-evaluated and new possibilities explored.

After a spinal cord injury, it may take several years to return to work. While people with SCI work in all kinds of jobs and professions, often excelling at them, only 30% of quadriplegics (and 40% of paraplegics) eventually return to full-time employment.[26] These percentages are increasing as government agencies and private businesses become more willing to modify worksites for people with disabilities.

While most people with mild brain injuries are able to return to work within three months — and half of those with moderate-to-severe TBI resume working in a little over two years — many of these people are given reduced responsibilities with little opportunity for advancement. Less than half of all TBI survivors hold on to their jobs for any length of time.[27] Once they're fired, they're unlikely to ever work again, making them dependent on their families or government subsidies — unless a claim for damages is large enough to financially support them.

The more highly skilled your pre-accident work was, the more difficult it may be to do after a brain injury. While some TBI survivors have re-entered the workforce for the first time after ten (or more) years, you're likely to find that returning to work becomes harder to do as time goes on. Potential employers may be reluctant to hire you, while you may not have the self-confidence needed to get (and hold) a job. Part-time employment, further schooling, and volunteer work may help you eventually find full-time work.

Family, friends, insurers and government agencies often encourage people with brain injuries to take menial or low-level jobs. This seldom works out well. TBI survivors tend to have less tolerance for tedious work than other people; they frustrate more easily; and they have a hard time following directions and functioning in busy environments. Moreover, they can't always monitor what they're doing well enough to know whether their work is progressing. They may also react negatively to advice or criticism. Emotional outbursts and altered social skills, in fact, are said to cause more job dismissals than long-term cognitive deficits.

If you have a brain injury, you should be assigned work tasks that won't frustrate you. You may also need a work environment that isn't too distracting or stressful. An occupational therapist can advise your employer on how to modify your work responsibilities and worksite. She can also help your co-workers understand your limitations and how to work with you most effectively.

The effect of returning to work on benefits from various sources: If you're able to return to work, but only in a diminished capacity at lower wages, any income you earn above $75 a week will be deducted from your *ICBC* wage-loss benefits. If you file a *WCB* claim and can only work in a diminished capacity at lower wages, you may be paid up to 90% of your net income losses in wage-loss benefits. If you return to work while getting a *CPP* disability pension, you'll have to repay any pension payments you get while working. Any employment income you earn while you're on *EI* will be deducted from your EI benefits. You can earn up to $400 a month without your *MHR* disability benefits being reduced. If you're on regular income assistance from MHR, any money you earn will be deducted from your payments. (See Chapter 6.)

Vocational Counselling and Retraining

Since insurers have a vested interest in claimants returning to work, they often pay for vocational counselling, re-education and retraining. If you can no longer do the work you did prior to your accident, a vocational counsellor can assess your current capabilities. When you're unlikely to be able to return to your pre-accident employment, alternative career choices may be suggested and you may be encouraged to enter a retraining program to develop new skills. (If you were unemployed at the time of your accident but intended to work in the future, a vocational counsellor can guide you towards a career that interests you and you can handle.)

ICBC prefers claimants to return to their original jobs after an accident even when this means doing alternative work. If you'll need retraining due to your injuries, this may be provided as an accident benefit. If you refuse to participate in a retraining program that an ICBC vocational adviser recommends, your accident benefits may stop. A recommended program should take your pre-injury occupation and present capabilities into account and be reasonably likely to return you to your pre-accident income level. When this is unrealistic, a recommended program should at least improve your earnings capacity and increase your independence. You'll normally continue to get wage-loss benefits while you're taking a retraining program or attending school. Job placement assistance may be provided as well.

WCB may begin their vocational rehab efforts once it's clear that you'll need help returning to work. You may be put into a work-conditioning program or provided with skill upgrading and refresher courses.

Whenever possible, the Workers' Compensation Board prefers people to return to their pre-accident jobs. If your company has a return-to-work program that your doctor feels you can handle, you'll be expected to comply with this. When selective light employment isn't available, WCB may have a work assessment done to determine your capabilities. (Assessments done prior to full recovery are usually part of a graduated return-to-work program.)

If you can't continue in your pre-accident job, WCB's next preference is for your company to find alternative work for you. Once your capabilities are assessed, the Board will consult with you, your employer, union "rep", doctors and other health-care providers to see whether your work responsibilities and worksite can be modified to accommodate your injuries. The Board may provide financial assistance for special equipment and site modifications. They may also help you acquire new skills and subsidize you while you get on-the-job training. You should be paid the same wages during your training period as you earned prior to your accident.

If your company can't find meaningful work for you in your present condition, a WCB vocational rehab consultant can help you explore other options in the same (or a related) field, where your existing job skills can be used. Along with job search assistance and other return-to-work support, you may be given individual or group counselling to motivate you and help you set appropriate goals. You may also be referred to private or government employment services and taught strategies to help you market yourself to prospective employers. While you're looking for a job or waiting to start a job you were offered, the Board may help you out financially. If a job requires you to relocate, reasonable moving expenses may be paid.

When there's no suitable work available in your field or a related one, a WCB vocational rehab consultant will help you find work in other fields that interest you. If you lack the skills to find a job, you may be put into a retraining program. Once you've completed your training, you should be given the other assistance noted.

Formal training to upgrade your qualifications and provide you with new work skills can take place at any time during the vocational rehab process. To improve your long-term employability and earnings potential, you may be trained in a trade or enrolled in a technical or academic program. Your interests, aptitudes, capabilities, and educational readiness will first be assessed to make sure you can benefit from this. Medical or rehab treatment you're undergoing or may need in the future will be taken into account as well. While you're enrolled in a full-time program, WCB may cover the cost of your tuition, books, equipment, and travel expenses. You should also receive an allowance equal to what you'd have gotten in wage-loss benefits. If you don't attend classes regularly or do well in them, WCB may stop paying for your continued participation. Should this happen, you'll normally be given job search assistance.

WCB won't help you change careers or undergo training that you'd intended to do anyway. However, they may cover part of your expenses if you want to participate in a program that's only partially related to your injuries, or is more expensive (or time-consuming) than needed for you to find work at your pre-accident income level. After the Board estimates what it would cost them to help you return to your previous income level, they may apply this towards the program you want to do. They may also help you start a new business or improve one you own, but they won't spend more money on this than they would for you to participate in a program to overcome the effects of your injuries.

If you have catastrophic injuries, WCB may pay for training or education to enhance your quality of life, even if this won't raise your income, or it goes beyond what's needed to return you to your earlier income level. They may also help your spouse, partner or another dependant find meaningful work.

If your spouse or partner is killed in a work-related accident and you weren't employed at the time, or your financial prospects are limited, WCB may provide you with job training to reduce the financial burdens on you and your family. (As a dependent spouse or partner of a deceased worker, you're not expected to use your survivor's benefits to upgrade your skills or education.) The Board may pay your tuition, book and material fees, as well as education-related travel expenses and child-care costs. You'll be expected to use your WCB (and other) pensions to cover your living expenses.

CPP provides vocational rehab to select CPP disability (CPPD) clients. If your medical condition is stable, you want to work, and your doctor agrees that it's all right to do this, you may be referred to a vocational rehab specialist in your community. She'll consult with you and your doctors in designing a return-to-work plan for you. Once your job skills and educational level have been assessed, you'll be helped to identify your needs, explore appropriate work goals, and figure out what work skills are currently in demand. If your education or skills have to be upgraded to find a job, CPP may cover this cost.

Once you've completed your skill upgrading or retraining, a vocational rehab specialist can help you develop job search skills, including how to prepare a resume, identify suitable companies, and locate available jobs. You may also practice interview techniques, and self-employment options may be explored.

Your CPP disability benefits should continue while you're participating in a vocational rehab program or looking for a job. Once you find work, you'll continue to get benefits for another three months. If you can't find a job, your disability benefits will stop at the end of the job search period. (Since you should be capable of working now, you'll no longer qualify for disability benefits.) If you have to stop work due to the same condition for which you'd gotten disability benefits, you should to able to get your benefits quickly reinstated if you meet CPP's disability criteria.

If you're on ***EI*** but you're capable of working, you'll be expected to look for a job. Various job search programs are available through local EI and HRCC offices. Some career counselling and education grants may also be available.

Human Resources and Skills Development Canada (HRSDC) co-sponsors a career centre with the BC Paraplegic Association. To qualify for this, you have to have a physical disability that makes it hard to find a job, be fluent in English, motivated to work, and able to travel to the BCPA offices in Vancouver to work with employment counsellors. You may also be referred directly to potential employers. BCPA's employment program has an extensive library of job search material and labour market information, and it's hooked up to HRSDC's national job bank resources. You may be taught basic computer skills and given technical computer support. You'll also have access to the internet, fax machines, phones and photocopiers. If you need funding for a training program or special equipment, or assistance making a worksite accessible, BCPA may be able to help with this.

Everyone who gets financial help from BC Employment and Assistance (BCEA) is encouraged to take advantage of ***MHR***'s employment programs. These are available at Employment and Assistance Centres throughout the province. You'll continue to get income assistance or disability benefits while participating in these programs. MHR may also cover part of your transportation and child-care costs. If a job requires you to re-locate, moving expenses may be covered.

The mandate of the Employment Strategy for People with Disabilities (ESPD) program is to help people who are getting MHR disability benefits gain the skills needed to find full-time employment. Once your capabilities are assessed, ESPD will help you identify appropriate career goals and develop a plan to reach these goals. If you're interested in self-employment, you may be referred to local organizations that can help with this.

To make it financially worthwhile for a company to hire you despite the expense of accommodating your disabilities, ESPD will try to give you a competitive edge over other people applying for the same job. You may be given on-the-job training, or short-term training in specific skills currently in demand. In some cases, you may be assigned a mentor who will work with you and advise you. You may also be given direct referrals to companies with job openings.

As an MHR disability client, you'll usually do volunteer work initially with a government or not-for-profit agency. This may help you move into part-time paid employment and eventually full-time work. ESPD will make sure that modifications to your worksite are made when needed and feasible. Adaptive furniture, technical aids, and customized computer software may be provided. Follow-up support may be given if you'll need extra time or help accomplishing assigned work tasks.

You'll be allowed to keep your PWD designation and enhanced medical coverage once you find a job. If your income level falls below what you'd get in disability benefits if you weren't working, MHR should make up the difference; you shouldn't be penalized for having a job. If you have to stop work for any reason, your full disability benefits should be immediately reinstated.

Vocational Rehabilitation Services (VRS) works with B.C. residents (16 or older) who have a permanent disability that hinders them from working. VRS offers access to training programs that prepare people for paid employment. They work with the institutes that provide this training to see that help is available when needed. Employment and Assistance Centres throughout the province, and community-based service providers under contract to MHR, provide all services. You don't have to be getting income assistance or disability benefits from MHR to be eligible for this. You'll first be assessed to make sure you have the potential to benefit from the services offered. Your doctor will also have to provide a medical assessment.

VRS offers vocational counselling, career planning, specific skill training and on-the-job training as well as educational help. Technical aids and disability-related goods and services may be available. Once you find a job, VRS will work with your employer to make sure your work experience is positive.

Advocacy support groups such as the BC Paraplegic Association and the BC Coalition of People with Disabilities can be contacted for information about vocational counselling and job search support for people with disabilities.

Education

When you enroll in an educational program that's oriented towards helping you find paid employment, your school tuition and related expenses may be paid in whole or part by ICBC, WCB, CPP or MHR.

If a permanent disability limits you from full participation in post-secondary school or the work force, you may be eligible for a Canada Study Grant of up to $5,000 a year to help pay education-related costs associated with your disability. (Canada Study Grants in lower amounts are available to students without disabilities who have dependants or are in financial need.)

VRS will work with your post-secondary or other educational institute to see that you get the help you need while you're in school. Loans and grants may be given as well as funds for tuition, books, transportation, and other education-related expenses, including attendant care and modifications to your classroom or car. You'll also have access to adaptive technical aids and equipment.

After a spinal cord injury, you're much more likely to be employed if you have a post-secondary degree. Most colleges, universities, and technical schools in the province have disability offices to assist students. You may be eligible for a scholarship or bursary from the BC Paraplegic Association if you live in the province, attend a post-secondary school here, and have a physical disability.

If you have catastrophic injuries, ICBC (or WCB) may pay for you to continue your education, even when this won't help you find a job, if they feel it's important for your psychological well-being and will increase your self-esteem. (You can request money for this as part of a claim for damages.)

If a disability prevents you from repaying your student loans, the BC Coalition of People with Disabilities can advise you on how to apply for loan forgiveness.

The G.F. Strong school program plays an integral role in the rehab process of adolescents in the province with spinal cord injuries, brain injuries and congenital disabilities. The program is funded by the B.C. Ministry of Education and run in partnership with the Vancouver School Board. Its goal is to help adolescents (under 19) with disabilities continue their secondary school education. Existing school programs may be revised to fit a student's needs.

Once an adolescent with a brain injury is assessed, she may be given remedial work to do. An adolescent with a spinal cord injury may take regular school courses or go into a long-distance educational program. Contact with her local school will be on-going while she's in rehab and an effort will be made to design an appropriate school program so she can eventually return to her local school. Both school accessibility and adaptive technology will be addressed. (The G.F. Strong school program also offers outreach educational workshops for family, friends and school staff.)

The Community Brain Injury Program for Children and Youth (CBICY) is part of the Vancouver School Board's Special Education services. It's run in partnership with provincial medical and rehab facilities, including G.F. Strong, Children's Hospital, Sunny Hill, and regional health authorities. Minors under the age of 19 with traumatic (or acquired) brain injuries, who aren't getting support services through ICBC or another third-party insurer, are given help after they leave the hospital (or residential rehab) and return to their local communities. If a minor receives compensation later for her injuries, her family will be expected to reimburse the program costs.

Housing Options

ICBC (or WCB) may pay for renovations to your home to accommodate your injuries. If you can't live on your own and don't have relatives or friends to live with, you may be able to move into an ICBC-funded transition unit or independent-living apartment for up to six months.

An ICBC rehab co-ordinator (or a hospital or rehab centre social worker) may be able to arrange for you to move into a group home. Since few group homes accept residents over 30, though, this isn't an option for everyone. Even if you get into a group home, this won't be a permanent housing solution for you unless you'll have enough money to cover the on-going costs through a claim for damages or other sources. (Residency in a group home can cost $4,500 to $9,000 a month. If ICBC covers this cost as an accident benefit, you'll soon use up the money in your accident benefits account.)

Advocacy support groups can be contacted for information on accessible housing. Several thousand independent (or assisted-living) housing units with varying degrees of support services are being set up throughout the province by BC Housing in partnership with regional health authorities. Both people with disabilities and seniors will be eligible for these. There are presently over 30,000 subsidized housing units in the province. While low income people with disabilities are eligible for these, there are long waiting lists.

Transportation

After being in an accident, you may be reluctant to resume driving. Even when you weren't at fault, if you were driving you may wonder what you could have done differently to prevent the injuries that you (or others) had. While well-meaning people may advise you to get behind the wheel again quickly to overcome your fears, this may not be wise. Check with your doctor first to make sure there's no reason why you shouldn't drive.

If you've acquired functional disabilities or have a brain injury, you may want to have a driving assessment done at the George Pearson Centre, which is connected to G.F. Strong in Vancouver. (Driving assessments can be done elsewhere in the province as well.) You'll need a doctor's referral for this. When warranted, remedial driving lessons can be arranged, and you can re-do your driver's test. Passing a new test will prove that you're capable of driving safely despite your disabilities. If you're involved in another accident, you won't want ICBC or another auto insurer to claim that you shouldn't have been driving, so your insurance is invalid. If ICBC won't pay for a driving assessment or remedial lessons up front, you should be reimbursed for this later as part of a claim for damages. (Even if you'll be fully responsible for the cost, you should do this to protect yourself and others.)

Even a mild brain injury can affect your ability to drive. In order to drive safely, you need to rely on your automatic pilot; keep track of multiple demands on your attention without getting flustered; and react quickly and appropriately to unexpected circumstances. These skills can be lost, or severely reduced, by a brain injury. If a health-care provider warns you not to drive and you continue doing this, your driver's licence may be revoked.

If you're 16 or older, you may qualify for a discount on your basic auto insurance if you can't use your lower limbs for driving, or your doctor certifies that a permanent impairment makes public transportation impossible. You'll first have to apply for a fuel tax rebate through the provincial government's Consumer Taxation Branch. Once you have a rebate claim number, you can take this to your Autoplan dealer, along with your driver's licence and insurance documents, and the disability discount should be applied to your policy. If you were eligible for the discount earlier but didn't apply for it, the money that you'd have saved (over a maximum 12-month period) can be credited to you retroactively and applied to your future insurance premiums.

If you have limited mobility, you should be able to get a SPARC parking placard from the Social Planning and Research Council (or a Disability Resource Centre). This will allow you to use handicapped parking spaces whether you're a driver or passenger. You'll need a letter from your doctor stating how long your disability is likely to last.

If you can't drive or use public transportation due to an accident-related condition, ICBC (or WCB) may open up a taxi account for you. If they don't, you should be reimbursed for your taxi costs in whole or part. (You'll have to get prior permission from WCB for these costs to be covered.) If you're entitled to damages from an at-fault driver, it's better to take taxis than to struggle with the bus or to only go to places you can easily walk to or easily reach in a wheelchair. You're unlikely to be awarded money for future taxi service if you don't use taxis regularly.

You may be eligible for the HandyDart service (or TaxiSavers). A health-care provider or social services official will have to verify your need for this. HandyDart is a shared door-to-door transportation service, and most trips have to be booked two to six days in advance. An attendant can travel with you at no cost. While people going to medical and rehab appointments, work, and post-secondary school are given first preference, HandyDart can be used for personal reasons as well. Waits and travel time tend to be long. (TaxiSavers allow you to use pre-paid half-price coupons for taxi rides.)

ICBC (or WCB) may pay your transportation costs to medical and rehab appointments. There are limits to what ICBC will cover as an accident benefit, though. While mileage and parking expenses are usually only reimbursed as part of a claim for damages, ICBC may cover these costs when you're sent to one of their medical advisers, or a medical-rehab appointment is part of a structured rehab program. They may also cover your mileage, parking and travel expenses when their rehab department agrees you need out-of-town treatment.

While ICBC (or WCB) may pay for modifications to your car to accommodate your injuries, this has to be pre-authorized. The one-time purchase of a specially-equipped vehicle may be authorized as well.

To make it easier for you to return to work, your transportation expenses to (and from) a job, school, or retraining program may be subsidized by the government agency you're working with to find paid employment.

PART II

Insurance and Legal Issues

CHAPTER 8

Bodily Injury Claims

Basic Auto Insurance in British Columbia

Everyone in the province who owns a car is required to buy basic Autoplan insurance from ICBC. (Vehicles owned, leased or operated by the federal government are exempt from this requirement.) Basic Autoplan insurance only covers accidents that occur in Canada or the United States.

Compulsory third-party liability coverage protects you from claims made against you. If you were at fault in your accident, ICBC will pay any claims against you up to the limit of your liability coverage. Basic Autoplan insurance gives you $200,000 in third-party liability coverage. Extended coverage of $1 million (or more) can be purchased through ICBC and other auto insurers. (Buses, taxis, limousines and heavy commercial carriers are required to have at least $1 million in liability coverage, or $2 million when dangerous goods are transported. Extended coverage is also available for these classes of vehicles.)

Compulsory accident benefits coverage provides all injured occupants of a B.C.-licenced and -insured car with medical and rehab treatment, wage loss (or homemaker) benefits, funeral expenses, and death benefits, regardless of fault. Your Autoplan coverage also provides you and other household members with accident benefits if you're hit as a pedestrian or cyclist. A pedestrian or cyclist who is hit by a B.C.-licenced and -insured car anywhere in Canada is entitled to these benefits as well.

Compulsory underinsured motorist protection (UMP) provides you with up to $1 million in coverage if you're injured (or killed) in an accident in which the at-fault driver doesn't have enough liability coverage to compensate you (or your family) to the degree that you (or they) are legally entitled. Additional UMP coverage can be purchased. Everyone in your household automatically has UMP coverage even when you don't own or lease a car if you have a valid B.C. driver's licence and don't owe money to ICBC. A stand-alone UMP policy can also be purchased.

Compulsory uninsured-unidentified (hit-and-run) motorist protection provides all B.C. residents with up to $200,000 in compensatory damages if they're injured or killed (or their property is damaged) by an uninsured or unidentified driver on a highway in the province. Any B.C. resident who has an accident in the Canadian territories or an area of the United States where no fund exists to cover these claims also has this coverage. (All provinces have funds that cover uninsured-unidentified accident claims.)

Compulsory inverse-liability coverage is also part of the basic Autoplan package but only applies to property damage, not bodily injury. To the degree that you weren't at fault in your accident, ICBC will cover the cost of repairing or replacing your car if the at-fault driver comes from an area of Canada or the United States where the right to recover losses is legally prohibited.

Optional additional coverage — including extended liability and UMP coverage; collision, comprehensive or specific-perils coverage; and various roadside protection plans — can be purchased from ICBC and other auto insurers.

You may not be covered by insurance if you were driving with an invalid or suspended licence; you're convicted of driving while impaired; you leave an accident scene without identifying yourself; or ICBC feels your claim is fraudulent or exaggerated. If you don't have valid insurance in place and ICBC pays out a claim against you, they may try to recover this money from you.

When an accident occurs outside the province but in Canada or the United States, the resulting court case (if any) is held in B.C. when all involved parties are entitled to ICBC coverage. Otherwise, it's held in the province or state where the accident happened.

Who Can File an ICBC Claim?

All auto accidents that occur in the province should be reported to ICBC — unless you live outside the province, you were in an out-of-province car, and no other car was involved. In this situation, only your own auto insurer has to be notified.

As a B.C. driver or resident, if you're in an accident outside the province but in Canada or the United States, your accident needs to be reported to ICBC to safeguard your right to accident benefits, Uninsured-Unidentified Motorist Protection, and Underinsured Motorist Protection (UMP).

Claims Filing Process

As the driver of a car involved in an accident or an injured passenger, pedestrian or cyclist, you should report your accident to the ICBC Dial-A-Claim centre as soon as possible, preferably within 24 hours. You'll be given a claim number when you call. (In some situations, the entire claims process can be handled over the phone.) If you're unable to report your accident yourself for any reason, someone can do this for you. While the police should notify ICBC if you were seriously injured, a relative or friend should contact them on your behalf as well.

As you describe your accident to the Dial-A-Claim staff, the information you provide will be entered into ICBC's computer system. In addition to where and when your accident happened, you'll be asked for the licence plate and driver's licence numbers of the cars and drivers involved; the police file number, if any; and the names, addresses and phone numbers of the drivers. (If you were driving, you may also be asked to supply contact information for witnesses and anyone injured.) When a driver is insured by a company other than ICBC, the name and phone number of his insurer and his policy number should be reported to the Dial-A-Claim centre as well. (Reporting your accident to Dial-A-Claim doesn't mean you've filed a claim for accident benefits or compensation. You'll still have to do this, when relevant. See Chapter 10.)

If you were driving and your injuries are relatively minor, the Dial-A-Claim staff will set up an appointment for you with an adjuster at an ICBC claims centre. A passenger, pedestrian or cyclist isn't required to go to a claims centre: an accident benefits application form can be mailed out upon request.

If you weren't solely at fault in your accident, a personal injury lawyer can advise you on initiating a claim for damages. If you don't agree with ICBC's assessment of liability, or they won't provide you with accident benefits, you may have to take legal action with regard to this. (See Chapter 14.)

CAUTION! If you're in more than one accident and plan to file a claim for any of them, you should file a claim for each accident. Otherwise, ICBC (and the courts) may decide that your injuries were caused by an accident for which you didn't file a claim, and you may not get accident benefits or compensation.

How Much Time Do You Have to File a Claim?

ICBC prefers to have an accident reported to them within 24 hours when it occurs in an urban area and within 48 hours in a rural area. You'll have to provide your adjuster with a written report within 30 days and submit a proof of claim within 90 days. Failing to follow these time limits may make it hard to get benefits.

You'll have one year from your accident date to take legal action against ICBC if they don't provide you with accident benefits, *or* one year from the date they stop providing these. If you get some benefits but not all you're entitled to, you have one year from the date that ICBC first refuses to provide the requested benefits to initiate legal action.

A tort claim for damages from an at-fault driver has to be initiated within two years of your accident. Legal action is initiated by filing a writ of summons with the court. Issuing a writ doesn't mean you have to start legal proceedings right away; it extends the time you have to do this.

ICBC will only accept a claim involving a hit-and-run accident that occurs in the province when the accident is reported to the local police within 48 hours. A hit-and-run accident that occurs outside B.C. has to be reported to the local police within 24 hours, and ICBC has to be given a sworn statement within 28 days, for the claim to be allowed. If you intend to file a claim for damages in connection to a hit-and-run accident, ICBC should be notified of this in writing as soon as practical — and always within six months.

If a municipality's negligence contributed to your accident — there may have been unmarked construction on the road, for example — you'll have to notify them within two months that you intend to file a claim against them, and legal action will have to be initiated within six months. (A municipality can be named as a third party to a claim for damages.)

When a minor is injured in an accident, the two-year time limit for filing a tort claim may be extended. However, ICBC will have to be notified in writing that a future claim may be made. A claim for accident benefits should always be filed within the statutory time limits. (The Public Guardian and Trustee's office can be contacted for more information about minors' claims.)

The two-year filing limit doesn't officially begin for someone who is in a coma (or *incompis mentis*) until he regains consciousness (or becomes mentally competent again). While the Public Guardian and Trustee is often involved in these cases, a relative or friend of the injured person may want to consult a personal injury lawyer to make sure all necessary documents are filed on time. The last thing a seriously injured person needs is to lose his right to accident benefits or compensation because legal time requirements aren't met.

CAUTION! **Unless an insurance claim is filed on time, you may forfeit your right forever to do this.**

What Happens Next?

The first thing ICBC will do when you file a claim with them is determine whether you're entitled to accident benefits and/or compensation. They'll make sure the car(s) involved in the accident are properly insured; the drivers' licences are valid; and the insured parties don't owe money to ICBC. (When a driver is in breach of his insurance, there may be limits to the damages paid.) An adjuster will then investigate the accident to determine liability (or fault). When this isn't clear-cut, the court may have to rule on it.

At your initial meeting with your adjuster, you'll be questioned about your accident and injuries, then asked to sign a statement verifying what you've said. (See the section on working with your adjuster in Chapter 9.) Before you sign the statement, you may want to take it home and review it or show it to a personal injury lawyer.

In order to get accident benefits, you'll have to fill out an application form. You may also be asked to sign a release form that will authorize ICBC to collect information about you from various sources.

If you haven't been examined by a doctor yet, your adjuster may suggest that you see an ICBC medical adviser. It's better to have your own doctor check you out. She'll be less concerned about limiting ICBC costs than making sure you get necessary treatment.

If you were on a job when your accident happened, you'll be advised to report the accident to the Workers' Compensation Board. This should be done even if you don't intend to file a WCB claim.

Once your condition stabilizes, your adjuster may make you a settlement offer. He's not legally obligated to inform you of your rights in doing this. A personal injury lawyer can advise you on what your claim is worth. (See Chapter 10.)

Unless you settle your claim very quickly, you'll usually have to sign a "final release of all claims" form. While a release signed on behalf of a minor doesn't prevent a future claim from being made, in most other situations it releases ICBC (and the at-fault driver, if any) from further responsibility. You may want a personal injury lawyer to review your release before you sign it to make sure you're not giving up your right to future accident benefits you may need.

When an Accident May Be Your Fault

ICBC carefully considers liability (or fault) in every accident. Liability is usually based on the statements made by the drivers and wit-

Salmon Arm Branch
Date (DD/MM/YY) : 27/01/10 01:42PM
Checkout Receipt

Auto accident survivor's guide for Brit 3
3132027117821 Due: 17/02/10

TOTAL: 1

Thank you for using the Library
Salmon Arm Branch 250-832-6161
Telephone renewals 1-250-860-4652
Web Site: www.orl.bc.ca

Library Hours
Monday 10:00 - 5:00
Tuesday 10:00 - 8:00
Wednesday 10:00 - 5:00
Thursday 10:00 - 5:00
Friday 10:00 - 8:00
Saturday 10:00 - 5:00
Sunday 12:00 - 4:00 (Oct - Mar)

Overdue fines are based on the
open days of the branch where you
BORROWED your items.

nesses; police reports and accident diagrams; photos of the accident scene; and weather or road conditions. When more than one driver files a claim for the same accident, the adjusters assigned to each claim go through the same process individually before jointly deciding on liability. This usually takes about two weeks. (Insurers sometimes wait until all examinations for discovery are done before deciding on liability. See Chapter 14.)

If you don't agree with your adjuster's assessment of liability, you can speak to his claims manager about this. He'll review the decision and discuss it with you. If you're still not satisfied, liability may have to be determined in court.

As an involved driver, if someone reports your accident to ICBC before you do, you'll be notified by mail that unless you contact them within two weeks, liability will be determined without your input.

Only ICBC or the court can decide who was responsible for an accident. You're not allowed to admit liability except at your own expense. If someone files a claim for damages against you, you'll be expected to co-operate with ICBC's investigation and defence of any legal action stemming from this. (Your insurance premiums will increase if ICBC has to pay out a claim against you.)

Even when a Traffic Court judge rules that a driver was solely at fault in an accident, ICBC doesn't have to accept liability on his behalf. They only have to do this if he pleads guilty to a traffic offence.

Hit-and-Run Accidents

A hit-and-run accident occurs when an involved driver leaves the accident scene without identifying himself. If you're in a hit-and-run accident, you'll be expected to make every effort possible to identify the driver. Besides writing down his licence plate number — or when this isn't possible, the make, model and colour of his car — you should try to get contact information from witnesses. Your accident has to be reported to both ICBC and the police.

It can be hard to prove that you were in a hit-and-run accident without a lawyer's help. ICBC will defend the unknown driver as vigorously as they defend an at-fault driver they insure. After first denying that your accident happened or an unknown driver caused it, they may claim that you didn't try hard enough to identify the driver, forfeiting your right to damages. To show that you did everything you could, you'll have to place ads in local newspapers; interview people who live (or work) near the accident scene; and post signs nearby, asking for witnesses to contact to you. This should be done as soon as possible. (The court determines liability in hit-and-run accidents.)

As a B.C. resident, you may be paid up to $200,000 in damages from ICBC's Uninsured-Unidentified Motorist Protection Fund if your accident occurred within B.C., the Canadian territories, or an area of the United States that doesn't have hit-and-run protection. If you and ICBC don't agree on whether you're entitled to damages in connection to an out-of-province hit-and-run accident, or you disagree on what your damages should be, this may have to be resolved through arbitration.

CAUTION! Leaving the scene of an accident you were involved in without identifying yourself is a criminal offence. So is making a false claim about a hit-and-run accident.

When a Driver Is in Breach of His Insurance or Uninsured

As a B.C. resident, if you're injured by an uninsured at-fault driver, you're entitled to damages through the Uninsured-Unidentified Motorist Protection Fund. As a condition of receiving payments from the fund, you'll have to support ICBC's attempt to recover from the driver any money they pay out to you. You may be required to initiate legal action. (The court determines liability in these cases.) If your claim is worth more than $200,000, the additional money may be paid to you through an UMP claim.

If your own insurance isn't valid and you have an accident, you need to get legal advice. A personal injury lawyer may be able to help you deal with coverage issues, and if you're denied coverage, help limit your liability and costs.

If anyone files a claim against you in connection to an accident that occurred while you were in breach of your insurance, ICBC will notify you by mail that you'll be held accountable for any money they pay out in damages. By not responding to this letter, you're essentially accepting full liability. If you don't feel you were solely at fault, you'll have three weeks to explain your side of the story. While ICBC doesn't have to pay out a claim until the court determines liability, accident benefits are usually provided, when needed. (An insurance breach doesn't affect a claimant's right to accident benefits.) If you're injured in an accident while you're in breach of your insurance, you'll probably have to sue ICBC to get accident benefits.

You'll only have to reimburse ICBC's expenses if the court assigns liability to you. While money paid out in accident benefits doesn't have to be reimbursed, you could be forced to sell assets other than your home to reimburse money paid out in damages. A lien may be placed on your home to ensure that ICBC will be paid back out of the sale proceeds if and when you sell. Your future earnings may also be garnisheed.

Different types of insurance breaches affect your coverage in different ways. If your car was being used for something other than the purpose stated on your insurance policy at the time of your accident, and you were paying lower premiums than you would to insure it properly, this is a ratings breach. (Using your car for personal reasons when it's registered for business use isn't a ratings breach since higher premiums are paid to insure a car for business use.) Likewise, if you moved to an urban area from a rural area — or to the lower mainland from elsewhere in the province — and ICBC wasn't notified of your move, you'll be in breach of your insurance as you'll have been paying lower premiums than required. Other ratings breaches include using your car for commercial use or carrying passengers for hire without being licenced under the Commercial Transport Act, and driving with more passengers than legally allowed. (If your car is outside the province for more than 60 days, or it should be registered and licenced outside the province, your Autoplan insurance won't be valid.)

Most ratings breaches can be forgiven upon payment of a penalty. You'll have 14 days from the date you're notified by letter that you're in breach to pay the amount due. If the penalty isn't paid, ICBC may refuse to cover you for personal damage or Underinsured Motorist Protection (UMP). You may also have to reimburse them for any money they pay out in claims against you.

Some insurance breaches may be waived for new drivers: driving outside permissible time limits; driving with more passengers than allowed; violating the zero blood-alcohol condition of the New Driver Program; and operating a motorcycle contrary to freeway restrictions or at a speed above 60 km/h. A new driver who drives without a qualified adult in the car, rides a motorcycle out of the sight of a qualified adult, or carries passengers on a motorcycle won't be covered by insurance.

Driving with a suspended licence (or without having a licence) and owing money to ICBC for Driver Penalty Points are automatic insurance breaches. If you drive someone's car without his consent, or you allow your own car to be driven by someone who isn't qualified to drive it, you'll also be in breach of your insurance. One exception to this is if your child was driving your car without your permission and he's convicted of theft (or given a conditional discharge) in relation to this. In this situation, ICBC may cover a claim that's made against you through your specific-perils coverage.

Various criminal offences are insurance breaches: dangerous driving; causing injury or death through criminal negligence; leaving an accident scene without identifying yourself; driving while impaired; and refusing to give the police a breath or blood sample upon request. Other automatic breaches include using your car for illegal purposes or to escape from the police; using it in a speed race; and deliberately trying to cause property damage or injury. Trying to deal with your accident privately without reporting it to ICBC also places you at risk of being in breach.

ICBC maintains a record of all uninsured drivers to ensure that they can't renew their licences (or purchase auto insurance) without fulfilling their financial obligations to the insurance company.

When a non-resident drives a B.C.-licenced car with an expired driver's licence from another province or state, the insurance on the car is normally valid as long as there's no reason why the driver shouldn't have a licence *and* she renews her licence within 30 days. If she's never had a licence, or her licence has been suspended, the insurance on the car won't be valid. (A student from outside the province who attends a B.C. college, university, or other educational institute may not need a B.C. driver's licence.)

Driving While Impaired

Every year, approximately 3,000 people in B.C. are injured in drunk driving accidents and over 100 people killed.[28] Driving while impaired is a criminal offence. If you face this charge in an accident in which anyone is injured or killed, you need to consult a lawyer as soon as possible.

You may be charged with impaired driving even though your blood alcohol level is within legal limits if the police don't feel you were in control of your car because of alcohol (or drugs). Refusing to give the police a breath or blood sample upon request subjects you to the same criminal penalties as a conviction for impaired driving. A conviction may result in a fine, the suspension of your driver's licence, and your insurance being invalid.

If you're convicted of impaired driving in an accident in which anyone is injured, you'll not only lose your licence for up to ten years (or for life with a third conviction), you may be sentenced to up to ten years in jail. If anyone is killed, you could spend up to 14 years in jail. Anyone convicted of impaired driving more than once in B.C. automatically serves jail time.

Driving while impaired may prevent you from getting accident benefits. You're also likely to be considered at fault in your accident. If ICBC has to pay damages to an injured person in connection to your accident, they may try to recover this money from you.

When Someone Is Killed

There's one traffic fatality (on average) in B.C. every day.[29] The most common causes are driving while impaired, driving without due care and attention, and speeding. Alcohol use alone accounts for almost 25% of auto accident fatalities. Weather conditions also contribute to a significant number of fatal collisions.[30]

When someone who is entitled to accident benefits is killed in an accident, ICBC normally pays his funeral and burial expenses, as well as death benefits to his survivors. Unless he was solely at fault, his family can also file a claim under the Family Compensation Act. (See Chapter 10.) If he was partially at fault, the damages they're assessed or awarded will be reduced by the same percentage as he was at fault. Liability may have to be determined in court.

ICBC will defend a deceased at-fault driver from claims made against him in connection to his accident.

> **CAUTION! If you may have been at fault in an accident in which someone was killed, contact a lawyer immediately!**

If You Were a Pedestrian, Cyclist or Passenger

Over 1,500 pedestrians (and nearly 1,000 cyclists) are injured or killed in auto accidents every year in the province.[31] If you hit a pedestrian or cyclist, you're legally required to remain at the accident scene to help her. If she's injured, the accident should be reported to the police as soon as possible.

If you're hit by a car as a pedestrian (or cyclist), ICBC may claim that you walked (or rode) into the car's path, making it impossible for the driver to yield the right of way. Uninvolved witnesses can be crucial in these cases. If the court accepts ICBC's interpretation, you'll be considered partially at fault.

Since cyclists in B.C. are legally required to use safety helmets, if you weren't wearing one at the time of your accident, you'll be considered partially responsible for any head injuries you have. (If you knowingly let your child ride a bike without a safety helmet on, you may be held partially responsible for her head injuries.) Cyclists also have to use headlights, reflectors and rear lights from

½ hour after sunset until ½ hour before sunrise. If you have an accident during this time and aren't using the required equipment, you may be considered partially responsible for your injuries.

If you're hit by a car anywhere in Canada or the United States as a pedestrian or cyclist, you're entitled to accident benefits if someone in your household has Autoplan insurance. (The car that hit you doesn't have to be insured by ICBC.) Any pedestrian or cyclist hit by a B.C.-licenced and -insured driver in Canada is entitled to these benefits as well. Since pedestrians and cyclists are rarely solely at fault in an accident, you can also file a claim for damages.

As a passenger in a B.C.-licenced and -insured car, you're entitled to accident benefits. You may also be entitled to compensation for your injuries even if the driver was solely at fault.

A pedestrian, cyclist or passenger isn't required to meet with a claims adjuster. However, ICBC should be given a statement about the accident within 30 days and a proof of claim submitted within 90 days. These documents should be sent by registered mail, or hand-delivered with a receipt requested.

Work-Related Accidents

When both drivers were working at the time of an accident, a claim can only be filed with WCB, not ICBC (or another auto insurer). If you were working but the other driver wasn't, you can file a claim with either WCB or ICBC — or, you can elect to get benefits from WCB while still filing a claim for damages against an at-fault driver. You'll have to decide what you want to do before filing your claim.

Even if you don't file a WCB claim, you'll have to submit an accident report to WCB if your accident happened while you were working. Only the Workers' Compensation Board has the right to decide whether your accident was work-related. (If you were travelling between job locations, the accident will probably be considered work-related. If you were on your way to work, it may only be a work-related accident if the trip was being made due to a work emergency.) If WCB rejects your claim, ICBC may dispute this.

When it's not immediately apparent that both drivers were

working, ICBC may provide you with accident benefits while waiting for the Board's decision on this. (This won't be done if you work for the federal government.) You'll have to sign a statement agreeing to pay ICBC back if the Board decides you're entitled to WCB benefits. (ICBC won't provide you with benefits you can get from another source.) You'll have to authorize WCB to send your benefit payments to ICBC until they've been fully reimbursed.

It's not always clear when it's better to file a claim with ICBC or WCB. Legal regulations change constantly, and each situation is unique. You may want to speak to a personal injury lawyer before deciding what to do. If liability is an issue and your injuries are relatively minor, you'll probably be advised to file a WCB claim. If you have serious injuries, you may be advised to file an ICBC claim. The best action to take will depend on how clear-cut the issues are. In general, when you're at fault in an accident you're better off with a WCB claim as their wage-replacement policy is more generous than ICBC's. You'll also get more on-going help. If you weren't at fault, you may be better off with an ICBC claim: you'll normally be paid damages for your pain and suffering, and you should eventually get back your full wage losses and total care costs.

If the Board considers your accident work-related, even if you don't file a WCB claim the only accident benefits you'll get from ICBC are those that exceed what the Board would have provided. You won't get wage-loss benefits from ICBC, nor have your medical and rehab expenses paid up front. If you weren't at fault, you should recover this money later in settling your claim. (Since ICBC prefers not to have the Workers' Compensation Board involved in claims, your adjuster may offer you an advance to cover your lost wages and medical-rehab expenses so you don't file a WCB claim.)

If you file a WCB claim and you have injuries with long-term consequences, you may want to consult a personal injury lawyer to make sure your disability payments are fair. If you appeal a Board decision, you'll probably want a lawyer to represent you.

If you weren't working when your accident happened, it doesn't matter whether another driver was. As with any auto accident claim, you should be able to get accident benefits from ICBC if you meet the requirements for this, and damages for your injuries if you weren't at fault.

Low-Velocity Impact Claims

For many years, ICBC had a "no crash, no cash" policy. When no more than $1,000 in damage was done to a car, it was generally assumed that a collision was too minor to cause injuries. Unless unusual circumstances existed, a claimant had to sue for accident benefits and compensation. ICBC's policy in these low-velocity impact (LVI) claims changed in 2003. While accident benefits are now provided, you're still unlikely to get damages in an LVI claim without taking legal action.[32]

If your claim is being treated as a low-velocity impact claim, an LVI Committee will decide whether the claim is accepted. Most decisions are reached within 30 days. If your claim is rejected, you can submit further information to your adjuster to show why it should be accepted. Or, you can initiate legal action. If most people wouldn't have been injured in a similar accident, the burden of proof will be on you to show the court that you were. (Juries tend to support ICBC in LVI claims.)

You'll only be paid damages after a low-velocity impact accident if you can prove conclusively that you weren't at fault; your injuries were objectively identified by a doctor and documented in detail; and there's a valid reason why you were more susceptible to injury than an average person would have been in a similar accident. If a pre-existing condition was aggravated by your accident, you're entitled to damages from the at-fault driver. (He's only responsible for the worsening of your condition, not for the fact that you have it.) Some physical conditions that may increase your susceptibility to injury are degenerative disc disease, osteoporosis, and muscle, joint or tendon weakness from an earlier injury. A pre-existing psychological condition can also be aggravated by an accident.

Accidents Involving Out-of-Province Drivers and Residents

When an accident occurs in B.C., the rules and regulations in effect in the province apply and B.C. law determines liability. If you live outside the province, no other car was involved and no one was injured, your accident should be reported to the police and your own insurer, not ICBC. (Phone the Dial-a-Claim centre for advice if a B.C. resident was involved.)

As an out-of-province resident, you'll only get accident benefits from ICBC if you were in a B.C.-licenced and insured car, or you were hit as a pedestrian or cyclist by a B.C.-licenced and insured car. If you were in a hit-and-run accident, the amount of compensation you can get will be the lesser of the amount that a B.C. resident would receive in the same situation in B.C. or the area where you live.

A B.C. resident can face both ICBC and an out-of-province insurer in court. If you're entitled to damages from an out-of-province driver, his auto insurer (if any) will be responsible for paying you compensation up to the limit of his liability coverage. If the court awards you more than this, the additional amount may be paid to you through ICBC's Underinsured Motorist Protection Fund.

When an out-of-province driver doesn't have auto insurance, you may be paid damages through ICBC's Unidentified-Uninsured Motorist Protection Fund, or a similar fund in the area where the accident happened. If you're hit as a pedestrian or cyclist by an out-of-province driver, you'll be eligible for accident benefits from ICBC if someone in your household has Autoplan insurance.

When liability is an issue in an accident involving an out-of-province driver, either party can initiate legal action. When an out-of-province driver sues a B.C.-licenced and -insured driver for damages, ICBC either defends the B.C. driver or pays out the claim.

CAUTION! **You may lose your right to UMP coverage if you don't get written permission from ICBC before settling a claim with an out-of-province driver or his insurer, or taking him to court.**

CHAPTER 9

Dealing with the Insurance Company

Bodily injury claims tend to be stressful. While ICBC is supposed to act in good faith with claimants, they often resort to harsh tactics to reduce damages. The reason for this is obvious: tens of thousands of bodily claims are made each year[33] and a single major-loss claim can cost over a million dollars.

Once you file a claim for damages, ICBC will put money into a reserve fund to cover their expenses relative to this. (Accident benefits are separately funded.) Enough money should be set aside to pay you reasonable compensation for your injuries and cover ICBC's costs in defending the at-fault driver. Their defence costs may include legal and investigative expenses, assessments, and medical-legal reports. If you develop problems that aren't initially apparent, or an accident-related condition worsens over time — an undiagnosed brain injury may leave you with permanent deficits, for example, or PTSD may become chronic, making full-time work impossible — the bodily injury claims department should alter their assessment of what your claim is worth and increase the money held in reserve for you. This often isn't done, though, and more money may be spent fighting your claim than you're offered to settle it.

If you hire a lawyer, he should handle all communications with ICBC. This will prevent you from saying anything that could place your claim at risk. However, your lawyer may not be as persistent as you would be in getting you accident benefits. It may also take much longer to settle your claim.

Working with Your Adjuster

Unless you hire a lawyer, you'll have to deal with one or more claims adjusters from the time you file your claim until it settles. Your adjuster isn't obligated to tell you about the accident benefits or compensation you're entitled to. His job is to minimize ICBC's costs, and your claim will be handled however he feels will accomplish this. If you have serious injuries, a tough adjuster with a proven track record in limiting damages in large claims may be assigned to your case.

You should always have a witness with you when you meet with your adjuster or other ICBC staff people. This can be a lawyer or other advocate, or a relative or friend. While one public advocate (a former ICBC official) suggests that claimants tape-record their meetings and phone conversations so there are no misunderstandings,[34] an adjuster may object to this. A personal injury lawyer can advise you on whether it's appropriate to request permission to do this.

It's important to take detailed notes of your meetings and conversations, *documenting everything*. ICBC employees will document their contacts with you, and you won't be able to effectively challenge their records without your own documentation.

Before your first meeting with your adjuster, you should give some thought to the questions you're likely to be asked. Besides having you describe your accident and what you think caused it, your adjuster may want to know who was with you, what your relationship to them is, where you were going (and why), where you were coming from, and what you'd been doing. Did you have the car radio or stereo on? Were you talking to anyone in the car, or were you on the phone? Was everyone in the car wearing seatbelts? How were your seatbelt and headrest adjusted? (An incorrectly-adjusted seatbelt or headrest can reduce the value of your claim.)

You may be questioned extensively about road conditions. Did your accident occur on a paved (or unpaved) road or a divided highway; at a curve in the road; or at the top (or bottom) of a hill? Was the road straight or hilly; wet, muddy, icy, or oily? Were there holes in the road or loose material (rocks, branches, cans, plastic bags) that may have contributed to your accident? Were you at a traffic light or intersection? How many lanes of traffic were there and were they clearly marked? How good was the visibility? Were the street lights on? Were your headlights and windshield wipers on?

Did you have prior warning of the accident? Relative to your car and a fixed point outside, where was the other car when you first saw it? What direction was it going in, and what was the driver doing or about to do? What safety measures did you take when you saw the other car? If you didn't do anything to avoid the accident, why didn't you?

Relative to a fixed point outside, where did the collision occur and where did the cars end up after the impact? Were there skid marks on the road? How long were they and what direction were they going in? If a pedestrian or cyclist was hit, relative to your car and a fixed point in the area, where was she on impact and immediately thereafter? Were there other cars on the road at the time?

What part of your car (and the other car) was hit, and what damage was done to it? If your car was towed, where was it taken and by whom? Were the police at the accident scene? Was anyone charged with a traffic violation or criminal offence? Did you or anyone else take an ambulance to the hospital?

You may also be asked about independent witnesses, and about other people's reactions to what happened. You don't have to repeat what anyone else said, nor do you have to provide information that could be used to reduce the value of your claim.

Your adjuster will try to minimize your injuries and their consequences. While you shouldn't exaggerate your problems, you need to tell him about everything that's bothered you since your accident, not just what seems most significant. What parts of your body were affected, when did you first notice this, and how do you feel now? Are you in a lot of pain, or do you have occasional discomfort? What time of day, and under what conditions, do you feel better or worse? If you have a whiplash injury, did you ever have headaches or back, neck, jaw or shoulder pain prior to your accident?

Did you hit your head or lose consciousness? If you went to the hospital, who took you there and how long did you stay? What diagnostic tests were done, and what medical treatment did you receive? How have your injuries affected your functioning level, if at all? If you've had to cut back on recreational activities, how often did you usually do these? If you feel that you've been under a lot of stress since your accident, or you're aware of changes in your thought processes, moods or behaviour, you need to let your adjuster know this even if he doesn't ask.

If little damage was done to your car, your adjuster may ask you a series of questions to figure out why you were injured. Was your car moving, parked or in gear? Was your foot on the brake? What did the car do on impact? Did you bang into anything inside the car? What part of your body was it and what part of the car? Did you tense up when you saw the accident coming, or were you relaxed? Do you have any explanation yourself for why a minor accident might have injured you? Did a doctor find objective evidence of an injury? Your adjuster may ask you to show him how you were sitting: the direction your body and head were in; how your seatbelt and headrest were adjusted; and how your body reacted on impact. A photo may be taken of you in the position you remember being in immediately after the collision.

You may also be asked about your pre-accident health and whether you have any pre-existing medical conditions. You need to be honest in responding to this, even though insurers often try to blame accident-related disabilities on earlier conditions a claimant has had.

Once you've described your accident and injuries to your adjuster, he'll prepare a statement for you to sign based on this. Even if you have a clear memory of your accident, and you've related this to him in a straightforward manner, he may manipulate what you've told him. You have the right to make any changes to the statement you feel are warranted. (These have to be initialled to be valid.) You can also ask for the statement to be re-written in your own words.

Before you sign your statement, take it home and read it over carefully, consulting a personal injury lawyer if possible. Even if your adjuster has accurately recorded what you said — and there's no guarantee he did — how he wrote the statement will be slanted towards protecting ICBC's interests, not yours.

(If you make any changes to the statement your adjuster prepares, he may claim in later legal proceedings that the original statement more accurately reflects what you told him than the amended statement. Or, he may tell you not to be concerned about the diagram he's drawn of the accident scene as it isn't to scale. In later legal proceedings, he may claim that his diagram portrays exactly what you said — and is basically an admission of fault.[35])

Since an accident-related condition may not become apparent for several months, the following clause should be added to your statement: "In addition to the injuries noted, my injuries include any other injuries that might arise from my accident, and any complications that might arise from my injuries."

CAUTION! Your adjuster may tell you that you were at fault in your accident to discourage you from filing a claim for damages. Before you accept liability, talk to a personal injury lawyer. Unless you were *solely* at fault, you may be entitled to some compensation.

Your adjuster may ask you whether you're married; what ages your dependants are; what your current salary is; and what your employment history has been. Were you ever in an auto accident before, or have you ever filed a claim for damages? Has anyone ever sued you for damages? If you're entitled to benefits from another insurer, your adjuster will want to know the details of this as well.

You'll usually be asked to sign a "general release of information" form for your adjuster. This will allow him to get information about you from various sources. He may want copies of your medical and employment records, WCB claims file (if any), past income tax returns, school records, and military records (if any). Your doctor may be contacted to confirm that an accident-related injury is preventing you from working, while your employer may be contacted to confirm your salary and the amount of work time you lose due to your accident.

In order to get your accident-related expenses reimbursed, you'll have to give your adjuster valid dated receipts for these. Keep photocopies of all submitted receipts until they're paid in full.

Protecting Your Rights

What you say at your initial meeting with your adjuster will have a large impact on how your claim is handled. Besides taking detailed notes of the meeting or tape-recording it, you'll need to be careful how you phrase your comments. While you'll want to make it clear that you're doing everything you can to recover, you won't want to give your adjuster a false impression that you're doing better than you are. Nor will you want to sound like you're complaining when discussing what's bothering you.

It's best to state simply and clearly what you're *presently* having difficulty doing, keeping in mind that you may be investigated. If there's evidence showing that you've lied to your adjuster, you'll lose your credibility with ICBC — and with the court, if your case goes to trial. Since your family, friends, neighbours and co-workers may be interviewed by ICBC investigators, make sure you don't say anything to your adjuster (or an ICBC defence lawyer) that someone else might contradict. Be honest and up front at all times, but brief and to the point, never offering more information than specifically requested. (For advice on how to phrase what you say, see the section on safeguarding yourself from insurance company tactics in Chapter 11 and the section on examinations for discovery in Chapter 14.)

If you're not sure of the best way to answer a question, you don't have to answer it. Never guess at an answer that you're not sure of, nor let yourself be pressured into saying anything you may later regret. You can tell your adjuster that you'll think about his question, and you'll get back to him about it in a day or two.

Instead of signing a "general release of information" form for your adjuster, you may want to sign separate releases for requested material. You'll then know what areas of your life are being explored. If ICBC wants to see your doctor's clinical records, you can ask her to send them to your lawyer (if any) first. He can then delete information that has no bearing on your insurance claim before ICBC has access to these documents.

You're not required to give your adjuster information that's irrelevant to your claim. If you had a whiplash injury in a low-velocity impact accident, for example, you may not want ICBC to see your full medical records. They may request other material that's not pertinent to your claim as well, looking for something that might prejudice a judge or jury against you if your case goes to trial. If you refuse to provide access to requested documents, ICBC can ask a judge in chambers to rule on whether the material should be released.

All communications from ICBC (and other insurers) should be sent to you in writing. You should never agree to a request that a claims adjuster makes over the phone. Before signing any documents or verbally agreeing to anything, always take a few days to consider the consequences. You may also want to consult a lawyer.

Will You Be Sent to an ICBC Doctor?

While you have the right to be treated by your own health-care providers, ICBC can insist on you being examined by their medical advisers. You should be notified of your appointments well in advance, and your transportation costs should be paid. If you refuse to undergo treatment that an ICBC medical adviser recommends, your accident benefits may stop.

Before you allow an ICBC medical adviser to examine you, you may want to check with a personal injury lawyer to make sure this is wise. You won't want to be examined by anyone with a reputation as a "hired gun" for insurers. Since ICBC sometimes ignores the recommendations of their own medical advisers, you may want to make it a pre-condition of your examination that the resulting report will be promptly passed on to your doctor and lawyer, if any. (You can file a "bad faith" action against ICBC if they don't fund the treatment their medical advisers have recommended.)

If You Have a Soft Tissue Injury or Subjective Condition

Over two-thirds of the injuries suffered in auto accidents are soft tissue injuries.[36] ICBC rejects many soft tissue injury claims, refusing to pay for rehab treatment as an accident benefit. In other situations, they may only cover short-term therapy. Unless you have other injuries as well, you may be referred to their Soft Tissue Injury Program. (See Chapter 4.) Adjusters are particularly suspicious of soft tissue injuries in low-velocity impact (LVI) claims.

If ICBC accepts that your accident caused a soft tissue injury, your doctor will be asked to grade the severity of it according to their criteria. She'll also be expected to use their soft tissue injury guidelines in treating you. Unless she feels that you should be evaluated by an orthopaedic surgeon, she's supposed to encourage you to resume your normal activities as soon as possible. Your adjuster may later ask her for a written report that describes how long it took you to return to normal (or restricted) activities; what medication she gave you; what rehab treatment you've had; and what specialists she's referred you to. If he doesn't feel you're recovering as rapidly as you should be, he may have an ICBC medical adviser assess you.

Since a soft tissue injury can worsen over time, it's important not to settle your claim too quickly. Before you release ICBC from further obligations towards you, you may want an orthopaedic surgeon or physiatrist (a rehab doctor) to advise you on whether you're at risk of having future problems. If you are, this should be taken into account in settling your claim.

A soft tissue injury that may cause future income losses is considered severe. If you do physical work, ICBC may agree to pay you wage-loss benefits for a longer time than if you work in an office.

A subjective condition is diagnosed primarily by what you tell the doctor, not what she observes. Subjective conditions include whiplash and other soft tissue injuries, mild brain injuries, chronic pain disorder, fibromyalgia, chronic fatigue syndrome, post-traumatic stress disorder, and other psychological conditions.

Proving that your accident has caused a subjective condition can be time-consuming, frustrating and expensive. It may take several months (or years) for symptoms of certain conditions to be recognized. Once they become apparent, an ICBC medical examiner may conclude that the underlying condition is unrelated to your accident. You may have to take legal action to get your medical and rehab treatment paid, and where relevant, fair compensation.

If you weren't at fault in your accident, you should be compensated for any accident-related condition that affects your ability to earn income. If you recognize yourself in the TBI symptoms noted in Chapter 7, you should consult a lawyer who specializes in brain injury cases before settling your claim. If you have chronic pain or fatigue, or an accident-related psychological disorder, talk to a lawyer who has experience in handling cases involving these issues before you settle your claim.

CAUTION! **If you take a subjective injury claim to trial, ICBC may try to discredit you in court. You need to be prepared for this. It won't be pleasant.**

If You're Unhappy with Your Adjuster

Once your adjuster forms an opinion about what your claim is worth, it may be hard to change his mind. (If he decided that your only injury is a broken arm, for example, he's unlikely to accept that you have a brain injury as well, no matter how compelling the evidence.) Getting upset with him about being denied treatment may make him harder to deal with. If you don't feel that your claim is being handled fairly or that you're being treated properly, you can speak to your adjuster's supervisor or claims manager about this.

You can also take your complaint to ICBC's customer relations department. After they've explained to you what you are (and aren't) entitled to, they'll make sure that you and your adjuster agree on the basic nature of your claim and what the unresolved issues are. If your adjuster doesn't have the information he needs to make a fair assessment of your claim, or there are unique circumstances he should be aware of, this will be passed on to him. He may be asked to consider whether his personal biases are interfering with his decisions, while you'll be encouraged to look at your situation more objectively. This may allow a compromise to be reached.

If you've hired a lawyer, he should deal with your complaints, not you. He can also contact the customer relations department if he's having problems with your adjuster. Since lawyers and adjusters usually communicate in writing, several months can go by before one of them responds to a letter from the other. By the time a few letters have been exchanged, a year may have passed and the underlying issues are forgotten. The customer relations staff may be able to get things back on track.

> **CAUTION! Complaining about your adjuster (or requesting a new one) may make your situation worse. If you and your adjuster can't work together amicably, you may have to hire a lawyer.**

Disputing an ICBC Decision

If you're unhappy with a decision made by your adjuster, the LVI Committee that rules on low-velocity impact claims, your rehab co-ordinator (if any), or another ICBC staff person or department, you can speak to a supervisor or claims manager at the office involved. If you're not satisfied with the outcome, you may be referred to ICBC's Fair Practices Review department, which combines their customer relations department with their freedom of information unit. Any decision you dispute other than liability or "quantum" (what your claim is worth) can be dealt with through this department. (Personal injury lawyers generally advise claimants *not to use* ICBC's internal review process to resolve disputes.)

The Fair Practices Review department will explain why the decision you're disputing was made. If your claim was denied because you're in breach of your insurance, you may be told how to get your coverage reinstated. If your accident benefits were denied or terminated, you may be given information on what you can do to get them. The suggested solutions may not be ones you want to follow. There may be valid medical reasons, for example, why you shouldn't undergo specific treatment or participate in a return-to-work program.

(All you may get from the Fair Practices Review department is an agreement to investigate a situation you feel is unfair. While you can also file a complaint with your local MLA or the B.C. government official who currently oversees ICBC, these people will contact the Fair Practices Review department to discuss your case. If an advocacy support group intervenes with ICBC on your behalf, they'll be referred to this department as well.)

After you've gone through the Fair Practices Review process, if you still don't feel you're being treated fairly, you can ask the ICBC Fairness Commissioner to review your situation. He won't review a dispute about liability, "quantum", or any matter currently being dealt with through court action or arbitration. (The Fairness Commissioner is independent to ICBC. He can act as a mediator or make recommendations which may be followed.)

You can also take ICBC to court as long was you initiate legal action within the required time. A dispute about what your claim is worth can only be resolved through negotiations or legal proceedings.

If you don't accept your adjuster's assessment of liability after his supervisor or claims manager has explained the reasons for this, you can apply for a claims assessment review (CAR) if you weren't injured. You'll have 60 days from the date of the liability decision to do this. The $50 application fee will be refunded if a decision is made in your favour. An independent examiner (often a retired provincial court judge) will review the written submissions that you and ICBC make before reaching a decision on liability. This will be binding on ICBC, but not on you. You'll still have the right to take legal action.

When Should You Settle Your Claim?

How long it takes to settle your claim will depend on various factors: the nature and extent of your injuries; whether liability is in dispute; whether you're entitled to damages; whether you've hired a lawyer; and whether your case goes to trial. While the average bodily injury claim takes six months to settle, when a lawyer is involved the average time is closer to 18 months. (Lawyers are usually hired in more complex cases and when claimants don't agree with an insurer's decisions.)

You shouldn't settle your claim until your injuries have stabilized and your doctors can predict with some accuracy what the expected outcome is. While most injuries heal within 6-12 months, some accident-related problems don't become apparent for several years. It can also take a few years before you realize that you have a permanent disability which may affect your future employment. Even if you returned to work fairly quickly, you may not have been able to continue in your job, or to advance in your career as you might have done "but for your accident". If you may have future income losses or future care needs, these will have to be evaluated before a fair settlement amount can be determined. Settling your claim too quickly may result in you being severely under-compensated.

Once your adjuster can estimate how much longer you'll be out of work (if at all), and how long you're likely to have accident-related problems (if at all), you may be asked to meet with him to discuss a settlement. At this meeting, you'll normally review all available medical reports together to make sure you agree on the nature of your injuries, where you are in your recovery process, and the probable outcome. You'll also have to agree on liability (or fault) and whether you're entitled to damages. If you don't agree on these basic facts, this will have to be resolved before a reasonable settlement offer can be made. (What your claim might be worth is discussed in Chapter 10.)

CAUTION! If you receive a cheque for a settlement amount that you've refused, don't cash it! If you do, you'll be considered to have accepted the offer, and your claim will be closed. Never cash a cheque from an insurer without documentation that clearly states what it's for.

❖

Can a Settled Claim Be Re-opened?

You'll usually be asked to sign a formal release when you settle your claim. This will free ICBC from further obligations towards you. While few settled claims can be re-opened, your release may be overturned if the nature of what you signed was misrepresented to you; you were misled (even unintentionally) into believing that you were only releasing ICBC from aspects of your claim that you considered irrelevant; you and your adjuster were both unaware of the seriousness of your injuries; or your settlement was clearly unfair.

If you were incapable of making an informed decision when you settled your claim, your condition has changed substantially since then, or you didn't get legal advice before signing a release, you can ask the ICBC customer relations department to re-open your claim. They'll only do this if you have new medical information that your adjuster didn't have when he made you a settlement offer. You'll have to prove that delayed-onset problems were caused by your accident and that your adjuster was unaware of these when you settled. (When ICBC wouldn't re-open a woman's claim after her condition worsened, the Fairness Commissioner recommended that they provide her with medical and rehab benefits, which they agreed to do.[37])

If you don't feel that the amount of money you agreed to accept is fair, you can ask the court to rule on whether your case should be re-opened. A judge will then decide whether it's appropriate to overturn your signed release. If she rules in your favour, ICBC will have to re-open your claim. A personal injury lawyer can advise you on whether you have a valid reason to request that a legally-binding document you've signed be overturned.

CHAPTER 10

ICBC Benefits and Compensation

Part 7 Accident Benefits

NOTE: To make sure the benefits in this section are still available, check with your adjuster, ICBC rehab co-ordinator (if any), or a personal injury lawyer.

Most people who are injured in auto accidents in B.C. are entitled to accident benefits — also known as Part 7 benefits or Part 7's. You may also be entitled to these benefits if your accident happened elsewhere in Canada or the United States and you were in a B.C.-licensed and -insured car. (To determine whether you're entitled to accident benefits as a pedestrian or cyclist, see Chapter 8.) You may have to sue ICBC to get accident benefits if you were in breach of your insurance. Your future insurance premiums won't be affected by the Part 7 benefits you receive.

ICBC may refuse to provide you with accident benefits if you didn't promptly notify them of your accident, give them a written statement within 30 days, and apply for accident benefits within 90 days. (Your benefits shouldn't be denied unless your failure to comply with these time limits has placed ICBC at a disadvantage in dealing with your claim.) If your adjuster requests a letter from your doctor outlining her findings, treatment and the expected outcome, and he doesn't get this, you may also be denied accident benefits.

To be eligible for accident benefits, your injuries or disabilities must arise and be documented by a doctor within 20 days of your accident. (In some cases, this time requirement may be waived.) You'll have one year from the date of your accident, or from the date that ICBC first refuses to provide you with benefits, to initiate a Part 7 legal action against them. (See Chapter 14.)

Unless you know what accident benefits you're entitled to, you may not get the help you need. While Part 7 benefits may not cover all your accident-related expenses after a catastrophic injury, an ICBC rehab co-ordinator can often authorize items and services that aren't available to all claimants.

Since it's often easier for a health-care provider to get paid than for a claimant to be reimbursed, whenever possible your rehab therapists and medical equipment suppliers should bill ICBC directly. While you should be reimbursed within 60 days for any accident benefits you pay out of pocket, in practice this may not happen until your claim resolves.

Any item or service that could be provided to you by another insurer (including WCB, an extended health-care plan, private surgical or dental plan, or private disability insurer) won't be covered as a Part 7 benefit. If the other insurer expects to be paid back when your claim settles, these costs should be reimbursed to you as part of a claim for damages.

You may want to get a copy of your Part 7 payment schedule every six months until your claim settles. This will show you what's been billed to your account to date. Unless errors in these records are corrected, you may not receive the benefits (or recover the money) you're entitled to. Your Part 7 payment schedule can be obtained through ICBC's freedom of information unit.

Medical, rehab and related benefits: Part 7 benefits should cover up to $150,000 in reasonable medical, rehab and related expenses. Included in this are medical, surgical, dental and hospital care recommended by a doctor; ambulance services; professional nursing (but *not* private in-hospital nursing); physiotherapy; massage therapy recommended by a doctor; chiropractic treatment; occupational therapy; speech-language therapy; prescription drugs; medical supplies and equipment (including wheelchairs, walkers, crutches, canes, hospital beds, raised toilet seats, assistive devices and prosthetic devices); and up to 12 hours a day of in-home attendant care. The cost of participating in an exercise program, or a gym membership if you didn't already have one, may also be covered. If you don't have medical insurance, ICBC should pay your hospital bills.

The Insurance (Motor Vehicle) Act states that Part 7 benefits include "funds for any other costs the corporation in its sole discretion agrees to pay." Any item or service that will help you return to work or school — or when this isn't possible, help you reach your optimal potential — may be provided at ICBC's discretion. In the past, this has included modifications to a claimant's home and car; the one-time purchase of a specially-equipped vehicle; driver retraining; exercise equipment; medically-prescribed bed, mattress or (custom-made) orthopaedic shoes; school fees, supplies and tutoring; sex and art therapy; vitamins and nutritional supplements; full-time attendant care; a one-on-one rehab worker; recreational programs; vocational assessments and retraining; work-hardening programs; pain-management programs; acupuncture; hypnosis; and psychological counselling. Some transportation costs may be paid as well.

Total disability (wage-loss or homemaker) benefits: Total disability means you're unable to work — or if you're a homemaker, perform your household duties. A disability may only last a few days, or it may continue throughout your life.

Total disability benefits don't begin until seven days after an accident. You should start receiving payments within four weeks of the date that ICBC receives your proof of claim. You'll continue to get payments at four-week intervals for as long as applicable. (Missed payments will be paid retroactively.) You'll have to provide your adjuster with the medical and rehab information he requests, and you may be examined by one or more ICBC medical advisers.

Total disability benefits are usually paid for as long as a disability continues. (If you were over 65 at the time of your accident, or you turn 65 while you're getting these benefits, they'll be paid for a maximum of two years.) ICBC may review your situation every 12 months and stop paying you total disability benefits on the advice of their medical advisers. If you're still getting these benefits two years after your accident, you may be referred to ICBC's rehab department. An ICBC medical or vocational adviser may assess you to determine whether specific treatment or retraining might help you return to work.

Before you can begin to get total disability (wage-loss) benefits, your adjuster will want proof that you were employed at the time of your accident — or, if you were unemployed, that you worked for at least six of the previous twelve months. (If you were on EI, a judge may be asked to rule on when you'd most likely have begun working again "but for your accident". You should receive wage-loss benefits from this time on.)

Your employer may be asked to fill out a Record of Earnings (R.O.E) form that shows your gross earnings during the year prior to your accident, the number of weeks you worked, how much time you took off work due to your accident, and how much pay you lost as a result of this, including over-time pay. If you're self-employed, own your own business, or work on a contract or commission basis, to support your wage-loss claim you may have to give your adjuster a letter from your accountant or bookkeeper, as well as past income tax records, business correspondence, projected sales figures, and a record of past (or current) orders. If you didn't file tax returns regularly or keep accurate records of your earnings, ICBC may refuse to pay you wage-loss benefits. (You may be able to validate work you did "off the books" by having your adjuster contact the people you worked for. Before you suggest that he do this, check with a lawyer or accountant to make sure you understand the potential tax implications.)

The maximum amount you can receive in total disability (wage-loss) benefits is the lesser of $300 a week or 75% of your weekly gross income, *minus* any wage replacement you're entitled to from other sources, including EI, WCB or a private disability insurer. Money you get from CPP (or the Quebec Pension Plan) will be deducted from your wage-loss benefits after two years. (Even if your CPP benefits increase, ICBC should only deduct the amount of your initial CPP payment.)

When a private disability insurer pays you less than 75% of

your gross pre-accident earnings, ICBC should make up the difference, up to their $300 weekly maximum. If you're able to work but only at a reduced salary, any money you earn in excess of $75 a week will be deducted from your wage-loss benefits. (Your combined weekly earnings and benefits can't exceed $375.)

Any income you lose beyond what you get in total disability (wage-loss) benefits can be claimed back later as part of a claim for damages. While ICBC would like to place a cap on the lost earnings per year that can be claimed back, this hasn't happened yet.

The purpose of homemaker benefits is to allow you to hire someone to perform household duties that you can no longer do yourself as a result of your accident. If you worked prior to your accident and live alone, you may be entitled to both wage-loss and homemaker benefits.

Homemaker benefits have a weekly maximum of $145. If a family member takes over your duties at home, you won't receive this money. Your adjuster may ask for cancelled cheques or paid receipts to prove you've hired outside help. If he's not sure you legitimately need this help, he'll discuss this with your doctor or arrange for an occupational therapist to assess you.

Death benefits and funeral expenses: When someone who is entitled to Part 7 benefits is killed in an auto accident, ICBC is obligated to pay death benefits to his survivors and up to $2,500 in funeral and burial expenses. (This amount may change.)

How much money is paid in death benefits will depend on the deceased's role in his household and how many surviving dependants he has. When the main financial supporter of a family is killed, his surviving spouse or partner (or when there isn't one, a dependent child) will be paid $5,000 in death benefits. Another $1,000 will be paid to each dependent child — or when there's no surviving spouse or partner, each dependent child in addition to the first (who will receive $5,000). Death benefits to more than one child are divided equally between them. (If the deceased had three dependent children and a surviving spouse or partner, each child will receive $1,000 in death benefits. When there's no surviving spouse or partner, one child will receive $5,000 and the other two children each $1,000. Since the money is divided equally between them, each child will receive $2,333 in death benefits: one third of $7,000.)

When the deceased wasn't the main wage earner in the family, his surviving spouse or partner will be paid $2,500 in death benefits. Another $1,000 will be paid to each dependent child. When both parents were killed in an accident, $7,500 will be paid to the first dependent child and $1,000 to each additional child. (If there are three children in the family, each child will receive $3,166 in death benefits: one third of $9,500.) The Public Guardian and Trustee will hold the children's payments in trust for them, releasing the money to each child as he or she turns 19. The family of a deceased minor will receive $500 to $1,500 in death benefits, depending on the minor's age at death.[38]

Additional death benefits will be paid weekly for two years. These should begin 60 days after the deceased's death. When there's only one survivor or dependant, $145 a week is currently paid. A further $35 a week will be paid to each additional dependant. Any total disability benefits the deceased received before he died will be deducted from his survivors' weekly death benefits. Weekly death benefits aren't paid to a deceased minor's family.[39]

Since death benefits are determined by legal statute, you shouldn't need a lawyer to get them. ICBC usually only disputes paying this money when the person claiming it may not have been living with (or financially supported by) the deceased; the death may have been a suicide; or the deceased was in a car that was being used for illegal purposes or to escape from the police. Death benefits may also be refused to the survivors of a deceased driver who wasn't authorized or qualified to drive the car involved.

Besides the death benefits guaranteed to a deceased person's survivors as a Part 7 benefit, they may be paid damages under the Family Compensation Act, which is discussed later in the chapter.

Applying for Part 7 Benefits

You'll have to fill out an application form for accident benefits. When describing your injuries on your form, you should try to be as accurate and thorough as possible. If you ever need treatment for an injury that you've neglected to mention, ICBC may deny that it was caused by your accident. Make sure you write on your form that your injuries include "any other injuries that might arise from my accident and any complications that might arise from my injuries."

The employment section of your application form will ask you what your occupation is, where you work, how long you've worked there, and what your salary is. You'll also be asked about your work history. If you didn't have a regular salaried job for the three years prior to your accident, you'll need to be careful what you write here. Your earlier work experiences don't have to be limited to paid employment. You can include volunteer work, unpaid work you did in a family business, and any other occupations you've had that might eventually be income-producing. You'll want to present yourself as someone who was capable of working prior to your accident and fully intended to do so. If you file a claim for damages and have a scattered work history — or you think you may have trouble proving past or future income losses or lost employment opportunities — you may want to discuss your situation with a personal injury lawyer before applying for accident benefits. He may have some suggestions to make on how you can support a claim for lost income.

If anyone fills out your accident benefits application form for you, you should review this carefully before signing it. The other person may not be aware of the full extent of your injuries or your complete work history. Don't change anything a lawyer has written without discussing this with him. He may have deliberately omitted information he feels might reduce the value of your claim.

If You're Denied Accident Benefits

If you were in breach of your insurance when your accident happened, or your adjuster feels your claim is fraudulent or exaggerated, you may have to sue ICBC to get accident benefits. Treatment for a subjective condition may also be denied.

You may have to go to court to prove that your injuries were caused by your accident, or go through arbitration to prove that the treatment your doctors recommend is necessary and reasonable in cost. If you have a claim for damages that's apt to be large, it may be hard to get accident benefits. Your adjuster may feel that if you have to pay your own medical and rehab expenses you'll accept a quick settlement, reducing ICBC's costs. If your claim is transferred to their head office or to an unsupportive adjuster, your accident benefits may suddenly stop. To get them reinstated, you may have to fire your case manager, if any, or change your rehab program to one your new adjuster prefers.

Your adjuster may refuse to pay for items or services he hasn't pre-approved, even when pre-approval isn't required. Or, he may agree in principle to pay your medical and rehab costs, but not pay for certain therapy your doctor recommended — or stop paying for it midway through your treatment. If you refuse to undergo treatment or retraining that an ICBC medical or vocational adviser feels is appropriate, your accident benefits may stop. You should be given 60 days notice in writing before this happens. During this time, you can apply for a court injunction against the termination of your benefits. If the suggested treatment or retraining is unlikely to be helpful or could have a negative effect on your health, you may have valid grounds for an injunction. (You may not have prior warning that specific treatment is no longer being covered.)

ICBC usually won't pay higher medical or rehab costs outside B.C. than they pay for this treatment in the province. It's not unusual for them to refuse to pay the full cost of physiotherapy in the United States, for example, claiming that it's exorbitant and unreasonable. (Costs in excess of their standard payment rates may only be reimbursable as part of a claim for damages.)

When you're not at fault in an accident, it's often to ICBC's advantage not to pay for your rehab. (See Chapter 18.) If you wait until your case settles to be reimbursed, though, you may have to pay a lawyer a contingency fee on this.

If you receive an accident benefits denial letter and you feel that you have a legitimate claim to Part 7 benefits, you can dispute this through ICBC's Fair Practices Review process. If you're notified that your benefits are going to stop (or you're not getting all the benefits you should be getting), this can be disputed through the same internal review process. You'll be given an opportunity to submit evidence showing why your benefits should continue. You can also initiate a Part 7 legal action or take ICBC to arbitration.

A personal injury lawyer may be able to get you accident benefits that you can't get on your own by providing ICBC with more convincing medical evidence than you've been able to give them. If your adjuster can't explain to his satisfaction why you're not getting accident benefits, he can threaten to sue for punitive or aggravated damages. This may be enough to get ICBC to start providing benefits. (Punitive and aggravated damages are discussed in Chapter 15.)

Financial Compensation (or Damages)

If you weren't solely at fault in your accident, you're entitled to be compensated for the harm that was done to you through someone else's negligence or wrong-doing. If you were partially at fault, you may still be entitled to compensation, but at a reduced level. Both liability and the amount of the damages you're entitled to may have to be determined in court.

You'll only be compensated for the losses for which you specifically request damages. General damages are intended to compensate you for your pain and suffering, which includes your loss of enjoyment of life and loss of functional abilities. Pecuniary damages are the past and future economic losses you can prove, which include your out-of-pocket expenses, lost income, and future care needs. Most claims for future economic losses end up in court.

The various types of compensation you may be entitled to are discussed in Chapter 15 along with other issues at trial. Even if your claim settles out of court, you should be compensated under each head (or category) of damages that applies to your situation.

How Much Is Your Claim Worth?

If you were solely at fault in your accident, settling your claim basically means being reimbursed for your accident-related expenses, and in some cases, buying out future accident benefits you'll need over time. Your Part 7 benefits will be discounted to a present-dollar value when you cash them out to settle your claim. If you have serious injuries, you may want to keep your Part 7's open, or hire an economist to determine a fair buy-out amount. (See Chapter 18.)

If you weren't at fault in your accident, you should be fully compensated for your injuries and their consequences. Your adjuster won't evaluate what your claim is worth in the same way as a personal injury lawyer. He may compare ICBC's costs if you don't initiate legal action with what it might cost them if you do. (Medical-legal assessments and reports alone can cost tens of thousands of dollars.)

A variety of factors influence what a claim for damages is worth. What someone with similar injuries was paid may have no connection to how much money you're offered or awarded in court. A 40-year-old neurosurgeon whose finger is amputated may get relatively little money for his pain and suffering, but have a multimillion dollar claim for lost income. Someone in a low paying job who was close to retiring may get little money for his lost earnings after a spinal cord injury, but a large sum for pain and suffering.

In deciding what settlement offer to make, your adjuster may take into account how credible a witness he feels you'd be in court. If his offer is too low and your case goes to trial, would a judge or jury be more likely to support your position or ICBC's? (The courts often side with ICBC in subjective injury claims and low-velocity impact accidents.)

While your adjuster's settlement offer is supposed to be "fair, objective and defensible",[40] he's under no obligation to offer you what your claim is worth, nor to make you the best offer he can. Based on your medical information and subjective complaints, how long you've been (or are apt to be) unable to work, and how your injuries affect your life, he'll decide whether your injuries are mild, moderate or severe, making you an offer that reflects this. (An injury is only considered severe when your symptoms are likely to persist indefinitely; necessary lifestyle changes may be permanent; you'll need on-going medical and rehab treatment; and you may never to able to resume your pre-accident work.)

After looking at your injuries and their consequences, your adjuster will place a monetary value on your pain and suffering.

(While you may be told about similar claims where people were paid less than this in general damages, these are likely to be the lower end of what was paid in the past.) He'll then estimate your economic losses, if any, and suggest a settlement amount he feels is fair. While most offers are negotiable to some degree, your final settlement will be expected to fall within the general range of what you're offered. If you and your adjuster are wide apart on what you feel your claim is worth, you'll probably end up initiating legal action.

The highest awards for pain and suffering are given to people with severe chronic problems that limit their ability to work. The maximum amount currently paid ($300,000) is only awarded in cases of severe catastrophic injury. ICBC rarely offers this much out of court.

Depending on how your injury affects you, a below-the-knee amputation is worth around $100,000 in general damages and an above-the-knee amputation around $125,000. Back injuries and disc problems with on-going consequences tend to be in the $50,000 range. A mild soft tissue injury may be worth nothing or a few thousand dollars at most, while a moderate-to-severe soft tissue injury may be worth $20,000-$35,000 or more. If you have massive brain damage, you may get little money for your pain and suffering if ICBC (or the court) feels you lack the awareness to be consoled by financial compensation of any amount. If you're aware of having on-going deficits from a brain-injury, a judge or jury may award you $150,000 or more in general damages, but you probably won't be offered this much out of court.[41]

Awards for pain and suffering (or general damages) vary most widely on claims involving subjective conditions. Unless ICBC accepts the existence of your condition and agrees it was caused (or aggravated) by your accident, you won't be offered any damages. If they accept that you're entitled to damages, they'll consider how severe or debilitating your condition is in making you an offer. How much pain do you have? To what degree have you had to restrict your daily activities? How much rehab treatment have you needed? How has your work situation been affected, if at all? (You may not get fair compensation for a subjective condition without initiating legal action and taking your case to trial.)

❖

Your general damages may be smaller than your economic losses. Since the maximum amount that ICBC pays in total disability (wage-loss) benefits is $300 a week, your additional income losses, if any, should be paid to you as part of your pecuniary damages. If your employment possibilities have been permanently diminished by your accident, your future net income losses should be extended to retirement age and discounted for your life expectancy. (How past and future income losses are calculated is discussed in Chapter 15.)

Unless you've fully recovered from your injuries, you may also be entitled to damages for your future care needs. Both future income losses and future care needs can substantially increase the value of a claim. (A minor who may never be fully employable due to an accident can receive a multi-million dollar settlement.) Rather than accepting what ICBC offers you under these heads of damages, you may want to hire an economist to calculate what's appropriate.

Your settlement should include the reimbursement of your out-of pocket expenses. You may be able to recover some of your costs in pursuing your claim as well. You'll have to negotiate this with your adjuster if you settle out of court.

If you don't accept your adjuster's offer, he may ask you what aspects of it you object to, what you feel would be fair, and what you're basing this on. While settlement discussions aren't legally binding, it may be a mistake to mention a specific amount that you'd be willing to accept. If your injuries end up being more serious than you realize, or any complications arise, the sum that you've agreed in principle to accept may not cover your future expenses or on-going care needs. You're unlikely to be offered more than this in out-of-court negotiations, though.

Adjusters have certain limits on how much money they can offer a claimant. Your adjuster may not be able to increase his offer to you unless the bodily injury claims department accepts that the nature of your disabilities has changed. (If your case goes to court, prior to trial the ICBC defence lawyer may make you a settlement offer that's much higher than your adjuster proposed paying you.)

Even if your adjuster's settlement offer seems generous, you may want to consult a personal injury lawyer before accepting it. If other people with similar injuries and work histories have been awarded much more money in court than you were offered, you'll want to know this. Moreover, unless ICBC has accepted full liability in writing on behalf of an at-fault driver, your adjuster's offer may be misleading. If you're considered partially responsible for your accident or injuries, the money that you've agreed to accept will be reduced accordingly. Money you were offered for your future care may also be reduced by the Part 7 benefits you're entitled to. (See Chapter 18.) Unless these issues can be resolved, legal action may have to be taken.

Negotiating a settlement on your own takes time, patience and skill. You may find Martin Zevin's book "How to Settle Your Own Personal Injury Case" helpful even though it's written from an American legal perspective.

TBI ALERT! If ICBC agrees to compensate you for a mild brain injury, they'll expect to do this at a large discount to what your claim may be worth. Your adjuster may warn you that it will be hard to prove the existence or consequences of your injury at trial. While he may be right, you should talk to a personal injury lawyer who specializes in these claims before accepting his offer.

Underinsured Motorist Protection (UMP) Claims

When an at-fault driver doesn't have enough liability coverage to pay the claims against him, Underinsured Motorist Protection helps to ensure that an injured person with UMP coverage will be fairly compensated. UMP claims are frequently made when several people are injured in the same accident. When the damages owed exceed an at-fault driver's third-party liability limit, UMP should cover the additional amount due, up to each claimant's individual UMP limit. Both pedestrians and cyclists are entitled to UMP coverage when someone in their household has a B.C. driver's licence.

(If ICBC denies that you're entitled to Underinsured Motorist Protection, or you don't agree with them on how much your UMP claim is worth, this may have to be resolved through arbitration.)

The total amount you can receive in an UMP claim, including court costs and interest, will be the lesser of the damages awarded in court (or assessed in arbitration) and the amount of your UMP coverage. Your UMP payment will be reduced by any benefits you've received (or were entitled to) from any source, including Part 7 benefits, payments from the Unidentified-Uninsured Motorist Protection Fund, WCB benefits, government (and private) disability benefits or pensions, and payments from other insurers.

If your accident happened in an area where suing for damages is prohibited by law, you won't be allowed to make an UMP claim. However, if it occurred in an area where third-party liability coverage is minimal or not required, but you're not *expressly prohibited* from suing an at-fault driver for damages, you can file an UMP claim. You can also file an UMP claim for an out-of-province accident when you don't have access to Uninsured-Unidentified Motorist Protection. When an accident involving an UMP claim occurs outside B.C., the laws in effect where the accident happened apply, but B.C. law determines how much money you're entitled to. (You may lose your right to UMP coverage after an out-of-province accident if you settle with an underinsured driver without written permission from ICBC.)

Compensation for the Death of a Spouse, Partner, Parent or Child

When a person who is killed in an auto accident wasn't solely at fault, his surviving spouse, partner or children — or if he's a minor, his parents, grandparents or step-parents — can file a claim under the Family Compensation Act. If he was partially responsible for his accident or injuries, the money his survivors are awarded will be reduced by the percentage he was at fault. When a deceased person's family doesn't file a claim for damages within six months of his death, the Public Guardian and Trustee may do this for them. Families rarely accept the settlement offers that ICBC makes, and most of these claims end up in court. (The Public Guardian and

Trustee will review any settlement offers that are made to the family to make sure they're fair to the surviving minors.) A judge normally decides how an award under the Family Compensation Act is to be divided amongst the various survivors.

The deceased's family should be reimbursed for any accident-related expenses he had prior to his death, as well as for on-going costs directly caused by his death, including child care, housekeeping services, and family therapy. Reasonable funeral expenses should be paid and each of the deceased's minor children should receive $20,000 to $30,000 for the loss of his love, guidance and affection.

The largest award usually paid under the Family Compensation Act is for lost earnings. The size of this award is based on how much income the deceased would likely have earned over the years if he'd lived. Determining this amount is subject to widely varying interpretations. Even if the deceased held a regular salaried job prior to his accident, his earnings might have increased over time due to raises, promotions, and new job opportunities. ICBC will try to minimize his lost earnings in calculating what they feel is an appropriate award amount, while his survivors will want to maximize these losses. A personal injury lawyer can be instrumental in seeing that the family is fairly compensated.

When an award under the Family Compensation Act exceeds an at-fault driver's liability coverage, an UMP claim may be made.

CHAPTER 11

Insurance Company Tactics

NOTE: The tactics discussed in this chapter are also used by WCB and other insurers. The assumption in the text, however, is that you've filed a claim for damages against an ICBC-insured driver, and your case may proceed to trial.

As a B.C.-government crown corporation, ICBC has a monopoly on basic auto insurance in the province. While it was originally set up to ensure that the needs of claimants would be met, adjusters often seem more focused on minimizing claims costs than on helping people. Despite ICBC having accumulated billions of dollars in surplus funds over the years,[42] the provincial government routinely proposes switching to a no-fault system to control claims costs. While major-loss claims might still be allowed to be pursued in court, most claimants would be prohibited from suing for damages.[43] Limiting tort claims would benefit ICBC at the expense of claimants. The fact that you can take legal action, when necessary, safeguards your right to reasonable compensation for your injuries.

ICBC often treats seriously injured people as if their claims are fraudulent or exaggerated. Your adjuster may decide that you've magnified your problems to gain sympathy and attention or be awarded large damages. Your accident-related disabilities may be blamed on medical conditions you haven't been bothered by for years, while psychological problems stemming from your accident may be blamed on earlier traumas or a pre-existing condition. As detectives investigate obscure aspects of your life, you may be denied accident benefits, placing you in financial hardship.

Independent Medical Examiners

In an attempt to diminish the value of your claim, your adjuster may send you to an independent medical examiner (or IME) with a reputation as a "hired gun" for insurers.[44] An ICBC-hired medical examiner may try to discredit you by offering an unsupported opinion in a medical-legal report that's unrelated to his area of expertise. One orthopaedic surgeon in the province, for example, frequently blames claimants' slow recoveries on non-existent psychological problems. Other ICBC experts rarely find anything wrong with anyone that they can't blame on a pre-existing condition, or they don't feel will spontaneously resolve once the person's insurance claim settles. A medical examiner who wants to be hired by insurers for assessments and medical-legal reports has to consistently downplay claimants' disabilities. This may mean distorting his own findings or ignoring evidence of a claimant's on-going problems.

Before you're assessed by an ICBC-hired examiner, you should find out as much as you can about him. If you've hired a lawyer, he may be aware of an IME's reputation or can get feedback on this from other lawyers. (The Trial Lawyers Association of BC maintains a database of expert witnesses. These may be clinical psychologists, neuropsychologists, occupational therapists, vocational counsellors or future care assessors as well as medical doctors.) You can also look up an IME's name in ICBC's "Blue Book": their annual *Statements and Schedules of Financial Information*. This notes every service provider to whom ICBC paid $10,000 or more in the previous year. (The Blue Book can be purchased for $5 from ICBC's head office.)

ICBC relies on a small number of medical examiners for the majority of assessments, medical-legal reports, and court appearances.[45] While the B.C. Supreme Court has criticized some of these people for being advocates for ICBC, not independent professionals — and little weight is sometimes given in court to the opinions of clearly biased experts — this practice regrettably continues.[46] If an IME's assessment of you results in you not getting necessary treatment, you can file a complaint with the appropriate professional organization, such as the College of Physicians and Surgeons of BC or the College of Psychologists of BC. (You may want to wait until your insurance claim resolves to do this.)

Can you refuse to go to an IME? You don't have to see every medical (or other) expert that ICBC wants to send you to. If you have any reason to believe that an appointment was set up for you with someone who won't be objective, your lawyer (if any) may be able to convince ICBC to send you to someone else. If they won't do this, and you're advised not to keep your scheduled appointment, ICBC can ask a judge in chambers to issue a court order requiring you to have the assessment done. Your lawyer will have to explain to the judge (or court master) why he feels a particular examiner's opinion is apt to be slanted in ICBC's favour. His arguments will have to be supported by evidence, such as a record of the work the IME has done for ICBC and other insurers in the past, and the nature of the opinions he's expressed. If the judge rules in your favour, you won't have to undergo the assessment.

If ICBC wins their motion in chambers, you'll have to be assessed by the selected IME. However, your objection will become part of the court record if your case goes to trial. This may, or may not, be to your advantage. While it will show the court that you didn't feel you'd be objectively assessed, it may also make them wonder whether you co-operated with an assessment you didn't want.

Disowning an IME's report: ICBC may send you to a series of IMEs until they find someone to support the position that there's little or nothing wrong with you: you've exaggerated your injuries and problems, assuming they even exist. When an IME's medical-legal report doesn't say what ICBC hopes it will, they may "disown" it, meaning they don't intend to use it at trial. While they may change their mind about this later, in the meantime you may not get to see the disowned report. (The only way to guarantee that you'll see an assessment report that ICBC commissions and pays for is to make it a pre-condition of undergoing the assessment that a copy of the resulting report will be promptly sent to your doctor or lawyer. ICBC's commitment to do this should be put in writing.)

The ICBC defence lawyer may share an IME's report with your

lawyer before a decision is made to disown it. If your lawyer thinks the disowned assessment might strengthen your case at trial, he can subpoena the examiner and require her to testify. Since she'll no longer be protected by the confidentiality rules that govern expert witnesses, he'll be able to question her outside court to make sure her testimony will help your case, not harm it.

TBI ALERT! ICBC may have you assessed by numerous IMEs in an effort to find someone who will state that you have no on-going brain injury symptoms; your symptoms, if any, aren't related to your accident; or they can be successfully treated with short-term therapy. If the court accepts this, you may not be compensated for your past and future income losses or future care needs.

How to protect yourself: The first thing you may want to ask an IME is what percentage of his income comes from medical referrals and what percentage comes from ICBC, WCB and other insurers. How many assessments does he do each year for insurers? How often is he hired by claimants' lawyers in auto (or work-related) accidents, and when did this last happened? His answers should give you some insight into how fair you can expect him to be.

Before proceeding with an assessment, make sure the examiner has copies of all relevant reports from your doctors and other experts who have assessed you. If he doesn't have reports that show the findings of your treating doctors and rehab therapists (or your own medical experts), you can ask him to phone the ICBC defence lawyer in your presence to request this. Having him verify in writing what documents he has, or has requested, may make it harder for him to ignore disabilities discussed in earlier reports.

You can also ask an IME for permission to tape-record your session. This may prevent him from probing into aspects of your life that are none of his business or from distorting what you say. While the courts have given examining professionals the right to decide when a session can be taped, an IME who intends to treat you fairly shouldn't object to this. (If an examiner refuses to allow you to tape your session with him, asking him to explain his reasons for this may embarrass him into changing his mind.)

Whether your session is taped or not, it's important to co-operate fully with the examiner. If you don't, and your case goes to trial, the court may question your credibility. At the same time, you should keep in mind that everything you say and do will be interpreted to ICBC's advantage. The purpose of the assessment is to limit the benefits and damages you're entitled to.

To make sure you provide the same information to everyone who assesses you, before seeing the first medical examiner ICBC sends you to, you may want to prepare a summary sheet of your injuries and recovery process. This can include the names of the health-care providers you've seen, the treatment you've received, and the nature of any functional, cognitive, behavioural or emotional problems you've had since your accident. While you may not be allowed to refer to your summary sheet list when you're with an examining professional, you can review it later and make a note of what you remembered to say and anything else you discussed. This may be useful later if you're assessed by other IMEs or when preparing your case for trial.

If you only know something because someone else told it to you, you need to make this clear to the examiner, especially if you have (or may have) a brain injury. Sounding like you remember what you don't actually recall, responding to questions you don't know how to answer with potentially damaging information, and confusing one accident or trauma with another — all common behaviours for people with TBI — could jeopardize your claim for accident benefits or damages.

Charges of Malingering and Fraud

"Malingering" means to intentionally invent (or exaggerate) physical or psychological symptoms for financial gain or to avoid work. Whenever someone who is sent for an assessment is involved in legal proceedings, *or* he may benefit financially from having a physical or psychological deficit, neuropsychologists and other defence experts look for signs of malingering.[47] An IME who assesses you may suspect that you're malingering before he meets you.

If you've refused treatment recommended by an ICBC medical adviser, an IME may conclude that you've made little effort to recover, even though your decision was based on your doctor's advice, and you underwent the treatment she suggested. An IME may find discrepancies between your complaints and his observations because he's ignoring relevant evidence. If you argue with him, or you seem disillusioned with the medical-legal-insurance system, an IME may feel that you're not being co-operative and are trying to mislead him. In fact, you may be argumentative because you have valid reasons not to trust him, while your frustration with the medical-legal-insurance system may be justified by your experiences. You may also be angry at being assessed by a series of IMEs whose reports ICBC then disowns. While most testing procedures have built-in validity components to show when someone isn't co-operating, an IME may ignore these if they disprove his opinion that you're malingering.

Unwarranted charges of malingering can usually be successfully challenged in court by a good lawyer. Nonetheless, it can be disturbing to read in a medical-legal report that you're exaggerating your problems when you've done everything you could to recover. The implication that you're malingering may also be used to deny you necessary treatment or to terminate your accident benefits.

Charges of fraud: ICBC has reported that fraudulent or exaggerated claims account for 10-15% of all claims dollars paid. This is very misleading. These percentages apply to *all* types of insurance fraud combined, not just auto-related claims.[48] Criminal charges are rarely made in bodily injury claims.[49] Despite this, ICBC continues to vigorously investigate these claims.

Instead of providing you with the accident benefits you're entitled to, and offering you fair compensation for your injuries, your adjuster may initiate an extensive investigation of you. You may be treated as if you're trying to defraud ICBC, even when you've understated the effect your injuries are having on your life.

Detective Investigations and Surveillance Efforts

ICBC claims centres have special investigative units that are responsible for "investigat[ing] suspicious claims with a view to laying criminal charges or obtaining evidence to justify denying fraudulent claims."[50] ICBC has one of the largest in-house investigative teams in Canada, and private detectives are hired as well.[51]

Your adjuster may have you investigated if he feels that you've made up aspects of your work history or embellished your employment records; you may have returned to work while claiming wage-loss benefits; or there's "any other reason to suspect fraud".[52] This last phrase gives adjusters a lot of discretion in when they can have a claimant investigated.

You're most likely to have your claims file tagged for special attention if you've made previous ICBC claims; you were a high wage earner prior to your accident; you can no longer work at your pre-accident income level; you were unemployed (or working part-time) when your accident happened; or you'd recently started your own business. If your lifestyle or work is unconventional, or you're outside the mainstream in any way, you're also apt to get your claims file tagged and every aspect of your life investigated.

Your relatives, friends, co-workers and neighbours may be interviewed by detectives and obscure aspects of your past explored. Investigators may not only interview people you know now, or knew at the time of your accident, they may talk to former employers, teachers or neighbours whom you haven't seen in years. Your early work (and school) records may be searched for unfavourable comments, instances of anti-social behaviour, poor coping strategies, and performance failures.

While investigators who work for ICBC are supposed to identify themselves before interviewing anyone, private detectives are specifically instructed to make it clear that they're *not* ICBC employees, but are conducting an independent investigation.[53] This may put your relatives and friends off-guard, allowing a detective to learn something that could be damaging to your case.

If you're no longer able to work the same hours (or earn the same income) you did prior to your accident, detectives may look for evidence that you'd been hoping to reduce your hours or work responsibilities for some time. If you can no longer pursue activities you used to enjoy, an effort may be made to find someone who *thinks* he remembers that you *may* have been planning to stop doing this anyway. If you've had emotional or behavioural problems since your accident, an investigator may look for prior evidence of this. Did an employer or teacher ever find you short-tempered, inattentive or uncooperative? Did you ever function at less than your optimal level? Have you ever been angry or aggressive, self-absorbed or self-pitying? Did you ever yell at a neighbour's child? While anyone might behave like this occasionally, if an investigator learns about specific instances that present you in a negative light, ICBC's lawyer can try to elicit this information from trial witnesses.

No matter how clear-cut the issues are in your case, or how weak ICBC's position is, their lawyer may try to imply the following at trial: you were at fault in your accident; your injuries were minor if they occurred at all; you've exaggerated your accident-related problems and fully recovered from them; there's nothing to stop you from working full-time; you've never been capable of holding a full-time job; you were about to be fired from your job prior to your accident; you've had psychological problems your whole life; and you've made little effort to recover. While the defence might not be able to prove what they imply, by the time your case goes to trial you may have been so thoroughly investigated that anything in your life that could prejudice a judge or jury against you will have been discovered. You and your lawyer will need to be prepared for this.

Surveillance operations: If your adjuster doesn't think that your injuries are as disabling as you claim, or he feels that your recovery is better than you admit, you may be put under surveillance. This often happens when a claimant has a subjective condition or injuries with permanent consequences. Even if you're wheelchair-dependent due to your accident, your daily activities may be videoed.

If you think you're being followed, you can report this to the police, telling them that you're concerned for your family's safety.

(It's usually best to have a woman phone.) This should stop most surveillance efforts. You can also ask your adjuster whether ICBC is having you followed or if this is something you should report to the police. While he'll probably deny that you've been under surveillance, questioning him about this may put an end to it. (Surveillance efforts are rarely effective when someone is aware of them.)

You may be under periodic surveillance for weeks, months or years, even during your personal injury trial. Surveillance efforts are supposed to be conducted in public, not in places where you can reasonably expect to have privacy. You shouldn't be videoed through a window in your own (or someone else's) home, nor should you be put under surveillance in, at or near places used predominantly by children. Investigators aren't supposed to enter your private property, nor is audio surveillance permitted. Illegally or improperly obtained information can't be used as evidence at trial.[54]

You should be given any surveillance videos that ICBC intends to present in court seven days before trial. You'll need to review these carefully with your lawyer and discuss anything that seems misleading. (An investigator may have turned off his camera while you were struggling up a flight of stairs, for example, then turned it on again when you reached the top — "proving" that you can climb stairs without showing how hard this is for you. If you haven't been able to drive since your accident, you may be filmed through the rear-view mirror of a detective's car, so it looks like you're getting into the driver's seat of a car, not the passenger seat.)

Your doctor may agree to review the surveillance videos. If she doesn't see anything on them that changes her opinion about the nature or severity of your injuries, this may be important testimony to have at trial.

CAUTION! It's illegal to tamper with surveillance videos. If the videos that will be shown to the court seem to have been altered in any way, or what's on them is misleading, make sure your lawyer knows this.

❖

Safeguarding Yourself from Insurance Company Tactics

One of the primary functions of surveillance efforts is to find evidence that contradicts what a claimant says. Even if your lawyer handles all communications with ICBC, there may be occasions when you have to deal directly with someone who works for (or represents) them. If an ICBC rehab co-ordinator is assigned to your case, you may see her on a regular basis. You may also be assessed by ICBC medical advisers and experts, and interviewed by the defence lawyer. How you phrase what you say in these situations is crucial in protecting your claim.

If you say that you can't do yard-work anymore and a surveillance video shows you raking leaves, the defence may use this to discredit you in court, one apparent lie implying others. What the video won't show is that you could only rake leaves for a few minutes, or that you were in a lot of pain afterwards. Since it's hard to predict how a physical (or psychological) condition will change over time, you should try to qualify what you say as much as possible so it can't be disproved later. Rather than saying that you can't work in your yard anymore, you can say that you're unable to do yard-work *at the present time*; that doing this causes you pain; or that you can only work in your yard *for a short time now*. These statements express your limitations without placing you at risk of appearing to have lied.

The less contact you have with ICBC staff people, the less opportunity you'll have to say something you may regret. A personal injury lawyer, case manager, relative or friend should be able to act as your intermediary in most situations. Whenever you have to deal directly with anyone who works for (or represents) ICBC, you may want legal advice. (Someone should always be with you as a witness when you meet with an ICBC staff person.)

You need to be careful when speaking to *anyone* about your accident, injuries, recovery process, insurance claim, or legal case. If you downplay accident-related problems so you don't sound like you're complaining, your relatives, friends and co-workers may think you're doing better than you are, and they may pass on this impression to someone investigating your claim.

❖

It's important to be truthful with ICBC and their medical advisers, experts and lawyers about earlier accidents or injuries you've had and pre-accident medical or rehab treatment you've received. An investigator can easily learn this on his own, and an attempt to mislead ICBC will reflect badly on you. Never provide more information than you're specifically asked for, though. You won't want to open up more areas of your life to be investigated, nor provide the ICBC defence team with the names of more people to contact. Keep your responses honest, brief, and to the point at all times.

Before you give your lawyer any documents or records, or authorize the release of this material, you may want to discuss the nature of it with him. Since he'll have to share any documents that are relevant to your claim with the defence lawyer before your case goes to trial, if he feels the material in question might harm your case, he probably won't want it.

All communications from ICBC should be sent to you in writing so you're clear about what's being offered or said. Even if you don't intend to have legal representation, you may want to consult a personal injury lawyer before signing any documents or agreeing to accept a settlement offer. Settling your claim without knowing what it's worth can be costly, and is usually irreversible.

CHAPTER 12

Hiring a Lawyer

While only a third of the people in the province who are injured in auto accidents hire lawyers, two-thirds of ICBC claims dollars are paid to people with legal representation.[55] People with serious injuries are more likely to hire lawyers, of course. Nonetheless, the comparisons made by one Vancouver law firm are telling: ICBC offered someone with a brain injury $10,300 and the firm got him $900,000. Someone with whiplash was offered $6,000 and received $56,000 through the firm's efforts. A claimant with fibromyalgia was offered $37,000 and the firm got her $300,000.[56]

Before you decide whether to hire a lawyer or deal with ICBC yourself, you may want to discuss your situation with a few personal injury lawyers. You'll want to make sure that you know what your legal rights are, what options you have, and what risks you may take by dealing directly with ICBC.

If you file a claim for damages from an at-fault driver, his auto insurer will hire a lawyer to defend him. If you want a lawyer, you'll have to hire one yourself. If your case is heard in Small Claims Court, you may be able to handle this on your own. Adjusters generally discourage claimants from hiring lawyers — it's more expensive for an insurer when someone does.

When a Lawyer Is Necessary

If you only have minor injuries and your claim is fairly straightforward, there may be little reason to hire a lawyer. Not only will it take longer to settle your claim, your legal fees will reduce the money you end up with. If you have serious injuries with long-term consequences, though, you should consult a lawyer as soon as possible. A claim involving future income losses or future care needs can be worth hundreds of thousand of dollars (or more) and ICBC is likely to vigorously challenge it. A good lawyer can help you get fair compensation.

Legal representation is essential when liability is an issue, especially when you or anyone else have serious injuries. If your accident involved a hit-and-run driver, the right lawyer can make the difference between your claim being rejected or you getting both accident benefits and compensation. If you're required to initiate legal action against an uninsured driver in order to get damages from ICBC's Uninsured-Unidentified Motorist Protection Fund, you'll probably want a lawyer as well. If you were in breach of your insurance at the time of your accident, a lawyer can help establish limits to your liability, and to the costs that ICBC is entitled to recover from you. Since Underinsured Motorist Protection (UMP) claims often go to arbitration, you'll want a lawyer to represent you in this as well.

If ICBC questions the existence or consequences of your injuries or disabilities, or your adjuster doesn't feel these were caused by your accident, you may have to go to court to get Part 7 benefits or damages. A lawyer is likely to be more successful than you in proving that your injuries or disabilities are accident-related, and where relevant, that they're continuing to affect your life.

If you're charged with driving while impaired in an accident in which anyone is injured or killed, you need to contact a lawyer immediately. While ICBC is obligated to defend any at-fault driver they insure, your insurance coverage won't be valid if you're convicted of a criminal offence in connection to your accident. You'll need a lawyer to defend you from these charges so you're not personally responsible for the damages owed.

When someone is killed in an accident in which he wasn't solely at fault, his survivors may not get fair compensation without a lawyer's help. Having legal representation is also important when an accident involves an out-of-province driver and when a claimant may have future economic losses.

If you intend to hire a lawyer, it's best to do this early on. Not only is it better for a lawyer to deal with ICBC than for you to do this, ICBC will start investigating your claim right away and someone should be doing this on your behalf as well.

Any time a tort claim for damages is filed, a case may proceed to trial. While lawyers are often reluctant to take claims worth under $50,000 to trial, your lawyer should do what's best for you, even if this means arguing a $15,000 claim before the B.C. Supreme Court.

Work-related accidents: If you were working when your accident happened, a lawyer can advise you on whether to file a claim with ICBC, WCB or both. Making the right decision on this can be crucial when you have serious injuries. While hiring a lawyer isn't necessary with all WCB claims, you may want legal advice on various issues, including the size of your disability payments. If you dispute a WCB decision, you'll probably want legal representation.

Difficult wage-loss claims: Past wage losses that can be documented by an employer are usually fairly easy to prove. If you're self-employed, work on a contract or commission basis, or own your own business, you may need a lawyer's help in supporting a claim for past or future income losses. If your tax returns don't accurately reflect your pre-accident income — you may have done income-splitting with your spouse or partner, for example, had large one-time business expenses, or failed to declare all your earnings on your tax returns — a lawyer can help prove what your accident-related income losses are (and may be in the future), so you can be fairly compensated for this. If ICBC doesn't accept that you've lost job opportunities due to your accident, a lawyer may have to argue this in court. High wage earners, in particular, often have a hard time substantiating lost income without a lawyer's help. (Since most claims for future income loss end up in court or arbitration, a lawyer is needed with these claims.)

Problems with your adjuster: If your adjuster isn't supportive, or you have trouble getting accident benefits, you'll probably want to consult a lawyer. (Personal injury lawyers don't recommend that claimants use the ICBC internal review process discussed in Chapter 9. The Fair Practices Review department is felt to be slanted towards getting claimants to accept ICBC's decisions, not to change them.) You may also want to consult a lawyer if you can't negotiate a settlement agreement with your adjuster. He can advise you on whether the offer you were made seems reasonable. If it isn't, you may want him to take over the negotiations with your adjuster or initiate legal action.

If you have catastrophic injuries, you (or someone on your behalf) should consult a lawyer who specializes in these claims as soon as possible. You'll want to make sure that no evidence supporting your claim is lost; that you don't do or say anything to place your claim at risk; and that all necessary action is taken to get you the care you need and the compensation you're entitled to.

Finding the Right Lawyer

You should only hire a lawyer whom you have confidence in and feel comfortable with. You'll want him to have experience in handling similar claims and be available to work on your case immediately. The majority of ICBC cases are handled by approximately 20 law firms. Some of these firms initiate as many as 100 legal suits a year, with the average claim around $35,000.[57] The firms that specialize in major-loss (or large) claims usually limit the number of cases they work on. A smaller firm, or a lawyer in private practice, may be just as capable of getting you a fair settlement.

The phone book probably isn't the best place to look for a lawyer. A large ad in the Yellow Pages may mean that a firm handles a lot of ICBC cases, not that their clients necessarily get good settlements. If no one whose opinion you trust can recommend a personal injury lawyer to you, the Lawyer Referral Services of the Canadian Bar Association (B.C. branch) can refer you to someone, whom you can consult for 30 minutes for $10 or less. (Most personal injury lawyers offer free initial consultations.) Many B.C. lawyers have websites that will give you an idea of the kinds of cases they handle.

If you have a brain injury, spinal cord injury, or another disability with lifelong consequences, you'll want to hire a lawyer who has special expertise in these claims. If ICBC or another insurer disputes the cause or extent of your disability, the necessity of recommended treatment, or the impact that an accident-related condition is having on your life, you'll want to be working with someone who is experienced in dealing with this. While disability organizations won't recommend a lawyer, they can get you in touch with local support groups whose members may be able to suggest a good lawyer in your area.

You'll probably want to interview several lawyers before deciding whom to hire. When setting up your initial interviews, make sure you won't be charged for these. You may want to find out over the phone whether a firm ever represents ICBC or other insurers. If they do, and this would make you uncomfortable working with them, ask them if they can recommend a lawyer who only represents injured plaintiffs.

Assuming your claim is valid, there are many good lawyers in the province who can represent you. A lawyer with the initials "Q.C." (Queen's Counsel) after his name has been honoured for his long service and distinction at the Bar.

Interviewing a Lawyer

Your initial interview with a lawyer should take about 1½ hours. The lawyer will try to learn as much as he can about your accident and injuries, while you'll want to question him about similar claims he's handled and get an idea of what it would be like to work with him. (You may want to see if you can phone a few of his clients to discuss their experiences with him. They'll have to agree to this.)

It may be helpful to prepare a summary sheet for your interviews that contains the relevant information a lawyer might want. Where, when and why did your accident happen? Who was at fault, who was involved, and who were the witnesses? What injuries were you initially aware of, and what showed up later (and when)? Who examined you, what treatment did you get, and what are your current complaints, if any? You should also include some personal information: your age and marital status; the ages of your dependants, if any; the type of work do you do; and how long you've done this. How many years have you been at your present job, what do you currently earn, and what did you earn prior to your accident, if different? How much work have you missed due to your accident? Photos or documents that might help explain your situation should be brought to the interviews as well, including the police report, medical records, and correspondence relating to your accident or injuries.

Once you've answered a lawyer's questions, he should be able to tell you how strong a case you have, what he estimates your claim is worth, what will be involved in pursuing legal action, and how long your case may take to resolve. He'll usually mention his fees before asking if you want to hire him. Before you can make a decision on this, you'll want to ask him some questions and interview other lawyers. While there's no harm in mentioning that you're interviewing other lawyers as well, it's none of his business who they are.

If you don't have enough time to ask a lawyer everything you want, you can set up a second meeting with him. Check first to make sure you won't be charged for this.

How a lawyer answers your questions will help you judge whether you'll be satisfied with him representing you. Do you feel he'll work hard for you and be attentive to your needs? Has he answered your questions clearly, with a minimum of legal jargon, making sure you understand him? Does he seem realistic in his assessment of your case and both its strengths and weaknesses? How flexible are his fees and other aspects of his legal contract? Are his fees similar to what other lawyers charge in similar cases? Does he seem more (or less) knowledgeable and experienced than the other lawyers you've interviewed?

How convincing do you feel the lawyer will be in presenting your case in court or in negotiating with ICBC or another insurer? Does he follow the professional guidelines set by the Law Society of BC (as described in Chapter 13)? How easy do you feel it will be to work with him over the many months or years it may take to settle your claim?

TBI ALERT! **If you have a brain injury of even mild severity, a relative or friend should be with you when you interview prospective lawyers. Your judgment may be impaired, and you may not have enough insight into your situation to provide accurate information.**

Questions to Ask a Lawyer

In evaluating a lawyer's experiences with similar cases, you'll want to find out how they're similar and what the outcome was. If you were in a hit-and-run accident, or you (or another driver) were uninsured or in breach of your insurance, how much experience has he had with these types of claims? When was the last time he handled one and what was the outcome? If several people were injured in your accident or you have serious injuries with long-term consequences, how familiar is he with current UMP regulations, when was the last time he handled an UMP claim, and what was the outcome? If your accident was work-related, would he suggest that you file a claim with both ICBC and WCB, assuming you have this option? What are the advantages and drawbacks of filing a claim with either — or both? Has he handled many work-related auto accident claims?

Does the lawyer usually negotiate out-of-court settlements for his clients or do most of his cases go to trial? How many ICBC cases has he argued in court in the last year? Is he prepared to take your case through the full court process if necessary? What does he feel your claim is worth, and what is he basing this on? What does he see as the major weaknesses in your case?

Unless you've already gotten this information over the phone, you'll want to find out how much of the lawyer's work is devoted to ICBC cases. Does he (or his firm) ever represent ICBC or other insurers? Is anyone in his firm currently doing this?

You'll also want to ask the lawyer what specific steps he'll take in pursuing your claim and what the time frame is for these. How many hours does he think he'll spend on your case, and how long does he think it will take to resolve? How many cases is he actively working on now, and how many does he usually handle at one time? When can he start working on your case? What initial actions will he take?

You may also want to clarify how involved the lawyer will expect you to be in your case. Will you make all legal decisions based on his advice, or are there certain decisions he'll make on his own? If he consults another lawyer about your case, will he cover any costs involved?

How often will you be updated on what's happening with your case? Will you have regularly-scheduled meetings or phone conferences with the lawyer, and will he make sure that you're promptly sent copies of all correspondence relating to your claim? How quickly does he usually return his clients' phone calls, and whom will you speak to when he's not around? If you'll deal with other people in his office occasionally, can he introduce you to them now? How long have they been with him, and how much experience do they have? What aspects of your case may be handled by his office staff, other lawyers in his firm, para-legals, or articling students? Will he accept full responsibility for their work?

Will the lawyer personally handle all negotiations and trial work on your case? Will he prepare you for your examination for discovery and court testimony, if any? Will he be at your discovery, and in court every day if your case goes to trial? If he's involved with another client on your court date, will your trial be postponed, or will another lawyer represent you until he can take over? Who will decide what course of action to take in this situation — you or him?

While there's no right or wrong answer to these questions, they should give you an idea of how accountable the lawyer will be to you, and what you can expect in working with him.

In addition to your lawyer's fee, what other costs will you be responsible for? Will the lawyer wait until your case has resolved to be reimbursed for his expenses? How often will you be sent an interim statement of accounts that shows what he's spent to date on your case? Will he pay for expert assessments and medical-legal reports up front or will you have to do this? Will you be informed before he incurs any major expense? (Depending on your comfort level, this can be anything above $500 or above $5,000.) If he earns $100,000 or more on your case — or another set amount, which could be more or less than this — will he split any expenses with you that ICBC (or another insurer) doesn't reimburse? Will he agree not to charge you more than the Registrar's rates for his expenses?

If you don't recover enough money to pay his expenses in full, will he absorb this cost himself or place a cap on how much money you'll have to pay him?

You'll also want to be clear about what services his legal fees cover. Besides filing legal documents for you, representing you in court and in other legal proceedings, and trying to negotiate a settlement, will he help you get accident benefits from ICBC, and when relevant, disability benefits from the government or a private insurer? If legal action has to be pursued to get you accident benefits, how will you be billed for this? If aspects of your case have to be brought back before the trial judge or argued before the Court Registrar after trial, will his contingency fee cover this, or will you be billed separately for it?

If your case is appealed, will he handle the appeal? How much appellate experience does he have and how successful has he been? If another lawyer represents you on appeal, will he pay the appeal lawyer's fee, or will you be responsible for this? Who will cover any appeal costs that ICBC (or another party) doesn't reimburse?

If you develop delayed-onset problems or end up with permanent disabilities, will the lawyer refer you to someone who has more experience handling claims of this size or complexity? If you decide to continue using him, will you be able to re-negotiate your fee agreement? If anyone in his office who works on your case starts to work for ICBC (or a legal firm that represents them) while your case is pending, will you be notified beforehand? What options will you have if you're concerned about a potential conflict of interest?

You may also want to ask the lawyer whether he's ever been sued for malpractice or brought before the Law Society of BC, or another professional organization, for unethical or unprofessional behaviour. Over last five years, how many clients have taken him to court to dispute his fees? Are his billing practices or professional conduct currently being contested? (While he may not answer these questions, you can ask them.)

To evaluate the lawyer's competency in court, you may want to ask for copies of trial transcripts of similar cases he's handled. You can also find out when he'll be in court next on an ICBC case so you can observe him in action.

Major-loss claims: If an accident-related disability may affect your ability to work in the future, you'll want to hire the best lawyer you can to make sure you receive enough money in damages to take care of yourself throughout your life. You'll need to be extremely thorough in questioning prospective lawyers. You (or a relative or friend) should take detailed notes of what each lawyer tells you.

If you have a spinal cord injury or brain injury, you'll want to find out how much of the lawyer's practice is devoted to these cases and how many years he's handled them. Does he have special training in neuro-law? If you have chronic pain or fatigue, fibromyalgia, post-traumatic stress disorder, or another accident-related psychological (or psychiatric) condition, how knowledgeable is he about this? Has he taken courses that deal with these disabilities or represented other clients with them?

You'll also want to make sure that the lawyer has the time and resources needed to devote to your case. Is he prepared to spend as much money as necessary to successfully pursue your claim? If liability may be an issue, will he hire an investigator to locate witnesses and an accident-reconstruction engineer to determine what caused your accident, paying for this up front? What expert witnesses does he anticipate needing to support your claim? Will he pay for medical, psychological, neuropsychological, occupational, vocational and future-care assessments up front, as needed? Will he hire an economist to estimate the present-dollar value of your future economic losses, if any, and pay for this up front? If you're not fully reimbursed for the fees his experts charge, will he deduct the non-reimbursed money from your award or settlement before he calculates his contingency fee? (This will reduce his fee and increase the money you end up with.)

If you won't be able to return to work for a long time (if at all), what action will he take to ensure that the financial pressures on you and your family aren't overwhelming? Will he help you apply for wage-replacement benefits, federal or provincial benefits, or disability benefits from a private insurer? If you need treatment that isn't covered by MSP, ICBC, WCB, an extended health-care plan or other insurer, will he pay for this up front and wait until your case resolves to be reimbursed? (Few personal injury lawyers still do this, but there's no harm in asking.) What is he prepared to do to ensure that you'll have the money you need for child care, attendant care, or household help? Will he hire a professional case manager for you? (Most lawyers who handle claims involving catastrophic injuries are focused on improving the quality of life for their clients and their clients' families, acting as advisers and advocates in all matters.)

After a catastrophic injury, it's particularly important to find out how much of the work on your case will be handled by the lawyer you're interviewing and how much other people in his office will do. Whom will you deal with on a daily basis, and how much experience do they have?

What You'll Have to Pay a Lawyer

While legal aid lawyers don't handle personal injury cases, if you face criminal charges in connection to your accident or you're having trouble getting income assistance or EI benefits, the Legal Services Society of BC can arrange for a lawyer to represent you in this. Your household income must be under $1,000 a month to qualify. If you recover money from a case that a legal aid lawyer represents you in, you may have to pay back some (or all) of the Legal Services Society's costs. (A personal injury lawyer may be willing to represent you in the above actions without having his fee paid until your insurance claim settles.)

Contingency fees: Most personal injury lawyers are paid on a contingency fee (or percentage-of-outcome) basis. You'll also be responsible for your lawyer's out-of-pocket expenses, most of which should be reimbursed to you when your insurance claim settles. While you won't owe your lawyer a legal fee if your claim is denied and you're not paid any damages, you'll still have to cover his expenses. (You may also have to pay court costs and ICBC's expenses.)

The contingency fee percentage you're charged should be negotiable to some degree. If a lawyer doesn't want to represent you for what you're willing to pay him, he won't take your case. You need to be realistic in your expectations, though. Depending on the circumstances, most personal injury lawyers in the province charge 15-30% of the amount recovered, with 25% the most common percentage charged in ICBC cases. (The Law Society of BC has set a maximum contingency fee percentage of 33⅓% in auto accident claims for personal injury or wrongful-death.) The percentage your lawyer charges you will reflect the risk he feels he's taking in representing you, how difficult he expects your case to be, and how much work he thinks he'll have to do.

In general, the more your claim is worth, the lower the contingency percentage you should pay. Other considerations that may affect the percentage charged are whether liability is an issue; whether there's a dispute about the cause, nature, or consequences of your injuries; and at what point the lawyer became involved. A lower percentage may be charged when a case settles before a lot of trial preparation is done. One Vancouver law firm that handles major-loss claims charges 15% when a case settles more than 60 days before trial; 20% when it settles within 60 days of trial; 25% when it goes to trial; and 33⅓% when it goes to appeal and the firm handles the appeal.[58] This applies to cases worth $500,000 or more, where neither liability nor the extent of a claimant's injuries are vigorously challenged. A lawyer may charge 10-15% in some situations and 30% in others, depending on the strengths and weaknesses of a client's claim. (When liability isn't clear-cut, a higher percentage is usually charged.)

A lawyer may agree to lower his contingency fee percentage if your award or settlement goes above a pre-determined amount. You'll have to jointly decide the level at which this reduced percentage is to go into effect. (This can be $100,000 or $500,000, depending on what you agree to.) While personal injury lawyers typically charge a higher percentage on appeal, if you hire an appeal lawyer and pay him yourself, you may not have to pay your trial lawyer a higher contingency percentage on appeal. (You'll have to negotiate this issue with him.)

Once your case resolves, if you don't feel that your legal fees are reasonable, you'll have the right to take your lawyer to court to dispute this. Your situation may have changed, making what initially seemed fair now seem unreasonable. The courts have been open to reducing contingency percentages that are too high, given the amount of legal work done.

Other percentage arrangements: If you were involved in serious settlement negotiations with your adjuster before hiring a lawyer, he may agree to only charge you a contingency fee on the money that exceeds what you were already offered. If an appeal lawyer argues your case before the B.C. Court of Appeal or the Supreme Court of Canada, he may base his fee on the money at risk, not your full award, or he may bill you by the hour or charge you a set fee.

Hourly-rate fees are usually charged by lawyers in everything but personal injury cases. If you expect to receive damages of several hundred thousand dollars or more, it may make sense to pay your lawyer by the hour instead of paying a contingency fee. Which payment method you choose will depend on your level of comfort. If your lawyer bills you by the hour you'll have to pay for his time even if your claim is denied or you don't recover enough money to pay his fee. Moreover, a lawyer who bills you by the hour may expect his time and expenses to be paid on an on-going basis.

What may work out best with a potentially large claim is to pay your lawyer a combination of an hourly-rate fee and a contingency fee. If you have injuries with lifelong consequences, you can discuss this payment option with the lawyers you interview to see what they suggest.

Any services not expressly covered by your contingency fee may be billed on an hourly-rate basis. This includes a Part 7 legal action as well as post-trial efforts to collect your money. If you hire a new lawyer, your first lawyer may bill you by the hour for the work he did on your case. (In practice, personal injury lawyers rarely keep track of the time they spend on a case. The new lawyer usually negotiates with the first lawyer to determine the size of the first lawyer's fee. This amount is then deducted from the new lawyer's fee.) If your case goes to appeal and you were already charged the maximum contingency percentage allowed, you may be billed by the hour or charged a flat fee for the appellate work your lawyer does.

Most personal injury lawyers in the province charge $100-$300 an hour for work they bill in this way. When they appear in court on a client's behalf, a higher daily rate is usually charged.

Fixed fees in a personal injury case are usually limited to appeals, WCB applications, and post-trial appearances before the Court Registrar. A lawyer generally only charges a fixed fee when he knows beforehand how much work he'll have to do. You should be told what you'll pay for any services billed in this way. If the fee quoted doesn't include the lawyer's expenses, ask him to itemize these for you up front.

A retainer is money you pay a lawyer in advance, which is held in trust until used. When the amount in trust falls below a certain level, you may be asked to place additional money on account. The only time a retainer is normally requested in a personal injury case is when a lawyer isn't sure that enough money will be recovered to pay his expenses.

In addition to your lawyer's fees (and the taxes on this), your legal expenses may include the cost of collecting evidence and examining the facts in your case; getting expert assessments and reports done; and anything else needed to successfully argue your case at trial. While many personal injury lawyers pay these expenses up front, they expect to be paid back when a case resolves. You may be responsible for court costs, filing fees, the fees charged by various experts, travel expenses for trial witnesses, and your lawyer's office expenses. If you're awarded costs and disbursements at trial, which usually happens unless a claim is denied, ICBC should reimburse most of your lawyer's expenses, but they may not pay all of them. (Disbursements are the expenses your lawyer has in conducting your case.) If your claim settles out of court, you'll have to negotiate with ICBC to determine what expenses they'll pay.

Your Legal Contract or Fee Agreement

Unless your contract with your lawyer clearly outlines the services he'll perform, the legal fees and other costs you'll be responsible for, and other issues that are important to you, your working relationship may become strained by the time your case resolves. Your lawyer's standard contract or fee agreement will protect his interests and limit his liability; it won't protect you in the same way. While you can use his contract as a starting point in your discussions with him, most contract terms should be negotiable.

A description of what you'll have to pay your lawyer is basic to your contract with him. The contingency percentages printed on the contract can be altered: what's appropriate in an average case may not be fair in your situation nor what you've agreed to. The simpler your case is, the more it's worth and the earlier it settles, the lower the contingency percentage you should pay. You may want your contract to outline different contingency fee percentages for different outcomes, based on what you and your lawyer have discussed. If your claim settles for over $100,000 (or another predetermined amount), your contract should state whether you'll pay a lower contingency percentage on your whole award or only the portion that exceeds the agreed amount. You may want your contract to state that if your case goes to appeal, your lawyer will only earn a higher percentage on the money in dispute, not your full award, and he'll pay your appeal lawyer (if any), not you.

Before you sign your contract or fee agreement, you should be aware of what other personal injury lawyers in the province charge in similar cases. You may want your contract to give you the right to re-negotiate your legal fees at a later date. (If an accident-related disability turns out to be more significant than you currently believe, substantially increasing the value of your claim, your lawyer may be willing to reduce his fee to keep you as a client.)

The only time it may make sense to hire a lawyer without agreeing to a specific contingency percentage or sliding scale is when you were seriously injured and how fully you'll recover is unknown. Until you and your lawyer know what issues will have to be argued at trial or in out-of-court negotiations, you won't know what terms are fair. Your lawyer may have to prove that your injuries were caused by your accident, that they're permanent in nature, and that they'll continue to affect your life and your ability to earn income. He may also have to present evidence at trial showing how much on-going care you'll need, how long you'll need this, and how large your future income losses will be. He may not want to commit himself to a contingency fee percentage or sliding scale until he can estimate how much work he'll have to do and what it will cost him to support your claim at trial.

Your lawyer's hourly rate and daily court rate should be noted in your legal contract. You'll also want your contract to state that you won't have to pay your lawyer's legal fees or expenses until your case resolves and you've recovered the money you're owed.

Since you may not be reimbursed for all your lawyer's expenses, you may want a clause added to your contract stating that non-reimbursed expenses will be deducted from your award or settlement before your lawyer calculates his fee. (He may only agree to this if his fee exceeds a pre-determined amount which can be noted in the contract.)

If your lawyer agrees to place a cap on the expenses you'll have to pay if your claim is denied, or you don't recover enough money to pay his expenses in full, your contract should note what this cap is. You may also want a clause in your contract stating that your lawyer will get permission from you prior to incurring an expense in excess of $1,000 or another set amount.

You may be able to negotiate with your lawyer to pay a reduced contingency percentage on out-of-pocket expenses (or special damages) that ICBC should have covered as a Part 7 benefit. (See Chapter 15.) While your lawyer will probably want his full fee paid on any special damages he has to argue in court or negotiate to get, he may agree to charge a smaller fee on uncontested special damages.

While some lawyers charge clients separately for the work they do getting them accident benefits, others don't do this. An independent Part 7 legal action is more likely to be billed separately than one heard at the conclusion of a tort trial for damages. To ensure that you're not charged for your lawyer's efforts in getting you accident benefits, your contract should state that he'll handle all necessary legal actions in connection to your insurance claim, *including* a Part

7 legal action and arguing costs and disbursements, without further cost to you. (He may only agree to this if his fee exceeds a set amount noted in the contract.)

If you'll be charged an additional fee for any services your lawyer performs, how you'll be billed should be spelled out in your contract. You may want a clause inserted stating that the money you pay for these services will be deducted from your lawyer's fee if his fee exceeds $100,000 or another set amount. Your contract should also state that if a second lawyer is hired in connection to your claim for any reason, your lawyer will deduct the second lawyer's fee from his fee.

When a lawyer bills a client on a contingency fee basis, his contract usually notes how he'll be paid if the client hires a new lawyer. Your legal contract may state that you'll have to pay your lawyer for the work he's done before he sends over your file to your new lawyer. He may let you change this to specify that his bill won't be due until your case resolves. You may also want your contract to state that your lawyer will send you his bill by registered mail within five business days of the date he's notified in writing that you're hiring a new lawyer. (See Chapter 13.)

CAUTION! Make sure your legal contract specifies that your lawyer's fee will be based on the money *recovered*; that you won't be charged more than the Registrar's rates for any item or service; and that you'll have the right to have the reasonableness of the contract reviewed by the B.C. Supreme Court.

Prior to finalizing your legal contract, it may be helpful to write down in your own words what you expect from your lawyer, what you understand your legal fees to be, and other issues you want covered in the contract. Your lawyer can then be asked to sign this. You can also ask him to write down in simple everyday language what services he'll provide in exchange for his fee and what expenses you may be responsible for paying.

Since conflicts with lawyers often revolve around a lack of

responsiveness to a client's concerns, you may want your lawyer to give you a written commitment that he'll return your phone calls within two to three business days; send you copies of all correspondence relating to your case within three to five business days; and mail you an interim statement of accounts every six months.

If your lawyer doesn't use a standard contract, he may compose a document on his firm's letterhead that outlines the terms you've discussed and agreed on. If his letter (or contract) contains terms that you haven't discussed, or it omits terms that you've mutually agreed to, this should be amended before you sign the contract. (Changes to a legal document have to be initialled by all parties.)

Any legally-binding document you sign should be written in a way that makes its intentions clear to an impartial outsider. To ensure that your legal contract protects your interests and that all negotiated terms are accurately reflected in it, you may want to review it with another lawyer before you sign it. He can explain the implications of each clause to you, including what you and your lawyer are each entitled to and what your respective obligations are. Don't expect the lawyer you're hiring to advise you on whether your contract with him is fair; get independent legal advice on this. The Lawyer Referral Services of the Canadian Bar Association (B.C. branch) can refer you to someone who does contract law, whom you can consult for 30 minutes for $10. Your business or personal lawyer, if any, may also be able to review your contract with you. If you re-negotiate or amend the terms of your contract later, you may want independent legal advice on this as well.

When a minor is injured in an accident, her parent or legal guardian can sign a contact with a lawyer on her behalf. The Public Guardian and Trustee may review this to make sure the terms are fair to the minor.

When a person is *incompis mentis* (or not of sound mind), someone with an enduring power of attorney for him, the Committee of his estate, or the Public Guardian and Trustee can sign a contract with a lawyer for him.

CHAPTER 13

Working With Your Lawyer

You're entitled to competence and consideration from your lawyer at all times. He should treat you with respect and keep you updated regularly on all aspects of your case. The Law Society of BC has set professional guidelines that all lawyers in the province are expected to follow. Your lawyer should prepare all legal documents and perform all legal tasks relating to your case promptly and properly; respond to all communications dealing with your case in a reasonable time; discuss all relevant information with you even when this reveals his mistakes or negligence; keep you reasonably informed about your case; provide progress reports when reasonably expected; answer reasonable requests for information; respond to your phone calls when necessary; and keep his appointments with you. If he tells you that something is supposed to happen by a certain date, that date shouldn't pass without him providing follow-up information. You should be told about all settlement proposals and have them clearly explained. The legal fees you'll be charged should be fully disclosed, and you should be informed in advance if your lawyer has a financial interest in any company to whom disbursements will be paid. He shouldn't accept compensation from anyone connected to your case without informing you of this, nor should he practice law while under the influence of alcohol or drugs.

The problem with these guidelines is that they don't define what "reasonable" is, and they leave it to your lawyer to decide when it's necessary to respond to your phone calls. Unless you can reach an agreement with him on what's reasonable or necessary, and this is put in writing and signed by you both, future conflicts may arise that interfere with your working relationship.

Your lawyer should advise you on legal matters, not make decisions for you. Your case should be conducted on the terms you feel are appropriate after listening to his advice.

You may have frequent meetings with your lawyer at first as he collects information from you, arranges for you to get accident benefits, and makes sure you're getting necessary treatment. Once these issues are taken care of, there may be long periods of time during which nothing much seems to be happening. Before your examination for discovery (see Chapter 14), you'll usually meet with your lawyer to prepare for this, then things will quiet down again. These interim periods can be very frustrating. While you're waiting for your lawyer to get pre-approval for accident benefits, he may have little time for you or your concerns. As your trial date approaches, you'll probably have a lot of contact with him again as he lines up his witnesses and makes sure he has the evidence he needs to support your claim. He may want frequent feedback from you in the weeks prior to trial as settlement negotiations become intense.

During the many months (or years) it takes to resolve your claim, you may have to initiate most contact with your lawyer. Since he may not respond to unexpected phone calls in a timely manner, if you want to stay informed about what's happening with your case you may have to schedule periodic meetings or phone conferences with him. Meeting him once a month may be reasonable at first, with this tapering off to once every few months thereafter, or as needed. Since you should be getting copies of all correspondence relating to your case and all documents filed on your behalf, anything you don't understand can be discussed with your lawyer at your next scheduled meeting, or a phone date can be set up to discuss this. If your lawyer isn't around to take your call at the prearranged date and time, make it clear to whomever you speak that you'll expect to hear from him within one to two business days.

You may want to keep a written record of your contacts with your lawyer and his staff, including what you talk about in phone conversations and meetings, what advice you're given, and what decisions are made. Your notes may be important later in clarifying what you've discussed or agreed to. You may also want a record of the dates (and times) you phone your lawyer and when he returns your calls. If you file a complaint against him later, your notes may help validate your position. Keep track of your lawyer's court appearances as well: there may be legal fees associated with this.

TBI ALERT! If you hire a lawyer before realizing you have permanent deficits from a brain injury, once this becomes apparent you should question him closely about his experience with these claims. You'll want to be working with someone who has special training in neuro-law, a working knowledge of the on-going effects of TBI, and a genuine interest in your problems. You may have to hire a new lawyer.

What You Can Expect Your Lawyer to Do

After you've decided what lawyer you're hiring, you'll usually meet with him so he can advise you on the benefits you may be entitled to through ICBC, WCB, other insurers or government agencies. If he's had other clients with similar injuries or disabilities, he should have a fairly good idea of the type of treatment you need and can hopefully see that you get this.

If you've already recovered from your injuries — or they've stabilized enough to know what to expect in the future — your lawyer may contact your adjuster to discuss a settlement. You should be informed of every offer made. Before your lawyer makes a counter-offer to ICBC (or another insurer), he should discuss this with you. Until you've accepted a formal Offer to Settle, he'll have to proceed as if a trial is inevitable.

Besides handling all legal proceedings connected to your case and filing all necessary documents, your lawyer should advise you of your legal rights and represent you in court and in out-of-court negotiations. He should act as your advocate with ICBC and other insurers, taking whatever steps are necessary to convince them of the nature and extent of your injuries and the level of care you need. (Once ICBC receives a Statement of Claim from your lawyer, they can only have contact with you in his presence.)

If your lawyer can't get you accident benefits, he may have to initiate a Part 7 legal action against ICBC to force them to fulfil their obligations towards you. (While a Part 7 action is usually filed automatically when a tort claim for damages is initiated, it isn't always pursued.) He should also make sure you get the disability benefits you're entitled to from other sources. This can be a complex process, especially when a condition is considered subjective.

If your claim for damages is apt to be large, and your lawyer has the financial resources to do this, he may pay for your rehab treatment up front if you can't afford to cover this cost yourself and ICBC (or another public or private source) isn't doing this. While few personal injury lawyers cover treatment costs anymore, a neuro-lawyer may do this, when warranted. (It's better for ICBC to pay for your treatment up front. See Chapter 18.)

If you were seriously injured, your lawyer may hire a professional case manager to oversee your care. If he feels that he can function in this capacity himself, make sure he has the time, knowledge and willingness to co-ordinate your rehab efforts and locate interim sources of financing for you, as needed.

If expert assessments have to be done to support your claim at trial, your lawyer may pay for these and wait to be reimbursed when your case resolves.

Your Role in Your Case

It's up to you to decide how involved you want to be in your case. Do you want to know about all actions and negotiations that take place or only the minimum necessary? While you can choose to remain relatively uninvolved, the more you help your lawyer understand who you are, what you were like before your accident, and how your accident and injuries are affecting your life, the easier it will be for him to protect your interests.

Your lawyer may want to discuss your accident with you in greater depth than he did at your initial interview. Photos of the accident scene will help him visualize what happened so he can judge whether you were at fault in any way. He'll expect to be told about any unique circumstances that might affect your case.

When you're discussing the details of your injuries and disabilities with your lawyer, make sure you include even minor problems that aren't being actively treated as these may have later repercussions that affect your claim. If a pre-existing condition was aggravated by your accident, your lawyer should be told about this. He'll want to know about any prior injuries or health problems you've had. It may also be helpful for him to have pre- and post-accident photos of you that show your overall changes as well as accident-related injuries or scars.

Your lawyer will want to know what medical and rehab treatment you've undergone due to your accident. He may ask you to update him whenever your condition changes; the nature or frequency of your therapy changes; or you're referred to a new doctor or rehab therapist. While he may not suggest that you keep a record of your medical and rehab appointments, or a diary of your recovery process, you may want to do this for future reference. (Functional disabilities, psychological or emotional issues, and behavioural changes, if any, should be included in your recovery diary. See Chapter 2.) This may help your lawyer in negotiating an out-of-court settlement or preparing your case for trial.

If you lose income as a result of your accident, your lawyer will need information from you to validate this. He may want a letter from your employer describing your pre-accident work responsibilities and how these have changed, if at all. If an accident-related disability prevents you from getting a promotion or raise, you'll have to be able to document this for it to be included in your claim for lost income. Your lawyer may ask you about your previous work history and want copies of your past tax returns. If your earnings during the three years prior to your accident were reduced due to specific life circumstances, you should discuss this with him.

The more complex your case and the more uncertain the outcome, the more thoroughly you and your lawyer will have to explore ideas together to support your claim. He'll need to rely on you for a clear picture of your pre- and post-accident life, including anything ICBC might use to discredit you. If there are aspects of your life that could be used to prejudice the court against you, your lawyer should be told about this early on.

When Problems Arise with Your Lawyer

Most complaints against lawyers have to do with poor communications and billing practices. You may also feel that your lawyer isn't handling your case in a timely manner; he's not looking after your interests; or he's guilty of professional misconduct. These are serious concerns that need to be dealt with promptly.

If your lawyer doesn't treat you with respect or he's verbally abusive, keep a record of the dates and circumstances so you'll have documentation if you file a disciplinary action against him. You can tape your phone conversations to back up your complaints.

You need to get independent legal advice immediately if the way your lawyer handles your case causes you financial losses. He may not have filed legal documents on time and your claim was denied, or he may have accepted a settlement offer without your consent. (You're legally bound by an offer he accepted even if you didn't authorize it.) Your only recourse in these situations is to file a complaint with the Law Society of BC or sue your lawyer for damages. Lawyers carry liability insurance that protects them if they act negligently, unprofessionally or not in good faith with a client, causing him financial losses.

If your lawyer can't get you accident benefits and he has no credible excuse for this, you may want to consult another personal injury lawyer to see whether your case is being handled properly and, if not, what options you have.

CAUTION! An articling student[59] may act as a liaison between you and ICBC, interview witnesses, obtain police or medical records, draft legal documents, handle motions in chambers, and do legal research. If you think your lawyer has given her work to do that's beyond her level of competency, discuss this with him as soon as possible.

Disputes about money: Since conflicts with lawyers over their billing practices are common, you may want your lawyer to send you an interim statement of accounts once or twice a year while your case is pending. You can then question anything you don't understand or agree with. Once your lawyer clarifies which expenses he anticipates ICBC reimbursing, you can try to work out a mutually acceptable way of dealing with non-reimbursed expenses, unless this was dealt with in your legal contract. The worst time to address this issue is after your case has resolved when you'll have little bargaining power.

Your lawyer's expense sheets and account statements should be carefully checked, especially his final statement of accounts. If you feel he's overcharged you, talk to him about this immediately. Unless you're able to reach an agreement on what's fair, you can apply for fee mediation through the Law Society of BC or "tax" your lawyer's bill. (See the next section.)

You have the right to challenge the reasonableness of the contingency percentage your lawyer charges you. Since you probably agreed to pay this in your legal contract, the court may only reduce your lawyer's fee if your situation changed dramatically, or you weren't capable of making an informed decision when you signed the contract. (You may have developed delayed-onset disabilities since then, or your judgment may have been impaired due to a brain injury, the stress you were under, or other circumstances.) You'll have to show the court why you feel your lawyer's fee is unfair. The courts often reduce contingency percentages to some degree, especially in cases that don't go to trial or when a minor is involved.

Resolving Conflicts with Your Lawyer

If your lawyer does anything that disturbs you, or he neglects to do something you think he should, you need to discuss this with him right away. When setting up an appointment to see him, make it clear that his behaviour is the only thing you'll discuss at your meeting. Once you're together, make sure you both stick to the subject at hand and don't get distracted by other issues. (A relative or friend should be with you as a witness and to take notes of what's said. You may also want to tape-record the meeting if your lawyer agrees to this.)

Regardless of the nature of your problems with your lawyer, if you don't feel satisfied with the response you get from him, or you don't feel comfortable discussing your complaints in person, you can write him a letter about what's bothering you. This will force you to organize your thoughts and figure out what you want to change. It will also give your lawyer time to think about your concerns and what he can do to satisfy you. If his explanations and assurances don't resolve the issues in question, ask him to write down what his position is, so you're sure you understand it.

If you can't settle your conflicts with your lawyer amicably, there are several options you have (as discussed below). The Lawyer Referral Services of the Canadian Bar Association should be able to refer you to someone whom you can consult for a nominal fee[60] to determine if you have a valid case against your lawyer; what's involved in pursuing it; how long this might take; and what it might cost. If your case is still pending, you may want to hire a new lawyer.

The Law Society of BC can help resolve disputes between lawyers and clients in several ways. While their fee mediation services are free, you have to apply for this in writing and your lawyer has to consent to it. An impartial mediator (usually another lawyer) will try to help you reach an agreement on the legal fees you should pay. Mediation is non-binding, and decisions have to be agreed to by both parties.

While the Law Society can't force a lawyer to reduce his fee or change his billing practices, if your dispute is about something else you can file a complaint with their Professional Conduct Department. As the governing body for the legal profession in the province, the Law Society not only sets professional standards for lawyers in B.C., it has the authority to discipline lawyers who don't meet these standards.

You may want someone to help you write up your complaint as you may be too close to the situation to explain it properly. Your complaint letter should contain a history of the problem to date as well as information about your current and past dealings with your lawyer. Any documents that might help explain the issues should be included.

The Law Society takes all complaints against lawyers seriously, and no lawyer looks forward to getting a letter from them asking him to respond to a client's grievances. Being asked to account for his actions may encourage your lawyer to resolve the problems you're having. When this isn't sufficient, or the allegations against your lawyer are particularly disturbing, your complaint will be passed on to the Society's disciplinary committee for investigation. If the committee issues a citation against your lawyer, this will normally lead to a formal hearing that's similar to a trial. The Law Society will be represented by its lawyer and governing board at the hearing, while your lawyer will have his own legal counsel. You won't be asked to appear, but the evidence you've provided will be used and additional information may be requested. If your lawyer is found guilty of the charges against him, he may be fined, reprimanded, temporarily suspended from practice, or permanently disbarred (expelled from the legal profession). He may also have to pay all costs related to the hearing. (Regardless of the outcome, you won't be responsible for any costs.)

The Law Society only has the right to take action against a lawyer for professional misconduct or incompetence. If your complaint relates to something else, or it's considered frivolous or without merit, you'll be notified of this. In some cases, you may be referred to another agency.

Taxing your lawyer's bill: Your lawyer's bill can be challenged before the B.C. Supreme Court Registrar. You may want another lawyer to represent you in this.

It usually takes about three months to get a date for the Court Registrar to review a lawyer's bill. If you haven't paid your lawyer yet, you'll have a year from the date of the disputed bill to apply for a review. If you already paid him, you'll have to apply for a review within three months of your payment. (Since proceeds from an insurance claim generally go to the lawyer who handled the case, his fee will be paid before you recover any money yourself.)

Both you and your lawyer will have to appear before the Court Registrar on the date of the taxation hearing. After your lawyer has tried to justify his bill to the Registrar, the Registrar will rule on whether it's reasonable or not. While most legal fees are reduced to some degree, unless the reduction amounts to at least one sixth of your lawyer's bill, you'll be responsible for paying all costs and disbursements relative to this action. If your lawyer's bill is reduced by more than one sixth, he'll have to pay all costs and disbursements. Either party can appeal the Registrar's ruling as long as this is done within 14 days.[61]

Suing your lawyer: If your lawyer's misrepresentation or negligence causes you financial losses, you can sue him for damages in the B.C. Supreme Court or Small Claims Court. His professional liability insurer will pay for a lawyer to defend him, while you'll have to hire your own lawyer. Few lawyers in the province handle these cases, and one of the best will probably defend your lawyer. A lawyer will only represent you in a malpractice suit when your financial losses are "quantifiable" (a monetary value can be placed on them), substantial and provable. Malpractice lawyers typically charge high contingency fees on the damages awarded or negotiated.

Suing a lawyer for malpractice is costly, stressful, and can take years to resolve. You may want to consider mediation or binding arbitration instead. Your lawyer and his liability insurer will have to agree to this.

Hiring a New Lawyer

If your lawyer is hostile or belligerent towards you, rarely returns your phone calls, doesn't answer your questions clearly, and makes no attempt to get your medical or rehab needs addressed, you may want to hire a new lawyer. This may also be appropriate if your situation has changed and you want someone with more experience in a specialized field. If you lose confidence in your lawyer or your relationship with him becomes strained, you need to get independent legal advice. The sooner your case is transferred to a new lawyer the easier the switch will be, and the less likely it is that your new lawyer will have to re-do work that was already done.

Your legal contract should outline the terms on which your first lawyer will be paid if you switch lawyers. Even if you're supposed to pay your first lawyer for his work and reimburse his out-of-pocket expenses before he's required to send over your file to your new lawyer, you'll have the right to have his bill reviewed by the Court Registrar. The Registrar will rule on whether the bill is reasonable and should be paid immediately.

In practice, the two lawyers usually negotiate the terms of the transfer between them. Your new lawyer may arrange for your first lawyer to send over his bill when he hands over your legal file. He'll agree to protect your first lawyer's interests by holding back what you owe him from the money recovered in your insurance claim. (You'll still be allowed to tax your first lawyer's bill.)

When negotiating a contract with a new lawyer, make sure you won't have increased legal costs because you're transferring your case to him. (Your costs might increase if he has to re-do work that was already done.) If your new lawyer agrees to absorb duplicate costs, if any, or costs you dispute in your first lawyer's bill, this should be included in your contract with him. Your new legal contract should also state that your first lawyer's fee will be deducted from your new lawyer's fee.

If your lawyer moves to a new firm, you'll have to decide whether to make the move with him or stay with the first firm. Whatever you decide shouldn't affect the quality of the legal help you get. You won't incur additional costs if your file stays where it is as your contract was probably made with your lawyer's firm, not him personally. If you decide to follow him to his new firm, there are established methods of dealing with this so you're not penalized financially or in any other way. You'll want to discuss this with your lawyer as soon as possible to make sure you're satisfied with whatever decision you make.

If your lawyer (or an articling student or other lawyer in his firm) moves to a legal firm that's handling ICBC's defence in your case, you can file an application with the court to have the firm removed as ICBC's counsel. A lawyer or articling student who worked on your case may also join ICBC's legal staff before your case resolves. Various adjustments may have to be made to avoid a potential conflict of interests. You may want to consult a lawyer who deals with conflict-of-interest situations. (The Lawyer Referral Services of the Canadian Bar Association should be able to refer you to someone.)

PART III

The Legal Process

CHAPTER 14

Legal Procedures

NOTE: Neither the information in this chapter nor in earlier or later chapters is intended to be taken as legal advice. Consult a lawyer before making legal decisions.

Tort Actions

You can only file a tort claim for damages if you weren't solely at fault in your accident. You'll have two years from your accident date to initiate legal action. In most cases, it's not ICBC you sue for damages; it's the at-fault driver, and the owner, leaseholder, or leasing company of the car he was driving, who are known jointly as the defendant(s). As a third party to your legal action, ICBC will act as (and for) the defendants at trial, in negotiations, and in all other legal matters. (ICBC is the defendant in a hit-and-run accident claim. No one is sued for damages in an UMP claim: you're paid through your own insurance coverage.) An out-of-province driver will be defended by her own insurer.

Most people want legal representation when litigation may be necessary. (Litigation is the process through which a law suit is carried out. The person who brings a case against another party into court is known as the plaintiff.) After an auto accident, the at-fault driver's insurer normally hires a lawyer to represent and defend her, while the plaintiff has to hire his own lawyer.

If ICBC doesn't make you a reasonable offer to settle when your lawyer contacts them, he may initiate a tort action by filing a writ of summons (a formal notice that legal action is being taken) and a Statement of Claim. The Statement of Claim will describe where and how your accident happened and what the defendant did to cause it. Various acts of negligence or wrong-doing may be noted that have nothing to do with your case but are included to cover every possibility that could potentially affect the damages you're entitled to. Your known injuries will be noted and should be said to include "any other injuries that might arise from [your] accident and any complications that might arise from [your] injuries." Every head of damages (or type of compensation) you may be entitled to should be mentioned, with no monetary value placed on this.

Your writ of summons and Statement of Claim have to be filed with the court and formally delivered to ICBC and the defendant. While they should file a Statement of Defence within 14 days, extensions are usually allowed to give them time to hire a lawyer. The defence lawyer then handles all negotiations with your lawyer, consulting with your adjuster on this.

The defence's statement may deny that the defendant did anything wrong, blaming the accident on you. After first denying the accident happened or you were injured, the statement may go on to claim that "even if" the accident happened, and "even if" you had injuries, it was your fault not the defendant's. Various ways in which you were responsible will be noted, none of which may have any connection to the facts. There's no need to be concerned about this: most defence statements are written this way. ICBC may later admit full liability on behalf of the driver you're suing.

Once your lawyer receives the defence statement, he'll set up the necessary examinations for discovery and apply for a trial date. Trials are generally booked a year or two in advance and may be postponed on one or more occasions. The issues at trial in a tort action are discussed in the next chapter.

Part 7 Legal Actions

You may have to sue ICBC to get accident benefits. You'll have one year from your accident date (or from the date ICBC first refuses to provide you with benefits) to initiate a Part 7 action. Once this is done, your lawyer will be able to question your adjuster under oath to see whether he can learn enough to apply for quick arbitration or a chambers ruling. These procedures remove ICBC from the decision-making process, allowing an impartial arbitrator or judge to decide whether you're entitled to accident benefits.

Most lawyers automatically file a Part 7 legal action when they initiate a tort claim. These are separate procedures, though, and either can exist without the other. While Part 7 actions are often heard at the conclusion of a tort trial, they can also be heard independently in either Small Claims Court or the B.C. Supreme Court.

If you pursue an independent Part 7 legal action, ICBC's written reply to your claim notice may deny that you were injured even if you were hospitalized after your accident or you've already received some accident benefits. After first denying that you're entitled to Part 7 benefits, they may claim that "even if" you are, you haven't complied with the terms of the Insurance (Motor Vehicle) Act, so they're not obligated to provide these. Their denials may have nothing to do with the merits of your claim.

When a tort claim for damages is likely to proceed to trial, the issues involved may be so similar to a claim for accident benefits that an independent Part 7 legal action is risky. To prove you're entitled to accident benefits, you may have to prove the main elements of your tort claim, giving ICBC information that you'd rather them not have prior to your tort trial. On the other hand, if your lawyer waits until your tort trial is over to argue your right to accident benefits, you may not get them for many years, placing you in financial hardship. The pros and cons of an independent Part 7 legal action is something you should discuss with your lawyer.

Even when a Part 7 legal action is successful, it doesn't mean ICBC will pay for future rehab treatment. At most, it confirms that you're entitled to accident benefits and that a particular type of treatment is warranted on the day the decision is made. ICBC may later argue that your situation has changed and you no longer require any rehab treatment or other accident benefits.

A lawyer who represents you in a tort claim may not charge you for the work he does getting you accident benefits. Or, you may be billed by the hour for a Part 7 legal action.

Chambers Hearings

Once legal action has been initiated, disputes may arise that can be resolved out of court by a judge (or court master) in chambers. If you've refused to be assessed by an independent medical examiner (or IME) selected by ICBC, for example, the defence can apply in chambers for a court order requiring this. Likewise, when one party to a legal suit won't release information the other side wants, a chambers motion can be made requesting this. The judge will decide what records should be released.

Only the opposing lawyers and the judge are normally present in chambers. After each lawyer has argued his client's position, the judge rules on this. His decisions are legally binding.

Small Claims Court Hearings

Only claims worth up to $10,000 can be heard in Small Claims Court. While you can bring a small claim before the B.C. Supreme Court, court costs may be awarded against you if the judge feels your case should have been heard in Small Claims Court. As the plaintiff, it's up to you to decide which court will hear your case. If you file a claim in Small Claims Court that you later realize is worth more than $10,000, you can transfer it to the B.C. Supreme Court. You can also transfer a case from the B.C. Supreme Court to Small Claims Court. (Plaintiffs sometimes do this to avoid a jury trial the defence has requested.)

Your notice of claim for Small Claims Court should describe where and when your accident happened, what injuries you had, and how much money you're asking for. (Notice forms are available from the Provincial Court, Small Claims Court division.) Part 7 legal actions are often heard in Small Claims Court. In some cases, filing a notice of claim may be enough to make ICBC start providing the requested benefits.

While many people represent themselves in Small Claims Court, you'll probably want to use a lawyer if there are complex issues involved, or a tort claim for damages may be heard after a Part 7 legal action is heard. Even if you don't think you need a lawyer, you may want legal advice on how to proceed.

The Small Claims Court Registry may require the opposing parties to attend a settlement conference with a judge. When this doesn't resolve the issues in dispute, a trial date will be scheduled. (Settlement conferences are discussed later in the chapter in the section on alternate dispute resolution.)

If you want witnesses to testify at your Small Claims Court trial, you'll have to arrange this yourself if you're not using a lawyer. While a summons[62] can be sent to anyone who is reluctant to participate, this has to be delivered within seven days of the trial date. If you plan on having medical or other experts testify, you'll have to give the opposing party a summary of the evidence they'll present at least 30 days before trial. (Letters or expert reports that you want to submit to the court also have to be given to the opposing party 30 days before trial.) If the other party wants to question your experts at trial, they have to inform you of their intention at least 14 days before the trial date.

Small Claims Court hearings are fairly informal, and less strict rules of evidence are followed than in the B.C. Supreme Court. Each judge conducts trials in her own way; there's no set procedure. The judge may frequently interrupt the proceedings to question the lawyers, plaintiff, defendant and witnesses. Once the witnesses on each side have testified, the opposing parties (or their lawyers) will explain their views of the issues in dispute. The judge will then announce her decision. While ICBC usually accepts the decisions made in Small Claims Court, both parties have the right to appeal.

If you lose your case in Small Claims Court, you'll have to pay the opposing side's costs. If the judge feels your claim is frivolous or without merit, you may also have to pay a penalty of up to 10% of the money you requested. (In some situations, ICBC may be ordered to pay a penalty.)

Examinations For Discovery

An examination for discovery is an out-of-court process in which one party to a legal suit (or his lawyer) can question another involved party under oath about issues relevant to the legal action. In addition to the plaintiff, the driver, owner or leaseholder of the cars involved, the legal guardian of a minor, someone who has power of attorney for one of the parties, and the Committee of someone who is *incompis mentis* may be examined in this way.

Your discovery may take less than an hour, or it may continue for several hours. Since this will probably be the first time you meet the ICBC defence lawyer, you'll want to make a good impression on him. Dressing neatly and conservatively will help you come across as someone who would be a credible witness in court.

You'll normally meet with the defence lawyer in a conference room in a neutral location. A court stenographer will be present to record the proceedings. While your lawyer should be there as well, he won't be allowed to advise you on what to say. He's there as a witness, to make sure the defence lawyer doesn't ask you irrelevant questions or take advantage of you in any way.

After the discoveries on both sides are done, the defence lawyer usually makes a recommendation to ICBC on liability and, when relevant, the size of an appropriate settlement. They may not agree with this. Your lawyer will be told what their position is, and he can submit a counter-offer.

You may meet with your lawyer a few times prior to your discovery to prepare for it. He should have a fairly good idea of the questions you'll be asked and can advise you on how to answer them. He may want to play the role of the defence lawyer in a practice session with you, asking you questions and listening to your responses. He can then help you re-think or re-phrase your answers, if necessary.

As the defence lawyer questions you during your discovery, you should keep in mind that his primary goal is to gain information to minimize ICBC's costs. He may seem very sympathetic and understanding to put you off guard so you'll reveal things you'd be better off not saying. You should try to keep your responses brief and only provide the information requested. If you're not sure how to answer a question, you have the right to say that you have no comment to make. You're under no obligation to respond to every question asked. If you only know something because someone else told it to you, you need to make it clear that you're relating second-hand information, not what you personally remember. Only your present accident and injuries should be discussed, not anything that happened in the past, and you should try not say anything that could be used against you or someone else might contradict.

What ICBC learns at your discovery will affect every aspect of your dealings with them. Since what you say under oath is admissible as evidence at trial, you'll want to qualify your statements as much as possible. Instead of stating, "This is what happened," it's better to say, "This is what I *seem* to remember happened." Then if a witness contradicts this, or you later recall events differently yourself, you won't appear to have lied. Saying, "I'm not able to walk without a cane *now*," or, "I'm not able to walk *long distances* without a cane" is better than saying, "I can't walk without a cane." By qualifying what you say, you won't look like you've exaggerated your problems if a surveillance video shows you walking without a cane. Statements like: "I *think* this is what happened", "as far as I remember", "other people tell me" are less likely to place your credibility in question later.

Once you've completed your discovery, you and your lawyer can review the implications of what you were asked and how you responded. You may also want to discuss the future direction of your case.

> **CAUTION! Be careful what you say in the defence lawyer's presence before and after your discovery. Idle chatter can reveal as much about you as your responses to questions under oath. No matter how nice the ICBC defence lawyer seems — beware! He's not your friend.**

If you have a brain injury of even mild severity, your lawyer and doctor will need to jointly decide whether you're capable of answering questions under oath. If your doctor doesn't think you can provide reliable information in a discovery, the defence lawyer may have to seek a court order requiring this. If what you say is later refuted, it will at least be on record that your doctor predicted this might happen, and it shouldn't be used to discredit you.

It's particularly crucial after a brain injury to be thoroughly prepared for your discovery. People with TBI tend to exaggerate, ramble, and make up answers to questions; they often mix up one accident or trauma with another; and they may confuse what other people tell them with what they remember themselves. Since these behaviours can have a negative effect on a claim for damages, your lawyer should carefully coach you on how to respond to the defence lawyer's questions. You'll want to review all aspects of your case together, practicing your responses until you can answer questions truthfully without providing damaging information. During the discovery itself, your lawyer may have to remind you to keep your answers brief and to only respond to questions you know how to answer. (While he won't be allowed to speak to you during the proceedings, breaks can be taken at any time, upon request.)

Traffic Court Hearings

If a driver who was involved in your accident pleads "not guilty" to a charged traffic offence, you may have to appear in Traffic Court to testify about what happened. ICBC only has to accept full liability for an accident when a driver admits fault, not when fault is assigned in Traffic Court. A Traffic Court judge's ruling doesn't determine liability in a claim for damages.

If you're charged with a traffic offence in an accident in which you or anyone else was injured, you'll probably want legal representation in Traffic Court. Being convicted of a traffic offence doesn't mean you were solely at fault, but it places your liability in question.

Traffic Court hearings are fairly informal and rarely take over an hour. Someone from ICBC is usually in court to observe the proceedings. There may also be other people present who have hearings scheduled for the same court session. If you've hired a lawyer to represent you in a tort claim, he or someone from his office may be in court as well.

As each case is brought before the court, a public prosecutor will try to prove that the person charged with a traffic offence is guilty of this. Evidence will be presented and witnesses may be called to testify under oath. The nature of the injuries that were suffered in an accident is irrelevant in Traffic Court. The only relevant thing is whether a traffic offence was committed. The judge normally rules on each case before she hears the next case.

A Traffic Court hearing can be unsettling if a witness says something that could place your claim for damages at risk. It's better to know about this before your tort claim goes to trial, though. Your lawyer can then try to address the issue at trial, if necessary, by presenting the court with opposing evidence. Testifying in Traffic Court will also give you some useful courtroom experience. This may make it less stressful when you testify later at your tort trial.

Criminal Court Hearings

If someone involved in your accident was charged with a criminal offence, you may have to testify in Criminal Court. Criminal charges are routinely made when someone is killed in an accident or a driver is intoxicated. Other situations where criminal charges are made include dangerous driving, failing to stop at an accident scene, and refusing to take a breath test (or supply a blood sample) when the police request this.

When the police don't feel they have enough evidence to prove a charge of dangerous driving, they often reduce this to a more easily provable offence such as driving without due care and attention. (Since this is a traffic violation, the case is heard in Traffic Court.) When someone dies due to accident-related injuries, the at-fault driver may be charged with involuntary manslaughter even though criminal charges weren't initially made.

If you're charged with a criminal offence in connection to your accident, you should get legal advice as soon as possible. (Some personal injury lawyers practice criminal law as well.) If you can't afford to hire a lawyer, the court will assign one to you. Being convicted of a criminal offence may result in a prison sentence, especially if this isn't the first time that you've committed this (or a similar) offence. It may also invalidate your auto insurance.

If you're injured in an accident in which the at-fault driver is convicted of a criminal offence, this shouldn't prejudice (or affect) your right to damages. The lawyer who handles your tort claim can help you prepare for your testimony in Criminal Court.

Alternate Dispute Resolution (ADR)

Alternate Dispute Resolution is a way of resolving disputes outside the court system. Four types of ADR are used in ICBC cases: standard mediation, fast-track mediation, arbitration, and settlement conferences. Statutory revisions passed by the B.C. government in 1998 encourage an increased use of mediation. While mandatory mediation isn't presently required, this could happen in the future. ADR is rarely used in low-velocity impact (LVI) claims.

Mediation is a non-binding process of settling disputes with the help of an impartial mediator. Either side in a dispute can apply for this. While mediation normally requires the agreement of both parties, a new Notice to Mediate regulation has been added to the Insurance (Motor Vehicle) Act. Either party to an auto accident claim being brought before the B.C. Supreme Court can now force mediation on the opposing party. If you refuse to participate, your court case may be postponed.

The majority of ICBC cases brought to mediation settle there.[63] When a claim doesn't settle in mediation, further negotiation efforts are usually unproductive and the case goes to trial. (In some situations, the concessions made in mediation may bring the opposing parties' positions close enough that an out-of-court settlement can later be reached.)

Your lawyer may prefer mediation to bringing your case to trial. Not only are trials stressful, the outcome is uncertain even when ICBC has accepted full liability on behalf of a driver. You'll have some control over your settlement in mediation; a judge or jury won't dictate the outcome.

Mediation shouldn't be applied for until you're aware of the ongoing consequences your accident and injuries may have on your life. All relevant evidence should already be gathered, and both sides should be prepared to settle. Prior to the mediation session, the opposing lawyers will exchange documents in support of their clients' positions, and preliminary offers and counter-offers may be made. Your lawyer will tell the defence lawyer how much money you're willing to accept and what other demands you have.

ICBC's mediation team should come to the session with the authority to settle your claim. If you ask for $50,000 in damages, they can't legitimately insist that they only have the authority to go up to $25,000, or that nothing they could possibly learn in mediation would make your claim worth what you're asking. Unless they're willing to negotiate with you on the terms you've established, they shouldn't be at the mediation table.

Mediation sessions usually take place at a neutral location. The defence lawyer may be joined by various ICBC staff people, including one or more adjusters. The mediator should already have a summary of the facts and a history of the negotiations to date, so he's familiar with the issues in dispute. The lawyers may also have given him written statements outlining their clients' positions.

The first thing the mediator will normally do is to make sure there are people present who have the authority to settle the case and both sides are willing to compromise. Once he's explained the mediation process to you, the opposing lawyers will orally summarize the facts as they see them. The mediator will then help them define the issues to be discussed and the order in which this will happen. The proceedings may be interrupted at any time so the mediator can meet privately with either side, or either party can talk in private.

> **CAUTION! Unless you tell a mediator that what you're discussing with him in private is confidential, he's free to share this with the opposing party.**

After the pertinent facts are discussed and the relevant evidence is reviewed, most information gaps between the two sides should be eliminated. At this point, an attempt may be made to reach a settlement agreement. ICBC's negotiators will make you an offer, explaining what this is based on and why they feel it's fair. Your lawyer will propose an alternative sum that you and he feel is fair. Each side's position may be supported by previous court-ordered awards in similar cases. If an agreement is reached, the mediator will write this up and both parties will sign it. Otherwise, the negotiations will continue until either side (or the mediator) feels that nothing more can be gained.

Since mediation sessions are confidential, no record is made of them. When no agreement is reached, neither side can use the concessions made in later legal proceedings.

Unfortunately, ICBC doesn't always enter into mediation in good faith. If your adjuster thinks they'll do better in court, his initial offer to you in mediation may be so low that there's no possibility an agreement can be reached.

While mediation costs are technically divided between the opposing parties, ICBC usually covers the full cost of this — *except* when they feel that a plaintiff's lawyer hasn't been co-operative. In this situation, they may only pay their half of the costs. Your lawyer may pay your portion up front and wait to be reimbursed when your case resolves. If you're awarded costs and disbursements at the conclusion of your tort trial, ICBC should pay your mediation costs without dispute.

Mediation typically costs $750 – $1,600 for a four-hour session. When a mediation conference is cancelled within one to eight business days of the scheduled date, a cancellation fee may be charged. You may be responsible for part of this cost.

Fast-track mediation is only used to settle disputes that can be resolved within an hour or two. It's not used when liability is in dispute, nor when there's a disagreement about the extent of someone's injuries. The two sides usually need to have agreed on all issues other than "quantum": what the claim is worth. ICBC always covers the full cost of fast-track mediation.

Arbitration is a method of settling disputes outside court with the help of an impartial adjudicator selected by both sides. This is usually someone knowledgeable about the issues in dispute. An adjudicator's decisions are legally binding and can rarely be appealed.

While arbitration isn't used to settle tort claims, both UMP claims and disputes about the reasonableness of requested Part 7 benefits are handled in this way. Arbitration is essentially a private, informal mini-trial, and the issues raised are often the same as those in a tort claim. The lawyers on each side have to argue their clients' positions as vigorously as they would at trial.

Once an adjudicator is selected, he'll meet with the opposing lawyers to determine what procedure to follow. (This differs from case to case.) Prior to the hearing, the lawyers will exchange statements outlining what they feel is the nature of the dispute. At the hearing itself, documents will be presented in support of each side's position and witnesses may testify. Once a witness has testified, the opposing lawyer can question her. You may be questioned as well.

Arbitration hearings can be complicated and expensive. Depending on the situation and outcome, you may be responsible for some of these costs.

Settlement conferences are basically non-binding mini-trials before a trial judge. Both sides usually have to agree to this. Sixty days before a scheduled trial date, a judge with mediation training will meet informally with the opposing parties. By this time, all aspects of the case should be known and all pertinent documents exchanged. (These hearings are closed to the public.)

Your lawyer will present your experts' reports and other relevant documents to the judge, summarizing and emphasizing what he feels is significant. He'll also support your claim with legal precedents. The defence lawyer will go through the same process in support of the defendant's position. The judge may ask for certain issues to be clarified before she makes her recommendations or suggests the range of money she feels your claim is worth. Neither side will be legally bound by this.

Since your lawyer will only present evidence to the judge that ICBC already has, he'll be less likely to reveal his courtroom strategy than in mediation. Assuming the defence lawyer is well-prepared, he should already be aware of the legal precedents your lawyer provides. While neither side normally learns much new in a settlement conference, it gives them a chance to see how a trial judge might rule on a case. This may allow an out-of-court agreement to be reached.

A settlement conference can also be requested before a trial date is scheduled. If your case has been drifting along aimlessly for a long time with no resolution in sight, negotiations have stalled, and outstanding issues aren't getting resolved, your lawyer can apply for a court order mandating a settlement conference. If ICBC is forced to participate in a hearing they don't want, though, they're unlikely to pay much attention to the judge's suggestions, which aren't legally binding.

Other Non-Binding Hearings

If your case has been bumped from the trial docket on more than one occasion, you may be given an opportunity to have a B.C. Supreme Court judge hear it on a non-binding basis in an open courtroom. Both sides have to agree to this. The judge's suggestions won't be binding on either party.

These hearings are very informal. The lawyers on each side briefly describe the issues to the judge and present their arguments. No witnesses are called, but relevant documents and reports may be summarized or presented. While the judge will only get a superficial overview of the facts, the opposing lawyers will have a chance to see how a trial judge views the issues in dispute. This may help the two sides reach an out-of-court agreement.

Fast-Track Trials

When a civil (or non-criminal) trial is expected to take two days or less to hear in the B.C. Supreme Court before a judge but not a jury, the parties can apply for a Rule 66 fast-track trial. This may bring a quick resolution to an uncomplicated case that only requires a few witnesses. When there are personal injuries or a death involved, both parties have to agree to a fast-track trial, or it has to be court-ordered.

A trial date has to be applied for within four months of the fast-track designation. A judge-only trial will then take place within four months of this. All examinations for discovery have to be done at least 14 days prior to trial, and no discovery can take more than two hours. This accelerated process can result in a court Judgment being obtained within eight months of a writ of summons being issued.

A claim being litigated through normal channels can be shifted to a Rule 66 fast-track trial when appropriate. Likewise, a case on the fast-track program can be shifted to normal channels when it's clear that more than two trial days will be needed.

NOTE: Hearings before the B.C. Supreme Court are discussed in Chapter 17, while hearings before the B.C. Court of Appeal and the Supreme Court of Canada are discussed in Chapter 19.

CHAPTER 15

Issues at Trial

Before your personal injury case can be resolved, a judge or jury will have to decide who was at fault (if this hasn't been agreed on); what the cause, nature and extent of your accident-related injuries and disabilities are (if this is in dispute); and what effect your accident and injuries have had on your life and may have in the future. The decisions reached on these issues will determine how much money you're awarded under each head of damages.

Liability

Since you can only claim damages for the harm that was done to you through someone else's negligence or wrong-doing, liability is fundamental to a personal injury case. The more serious your injuries are, the more likely it is that an effort will be made to place some of the responsibility for your accident or injuries on you. If a judge or jury decides you were solely at fault, you won't receive any compensation. If you were partially at fault, your award will be reduced by the same percentage as you're judged to have been responsible

To determine liability at trial, police officers, independent witnesses and expert witnesses may be asked to testify for either side. The lawyers may also refer to Traffic Court transcripts (or if anyone was killed, to the Coroner's Inquest report). While Traffic Court rulings don't determine liability in tort claims, a witness' testimony in Traffic Court may be referred to at a tort trial.

The court always determines liability when an uninsured or unidentified driver is involved in an accident. If you didn't have valid insurance in place when your accident happened, your lawyer may be able to establish limits to your liability and the costs ICBC is entitled to recover from you.

As a passenger in a car, if you knew the driver was intoxicated (or that he intended to speed or engage in another reckless activity), you may be considered partially responsible for your injuries. ICBC will have to prove that you were aware of the driver's mental state (or intentions) for your award to be reduced.

Not wearing a seatbelt won't automatically reduce the compensation you're entitled to, but it places you at risk of this happening. ICBC may try to prove that you were partially responsible for your injuries, while experts hired by your lawyer will try to show the court why a seatbelt wouldn't have protected you from the particular injuries you had.

Reductions in compensation are determined in court on a case-by-case basis. Not wearing a seatbelt (or getting into a car with a drunk driver) generally reduces an award by around 25%. Awards can also be reduced by as little as 10% or as much as 40%. (On rare occasions, the courts have reduced an award by as much as 80%.)[64] An incorrectly-positioned headrest may also reduce your award if it can be shown to have caused or contributed to your injuries.

Determining the Cause, Nature and Extent of Injuries and Disabilities

ICBC may deny that your disabilities were caused by your accident or dispute the existence and severity of an injury. Even an objective injury can be disputed. Your leg can be broken in one or more places. You may have a hairline fracture, or the bone may be shattered. You may need a cast on your leg or require a bone graft or surgical implants. A fracture can weaken a joint or cause life-threatening complications. Regardless of the circumstances, you may be offered the lower end of the current rate for a broken leg — as if all broken legs are equal.

ICBC vigorously challenges most claims involving subjective conditions, whether these are soft tissue injuries, mild brain injuries, psychological problems, or somatic disorders such as chronic pain or fibromyalgia. Your lawyer may have to prove that your condition exists; that it was caused (or aggravated) by your accident; and when relevant, that you have permanent deficits stemming from it. Since a subjective condition is diagnosed primarily by what you tell the doctor, if the court doesn't feel that you're a credible witness, they may decide that you've exaggerated your problems and reject your claim.

People with similar injuries react differently to them. You may have chronic pain when another person wouldn't, or you may cope well with a condition that would permanently disable someone else. The reluctance of insurers to accept that injuries affect people in different ways often makes it necessary to go to trial on a claim that should settle out of court.

In preparing their case for trial, the ICBC defence team may review your medical records to see whether your disabilities can be blamed on earlier conditions. Pre- and post-accident injuries or other life circumstances may be used to explain why you're having problems. If there are discrepancies between your reported complaints and what's documented in your medical records, these may be brought to the court's attention even when the inconsistencies are minor and can easily be explained. Your lawyer may have to prove to a judge or jury that your injuries and disabilities were directly caused by your accident.

The *thin skull rule* in personal injury law holds a person responsible for the injuries he's caused even when these are unexpectedly severe due to a pre-existing condition. The defendant has to accept you the way you are; it's irrelevant how your injuries would have affected someone else. The *crumbling skull rule* recognizes that a pre-existing condition is an inherent part of a person. While you're entitled to be compensated for the harm that was done to you, the defendant isn't responsible for making you better than you were, nor does he have to compensate you for your condition worsening if this would have happened anyway. If there's a measurable risk that a pre-existing condition would have worsened even if you weren't in an accident, the court should take this into account by reducing your overall award.

❖

Heads of Damages

If you're injured as a result of someone else's negligence or wrongdoing, you're entitled to enough financial compensation to restore you as fully as possible to the condition you'd have been in if the negligence hadn't occurred. The court will be asked to compensate you for both your non-economic losses and your economic losses (or pecuniary damages). The latter includes special damages, past and future income losses, and future care needs.

General damages (also known as non-pecuniary damages or "non-pecs") are your non-economic losses. These include pain and suffering, loss of enjoyment of life, reduced life expectancy, and loss of functional abilities. These losses are jointly referred to as an award for pain and suffering. In some situations, a lawyer may argue each loss separately.

A fair award for pain and suffering is one that will make your life more bearable and be some comfort to you. If your accident caused a disability with lifelong consequences, you may not be able to reach an out-of-court agreement on your general damages. (These are currently capped at $300,000.)

If you can no longer pursue activities you used to enjoy, or your accident prevented you from attending an important event in your life, you should be compensated for this as part of your general damages. A serious amateur athlete who will never play competitive sports again should get more compensation for his pain and suffering than a non-athlete with the same injury.

Special damages (or "specials") are the reimbursement of accident-related out-of-pocket expenses for which you have valid dated receipts. Whether your case goes to trial or settles out of court, your specials should be part of your final settlement. When a claim takes years to settle, the specials can be sizeable.

Special damages you should be able to claim without dispute include rehab treatment; over-the-counter drugs, bandages, heating pads and neck collars; transportation and parking costs to medical and rehab appointments, assessments, court hearings, and your lawyer's office; replacement or dry-cleaning of clothing ruined or soiled in your accident; long-distance phone calls to your family immediately after the accident; parking expenses for family members (and TV rental for you) while you're in the hospital; child care, babysitters and housecleaners needed as a direct result of your accident; psychological counselling; case management services; attendant care that exceeds the amount covered as an accident benefit; and modifications to your home, or the purchase of a specially-equipped vehicle, to accommodate your injuries. Money a rehab therapist charges you in excess of ICBC's standard rates can also be claimed back as part of your special damages. If another insurer expects to be reimbursed for the medical or rehab treatment they've covered, you'll need documentation of this to include it in your special damages.

ICBC may argue against paying for extensive psychotherapy, alternative therapies, exercise programs, pain-management programs, medication you might have needed anyway, and other items or services. Unless the opposing lawyers can negotiate an agreement on your specials, the trial judge will rule on this. Your lawyer may have to present evidence justifying the expenses that ICBC disputes paying.

Past income loss is relatively easy to assess when an employer can document this. If you weren't at fault in your accident, you should be fully compensated for any income losses you have in excess of what you've received in wage-loss benefits from ICBC and other sources. Unless you returned to work prior to trial, your past income losses are usually calculated from the date of your accident to the date of the court Judgment. When this money isn't paid to you right away, you should receive interest on it. (Past income loss is paid as after-tax income loss.)

Since there's currently no cap on an award for past income loss, if you were a high wage earner prior to your accident and haven't been able to work full time (or at all) since then, your award in this category can come to hundreds of thousands of dollars or more. In order to find a reason not to pay you damages for your lost income,

ICBC may have you extensively investigated. Even if their efforts don't turn up anything to reduce your award for past income loss, you may have to go to court to get this.

An award for past income loss is generally based on your average net earnings during the five years prior to your accident. If your income had been steadily decreasing, though, ICBC may use your most recent pre-accident earnings to calculate your lost income, not your average earnings. Likewise, if your income had been steadily increasing, your lawyer may argue at trial that this pattern would have continued "but for your accident", so your lost income should be based on your latest pre-accident earnings.

If you're self-employed, own your own business, or you worked on a contract or commission basis prior to your accident, your past income losses may be hard to prove to ICBC's satisfaction in out-of-court negotiations. Even if your tax returns clearly show what you earned in the past, and you can document the work you've had to turn down due to your accident, you may have to take your case to trial to be fairly compensated.

You may be entitled to an award for past income loss even if you were unemployed when your accident happened. Your pre-accident earnings power will be examined to calculate your potential lost earnings. The trial judge may be asked to rule on when you would most likely have returned to work "but for your accident". She'll base this on what seems most probable under the circumstances. If you didn't earn money in the years prior to your accident, but there's evidence showing that you were planning to work — you might have been attending school, for example, staying at home with a pre-school child, or starting a new business — your lack of earnings shouldn't be enough to deny you an award for past income loss. Your lawyer will have to show the court what you would have been capable of earning "but for your accident" and how likely it is that you'd have earned this. Meanwhile, the defence lawyer will try to prove that you wouldn't have worked even if you hadn't been in an accident.

If an accident-related condition prevented you from being hired for a job that you would have otherwise gotten, or from advancing in your career as you might reasonably have expected to do, you have a right to be compensated for this as part of your income losses.

Future income loss is harder to determine since it's a potential that's being assessed, not what has already happened. Your lawyer will first have to prove that you can't work as a result of your accident, or that you can only work part-time or in a lower paying job. He'll then try to place a monetary value on your loss through the testimonies of expert witnesses. (These may include your treating doctors and rehab therapists as well as an occupational therapist, vocational counsellor, economist, and professionals from the field you were in, or were training for, prior to your accident.)

Future income loss or loss of future earnings capacity isn't based solely on what you've earned in the past. Since the ability to earn income is a capital asset, if the court can be shown that this asset was lost or diminished as a result of your accident, you should be awarded money that represents a fair evaluation of your loss. Lost job opportunities that can be "quantified" (or have a monetary value placed on them) should be included in this.

If your accident interrupted your career, you should be compensated for your loss of future earnings power. If you were able to return to work, were you given reduced responsibilities, demoted, or fired as a result of an accident-related condition? Have you advanced in your career as well as you might have done "but for your accident"? If you were in school when your accident happened, did your grades get worse, forcing you to lower your career goals? If the court can be shown that your accident had a negative effect on your future income level, you should be awarded damages to compensate you for this, even if you were unemployed at the time of your accident or you've never had a job.

If you're unlikely to ever earn the income you might have had "but for your accident", your future income losses should be extended to retirement age. (There's currently no cap on this award.) In an effort to reduce the damages you're entitled to, ICBC may have you put under surveillance and thoroughly investigated. You may be sent to various independent medical examiners (IMEs) and other experts until the defence can find someone who will go on record stating that there's no reason why you can't work full-time and earn your pre-accident income.

Whenever future income loss may be an issue in a case, ICBC looks for evidence that the person can benefit from vocational retraining. If they take the position at trial that you'll be able to find alternative work in another field, they should offer to pay for any re-education or retraining you'll need.

Under current law, you're considered to have suffered a loss of future earnings capacity if the following conditions are met: you're less capable of earning income from any type of employment; you're less attractive as an employee to potential employers; you've lost the ability to take advantage of job opportunities that might otherwise have been open to you; and you're less valuable to yourself as a person who is capable of earning income in a competitive labour market.[65] Since these circumstances reduce your employment possibilities, you should receive damages for your loss of future earnings capacity even if you've never had a job. The court will take into account how likely it is that you'd have worked in the future "but for your accident".

You're at the greatest risk of being inadequately compensated for future income losses if you have an inconsistent work history; you worked at an unconventional job prior to your accident; you didn't declare all your income on your tax returns; you were in the process of starting a new business (or new career) at the time of your accident; or you were self-employed, unemployed, or under-employed. Your lawyer may be reluctant to include money you earned "off the books" in calculating your income losses.

If you're entitled to an award for future income loss, lost employment opportunities, or a lost capacity to earn income, the opposing lawyers may each hire an economist to calculate what you should receive under this head of damages. While both estimates should be based on the same factors, the experts on each side may reach very different conclusions. The court will decide which estimate is more credible or compromise between the opposing opinions.

If you've had little (or no) paid employment history, your future income losses can be estimated by referring to Statistics Canada records for workers in the province. Whether you were working at the time of your accident — even in a non-paying job: doing volunteer work, starting a new business, apprenticing or interning, pursing a career in the arts — should be taken into account, as should the average income of people your age, gender and education when they work full- or part-time. Your anticipated earnings "but for your accident" will normally be reduced by standard labour force risks. These include labour-participation rates (whether you'd have chosen to work), unemployment rates (whether you'd have found a job), and part-time factors (whether you'd have worked full- or part-time). Participation rates differ according to age, gender and education, and take into account illness, premature death, and other factors. A vocational counsellor may be asked to provide the court with average salary ranges for any jobs you might reasonably have expected to do "but for your accident".

*Loss of marriageability: S*ince there are financial benefits to being married, if your marriage breaks up as a result of your accident, or you're unlikely to get married due to accident-related disabilities, you should be paid damages for this as part of your future income loss.

Future care: If you still have on-going disabilities when your case settles or goes to trial, you may be paid damages for your future care. This can be the largest award in a personal injury case. (There's no cap on this award.)

The purpose of a future care award is to provide you with the on-going help you'll need as a result of your accident. This may include medical and rehab treatment, psychological counselling, exercise and recreational programs, vocational retraining, continuing education, modifications to your home or car, transportation expenses, housekeeping services, attendant care, and other items or services that will make your life more manageable. If you weren't able to undergo treatment your doctor recommended because you couldn't afford to do it, you may be awarded money for this purpose. (Your doctor may have to address your need for this treatment in her testimony at trial.)

You may only require certain items or services once, while you'll need others throughout your life. Even an inexpensive item that will have to be purchased frequently can add up to a lot of money over time. While future income loss is rarely extended beyond age 65, a future care award may have to be extended to your statistical life expectancy, which could be 84 or older. All other things being equal, the younger you are, the larger your future care award normally is.

If you're expected to have long-term future care needs, the opposing lawyers may each arrange for a future care assessor to evaluate you. While both assessors should base their recommendations on the same medical-legal reports, ICBC's expert will rely more heavily on reports that diminish your future care needs, while your expert may assume that your care needs will increase over time. The court may prefer one assessor's approach, or compromise between two or more assessors' opinions.

Instead of awarding you a specific sum for your future care, the court may decide what items and services you'll need, how often you'll need them, and what a reasonable one-time cost is. An economist can then calculate the present-dollar value of your future care award. A discount factor may be used to balance future uncertainties like the statistical likelihood of you dying prematurely. Inflation may be taken into account as well. An economist who calculates the present-dollar value of your future care award may have to defend his calculations in court.

If you have catastrophic injuries, as part of your future care award you should be compensated for the work your family does taking care of you. Household help may be covered as well as personal and attendant care. While compensation for these services is paid on an arbitrary basis, the courts usually award most requested amounts that are backed up by evidence.

Other Money You May Be Awarded

If your future economic losses are sizable, you may be entitled to a "tax gross-up" to offset the taxes you'll owe on the investment income your money earns. You may also receive management fees to help pay for professional financial advice. Your lawyer will have to specifically requests these awards. (See Chapter 18.)

If members of your family missed work as a result of your accident, their lost wages can be claimed back as part of an "in-trust" claim. After a serious injury, funds for family therapy (or individual counselling for family members) may also be awarded as an "in-trust" claim. The need for this treatment will have to be established at trial and a set amount of money requested.

While punitive and aggravated damages are rarely requested in ICBC cases, lawyers sometimes threaten to ask for them when an adjuster isn't co-operative, or he refuses to provide a claimant with accident benefits. Punitive damages are dealt with through a "bad faith action", which is separate from a tort claim. You may be paid punitive damages if the judge feels that ICBC's conduct towards you has been so "malicious, oppressive and high-handed that it offends the court's sense of decency."[66]

Aggravated damages are meant to compensate you for the pain, anxiety and mental anguish the defendant's conduct caused you. While these damages are rarely granted in ICBC cases, in 1995 the B.C. Supreme Court awarded aggravated damages to someone whose disability insurer refused to pay him benefits.[67] Since there's no essential difference in law between ICBC and a private insurer, you may be awarded aggravated damages if your lawyer can show the court that ICBC's refusal to pay for necessary treatment caused you increased pain and anguish, negatively affecting your life. (A claim for aggravated damages in an ICBC case is part of a Part 7 legal action.)

When the Injured Person Is a Minor

When a settlement offer to a minor is for under $50,000, the Public Guardian and Trustee either approves it or rejects it. If the offer is rejected, the case is referred to the courts. On offers above this amount, the Public Guardian and Trustee makes a recommendation to the court and the court determines an appropriate award amount.[68]

A seriously injured minor can receive several million dollars in damages. Structured settlements are often arranged in these cases. (See Chapter 18.) Depending on the minor's age, life expectancy and other factors, a $1 million award can translate into a $15 million structured settlement, with tax-free payments spread out over the minor's life.

When the legal fees charged to a minor are under $10,000, the Public Guardian and Trustee has to approve them. Higher legal fees require the court's approval.[69] The courts have sometimes cut legal fees by more than half in out-of-court settlements for minors.

Settling an insurance claim on behalf of a seriously injured minor should always be delayed as long as possible. While ICBC may want to settle the child's claim quickly, her lawyer should try to postpone this for at least four to six years. The older she is, the easier it will be to predict how well she'll do throughout her life. This is particularly important when an injury may affect future employment possibilities.

Determining an appropriate award for future income loss for an injured minor is always difficult. Her award may be based in part on the earnings of her parents and siblings, and her pre-accident academic ability, if known. It's usually assumed that a child with a high IQ, good grades, and parents in highly paid professions would earn more income as an adult than a child with a low IQ, poor grades and parents in minimum-wage jobs. An economist can evaluate the child's probable future income loss based on these and other variables. While ICBC may look for evidence that the child would never have earned much even if she hadn't been injured, her lawyer may try to prove that her income would have exceeded that of family members "but for her accident".

Proving the presence, extent or permanence of brain injury symptoms in children and adolescents is particularly hard. A child with a brain injury may be able to struggle through the first eight years of school without too many problems, only to find the academic challenges of high school beyond her reach. Since TBI symptoms often mimic normal teen behaviour, ICBC may claim that an adolescent's problems have nothing to do with her accident. Her lawyer may have to prove that her deficits and behaviour are the direct result of an accident-related disability.

Before a minor's future income loss can be calculated, the court will have to decide whether she's permanently unemployable. If ICBC can convince the judge or jury that she'll eventually be able to earn income at some type of job, her award for future income loss will be reduced accordingly.

CHAPTER 16

Preparing For Trial

It usually takes two to five years from the date of an accident before a case goes to trial. The wait is generally longer for minors, people with serious injuries, and claimants who have more than one accident. While an initial trial date may be set up before this, most cases are bumped from the trial docket at least once. The judge assigned to your case won't decide until the morning of trial which scheduled case(s) she'll hear. Her decision will be based in part on how much available time she has and how long the cases before her are estimated to take. If your case has already been bumped a few times, the judge may give it priority over other scheduled cases. While lawyers expect a case to be bumped at least once, they should be prepared for trial on the first scheduled date.

Your lawyer can apply to the court to postpone your (or your child's) trial if your doctors advise this. He'll have to persuade the court that there's a valid reason why the case shouldn't be heard at this time. Judges are usually open to postponements while medical conditions and opinions are still changing. They don't want trials held prematurely, particularly where minors are concerned.

Prior to the trial date, the lawyers will estimate how much court time they'll need to present their clients' side of the case. Depending on how complex your case is and how far apart you and ICBC are, your trial may take several days, weeks or longer to complete. (When a judge has other commitments, a trial may be broken up into two or more segments, with long recesses between them.)

All documents that will be submitted to the court have to be exchanged between the two sides at least 60 days before trial. This includes any experts' reports that will be used at trial. In the weeks prior to trial, the lawyers normally renew their efforts to negotiate an out-of-court settlement.

Requesting a Jury

Within 30 days of the date your lawyer files a Notice of Trial, you'll have to decide whether you want a jury. Either party can request this. While jury trials are postponed less frequently than cases heard solely before a trial judge, they generally take longer to complete. (A jury trial may have to be interrupted from time to time so the judge can explain various points of law to the jury, or describe how the law applies to a particular situation.)

You'll probably want a jury if your lawyer feels they'll be more sympathetic to you than a judge. Judges are more impartial than juries and less likely to be swayed by emotional issues. Judges also have to base their rulings on legal precedents, while juries can ignore this.

ICBC often requests a jury when a claimant's disabilities are subjective or may not have been caused by his accident. Juries tend to be suspicious of subjective conditions and are less likely to award reasonable damages in these cases than judges. A jury may also find it hard to believe that someone was injured in a minor accident that caused little damage to the cars involved. (ICBC generally prefers *not* to have a jury when someone has serious injuries with lifelong consequences.)

You can avoid having a jury trial that ICBC requests by transferring your case to Small Claims Court. Or, your lawyer may be able to convince the court that your case is too complex for a jury to understand.

TBI ALERT! **Since juries often react negatively to people with obvious brain injury symptoms, giving them low awards, ICBC frequently requests a jury in these cases. A judge is more likely to realize that a plaintiff's unusual behaviour stems from an accident-related injury.**

Most jury awards are hard to appeal. It's easier to prove that an award is too high (or low) when a judge has explained why she's awarded this amount and what legal precedents she's relied on. The B.C. Court of Appeal can only reduce (or increase) a jury award under any head of damages when the amount awarded is excessively high (or low) given the other findings in the case. When a jury awards more than the upper allowable limit for general damages, this is automatically reduced on appeal.

Juries sometimes refuse to award general damages in low-velocity impact (LVI) accidents even when they've found enough evidence of an injury to compensate income losses and reimburse out-of-pocket expenses. The juries' decisions in these cases have been upheld by the appellate court.

Assembling Evidence and Providing Documentation

As your lawyer prepares your case for trial, he'll collect evidence of your accident, injuries, recovery process, past (and present) life circumstances, and future care needs, if any. When relevant, he'll also look closely at your work history and future employment outlook. He may need your help in filling in information gaps so he's in the best position to support your claim.

Even when ICBC has accepted full liability on behalf of an at-fault driver, your lawyer may want copies of police and ambulance reports, statements from witnesses, and photos of the accident scene. If you took notes of your accident when it first happened, he may want you to review these so you can discuss the accident in detail with him.

If there was a Traffic Court hearing in connection to your accident, your lawyer may request a transcript of this. If a witness contradicts what she said in Traffic Court when she testifies at your personal injury trial, he may want to bring evidence of this to the court's attention. Traffic Court transcripts will also remind you of what you said yourself under oath.

Since your examination for discovery can be used as evidence at trial, your lawyer may want a transcript of this as well. If what you said at the time no longer seems accurate, you may want to clarify this in your court testimony.

To prove the nature and extent of your injuries, your lawyer may want copies of all medical and rehab records relating to your accident. He may also want to review your complete medical records, as well as the clinical records of any mental health professionals who have treated you since your accident — or prior to it. If ICBC vigorously challenges your claim, the defence will probably review these records closely, looking for evidence to reduce or eliminate your damages.

Your lawyer may ask you for a list of every health-care provider who has assessed or treated you since your accident, including when (and how frequently) you saw them. He probably won't need specific treatment dates as much as an indication of how long you were under someone's care and whether you still require treatment. Your treating doctors and rehab therapists may be asked for medical-legal reports.

You may be asked to write a detailed account for your lawyer of a typical day in your life. How are accident-related disabilities still affecting the way you function, if at all? Are you still having pain or discomfort from an accident-related injury? How have your moods or behaviour changed since your accident? Are there social or recreational activities you can no longer do? Have your relationships with others been affected by your accident? Have your sleep patterns changed?

If you kept a diary of your recovery process, your lawyer may ask you to relate anecdotes from this to him that highlight the changes you've gone through. Your experiences can help him personalize for the court how your accident has affected your life. If you had to miss an important event — your sister's wedding, son's graduation, a planned holiday — your lawyer should be told this.

To place a monetary value on the income you've lost as a result of your accident, your lawyer may need documentation of your pre-accident salary and income; the number of hours a week you normally worked; the amount of time you took off work as a result of your accident; and whether sick days or vacation time were used. He may want your complete employment records, including performance evaluations; pre-and post-accident job descriptions that outline your work responsibilities; personnel records that show your pre- and post-accident behaviour; a record of the amount of time you've taken off work pre- and post-accident; when and why you were ever laid off work; and the nature of any WCB claims you've made. If you didn't get a raise or promotion that you'd probably have gotten "but for your accident", your lawyer will need documented evidence of this for it to become part of your claim for damages. If you were unemployed at the time of your accident, and you may not be employable in the future due to accident-related disabilities, your lawyer should be told about every type of work you've done in the past or have been trained to do. This information can be used in calculating your lost capacity to earn income.

Your lawyer may want support letters from your past or present employers, union "rep", or professionals in your field of employment. Unless someone who writes a letter on your behalf is willing to testify at trial, the defence may not allow her letter to be submitted to the court. If she's unable to attend the trial, she can be questioned on camera by the opposing lawyers, or by lawyers hired to act in their place, and her evidence added to the trial records. (Since this process is expensive, it may only be authorized if her evidence is crucial to your case.)

If you own your own business, your lawyer may want copies of your company's financial statements for the three years prior to your accident and the years since. He may ask your accountant to outline the relevant facts in this. If you're self-employed or work on a contract or commission basis, your lawyer will need to know the full details of your employment, contract or commission history, including whether your income was increasing, decreasing or relatively stable during the years prior to your accident. The better you are at documenting your pre-accident profits and post-accident losses, the more likely it is that you'll be fairly compensated.

Your lawyer may want copies of your school records to show the court how your present functioning level compares to your school grades and early aptitude or IQ tests. He may ask for your legal records as well, including documentation of any prior claims you've made for damages. You may also be asked for pre- and post-accident photos of yourself. If you've had to use prosthetic devices since your accident — or metal plates and screws were used to hold a broken bone in place as it healed, then surgically removed — your lawyer may want to show this to the jury as evidence of the severity of your injuries.

Expert Witnesses and Assessments

Both your lawyer and the ICBC defence lawyer may have various assessments done of you prior to trial. The reports and court testimonies of the experts they hire, along with the medical-legal reports and testimonies of your treating doctors and rehab therapists, will help the court decide how much money to award you under each head of damages. Experts may be asked for their opinions on liability; the cause, nature and extent of your injuries; your functional deficits, quality of life and employment possibilities; your future care needs; and whether (or how much) you should be compensated for future income losses.

When ICBC pays for an assessment, they own the rights to the information obtained. They'll only have to show the resulting report to your lawyer if they intend to use it at trial. If your lawyer arranges for an assessment that doesn't support the position he intends to take at trial, he won't have to show the resulting report to the defence lawyer. (In this situation, though, you'll be responsible for the cost of the assessment and report, even if you're awarded costs and disbursements at trial.)

Defence experts will try to refute the findings and opinions of your experts in their reports and court testimonies. Likewise, your experts may be asked to comment on the defence experts' reports and testimonies. (You'll know who the defence lawyer's expert witnesses are 60 days before trial, when all experts' reports have to be exchanged between the two sides.) Either lawyer may send you to more than one expert in the same field if he's unhappy with the first expert's report.

If you're no longer able to do the same work you did prior to your accident, your lawyer may have a vocational counsellor or occupational therapist assess you to see what kind of work you're capable of doing, if any. Recognized experts in your pre-accident employment field may be asked to estimate what your future income might have been "but for your accident". If liability is in dispute, your lawyer may have an accident-reconstruction engineer do an analysis of what happened. He may also hire an economist to calculate the present-dollar value of various aspects of your claim. The experts your lawyer hires should be comfortable in court and able to effectively defend their opinions when challenged.

How much time an expert spends assessing you, and the length and complexity of her report, will generally determine what she charges for this. While a brief medical-legal report that deals with a simple issue may cost under $100, a neuropsychologist, vocational counsellor or occupational therapist might charge $5,000 or more, and a future care assessor twice that. In a complex brain injury case, a top expert in the field may charge over $10,000 for a comprehensive assessment and medical-legal report. As costly as this is, an assessment is usually worth doing when it's needed to support a claim for future economic losses.

Unless the court denies that you're entitled to damages, you should be reimbursed for the expenses your lawyer has in supporting your claim. However, ICBC may argue that a particular expert's assessment was unnecessary or too costly, refusing to pay for this without a court order. If an aspect of your claim is denied, expenses that solely relate to this won't be reimbursed.

If there are major disagreements between you and ICBC, your lawyer could spend tens of thousands of dollars on experts' assessments and reports. Since you may be responsible for some of these costs, prior to having an assessment done you may want to ask your lawyer what he thinks it will contribute to your case; how successful the expert has been in the past in defending her opinions in court; what she's likely to charge; and whether ICBC has paid her fees in other cases. If her fees are higher than those of other experts in her field, is there someone else who might be equally as good? (If your lawyer can't explain to you why an expert's fee is warranted, he may not be able to justify this later to ICBC or the court.) You may want to ask your lawyer to split the difference with you if an expert's fee isn't fully reimbursed. Will he at least deduct the non-reimbursed portion from your award before calculating his legal fee? (Whatever you agree to should be put in writing and signed by you both.)

When an out-of-town expert comes to court to testify on your behalf, you'll usually have to cover his travel expenses and pay for his time. If the court rules in your favour, you should be reimbursed for this — unless the judge feels that the expert's testimony wasn't needed to support your claim.

> **TBI ALERT!** **Expert witnesses are crucial in brain injury claims. Besides having a neuropsychological assessment done, your lawyer may have you assessed by a neurologist, physiatrist, physiotherapist, occupational therapist, speech-language therapist, vocational counsellor, and psychologist (or psychiatrist). He may also want you to be assessed at a brain injury clinic in Washington State so their recommendations can be built into your future care award. (There are no brain injury clinics in B.C. at this time.)**

Future care assessors: If you have disabilities with on-going consequences, the future care assessor hired by your lawyer will try to evaluate your future care needs according to a worst-case scenario. The lawyers may ask her to justify her recommendations in court. If your own experts don't feel that you'll require many of the items and services your future care assessor recommends, the judge or jury may question her analysis of your needs.

You may want to review your future care assessor's report before it's submitted to ICBC or the court. If her recommendations seem excessive, ask your lawyer to explain why you may need these things in the future. (An inflated future care assessment might make the judge or jury skeptical about other aspects of your claim.) You'll also want to make sure that all your future care needs are taken into account, including medically-recommended treatment you haven't pursued for financial reasons.

Based on the reports and court testimonies of the future care assessors on each side, the court will decide what items and services are appropriate for you, how often you'll need them, and for how long. A present-dollar value can then be placed on your future care award.

If you have catastrophic injuries, a comprehensive medical-rehab program will have to be set up for you before a future care assessor can determine the cost of your on-going care needs. Future changes that may occur should be factored into this. Your assessor's report should be reviewed by someone involved in your care on a daily basis, and your accident-related expenses to date compared to the assessor's recommendations. An estimate should also be made of the amount of time family members spend taking care of you, so compensation for this can be included in your future care award.

Lay Witnesses

Lay witnesses help your lawyer paint a sympathetic picture of you in court. This is particularly important when a claim involves a subjective condition. The decision about whether you're entitled to damages and what these should be may rest on how much the court trusts your lay witnesses.

Since you know your own life better than your lawyer does, you may have to give him the names of people who can be asked to testify on your behalf. He'll want to know what issues they can each address and what they'll contribute to your case. If your accident had a negative effect on your career, he may need lay witnesses to attest to this. He may also want lay witnesses who can comment on functional or behavioural problems you're having at home, work, school or elsewhere.

If your child was injured in an accident, her lawyer may want a few of her teachers to testify at trial. The courts usually give more weight to the evidence presented by a minor's teachers than to the testimonies of relatives and family friends. Changes in your child's functional level or behaviour will be of particular interest to the court. If she's had to lower her educational goals or change her career plans, the court will expect her teachers and school guidance counsellors to address this.

As you talk to your lawyer about who your lay witnesses should be, you need to keep in mind the possibility that you may have been extensively investigated. If there are aspects of your life that might create a negative impression of you in court, there's a good chance the defence lawyer knows about this and will try to use it to discredit you. To limit the harm this might cause, your lawyer should be told about any damaging evidence that could be uncovered. You can then help him locate credible lay witnesses who can neutralize this evidence or place it in a more positive light.

Before your lawyer contacts your lay witnesses in the weeks prior to trial, you may want to phone them yourself to see whether they're willing to testify. They may be more open to a request from you than one from your lawyer. Since people are often reluctant to say anything negative in public about someone they like, you may have to assure potential witnesses that you have no objection to them speaking frankly to your lawyer and the court about the changes they've noticed in you. Their honest observations of your post-accident behaviour can help you receive fair compensation. Warning them to expect your lawyer's call will also give them time to think about what they're prepared to say in court.

It may be helpful to give your lawyer a brief summary of how long (and how well) you know each suggested lay witness and what aspects of your life each is qualified to comment on. This can include specific questions to ask each witness at trial. While there's no guarantee that your lawyer will ask these questions, it may help him plan his courtroom strategy.

Your lawyer will normally arrange to spend time with each of your lay witnesses prior to their court appearances. Before he calls someone to the witness stand, he should know how she's going to respond to his questions. He'll need to be prepared for any damaging evidence a witness might give so he knows what topics to avoid and how best to elicit information.

The opposing lawyers don't have to share the names of their lay witnesses prior to trial, but this is usually done as a matter of courtesy. Thus, you should know shortly before your trial date whom the defence plans to call as lay witnesses. While someone who has refused to testify for ICBC may be on their witness list — she can be subpoenaed and forced to appear — uncooperative witnesses are rarely called on. Even if you're sure that the defence lawyer is bluffing about someone testifying for ICBC, your lawyer will need to take this seriously. He may have to find additional lay witnesses who can refute potentially damaging evidence.

Negotiating a Pre-Trial Settlement

As the lawyers renew their efforts to negotiate an out-of-court settlement, they'll each try to place a realistic value on your claim by comparing it to earlier settlements and court-ordered awards in similar cases. (Only court-ordered awards can be referred to in a lawyer's closing arguments at trial.)

Prior to your trial date, ICBC may make you a formal offer to settle. For this to be used as the basis for awarding costs after trial, the offer has to be made on a legal document that clearly states: "Offer to Settle in accordance with Rule 37". An offer can also be made in the form of a "Calderbank letter" that states the legal precedent (*Calderbank vs Calderbank*) that allows this to be substituted for a formal Offer to Settle, and notes the circumstances that make this necessary. Calderbank letters are typically used when liability and "quantum" (the value of an award) are dealt with in separate trials; when liability may be divided between two or more parties; and when a third party (such as WCB) may have a legitimate claim on a settlement.

(If your case is being heard in the B.C. Supreme Court and ICBC feels that it's worth under $10,000, a Calderbank letter may prevent them from being responsible for court costs. A Calderbank letter may also be used to make you a settlement offer before you've initiated legal action against an at-fault driver, or when you have a second accident but haven't taken legal action yet with respect to this.)

Both a formal Offer to Settle and a Calderbank letter will state that the offer being made isn't an admission of liability; it's being made without prejudice except in relation to costs; and it's only binding until the beginning of trial, or until cancelled by written notice. Costs and disbursements won't be included in the offer. You'll have to deal with these separately.

Once you've received a formal offer from ICBC, your lawyer can present a written counter-offer, stating how much money you'd accept to settle your claim. If you're awarded more than this in court, you'll be paid "double costs" at the conclusion of your trial. If ICBC's offer to you is higher than what you're awarded at trial, you may have to pay part of their costs. The judge won't learn of the offer or counter-offer until after the court rules on your case.

While you and your lawyer are discussing an appropriate counter-offer, it may be a good time to ask him whether he'll reduce his contingency fee percentage if your case settles out of court. You'll both have a better idea of the value of your claim at this point than you had when you originally negotiated your legal contract. If the fee percentage you agreed to pay doesn't seem fair now, you may be able to re-negotiate this. (Your new fee agreement should be put in writing and signed by you both.)

> **CAUTION! While being awarded double costs can have a significant effect on how much money you end up with, making a counter-offer for a lower amount than you feel you'll be awarded at trial could backfire on you. If ICBC's case is weak or they're not happy with the assigned judge, they may accept your counter-offer.**

Personal injury cases sometimes settle on the morning of trial. If ICBC's last-minute offer to you is fairly close to what you feel you'll be awarded in court, you may want to accept this. No matter how strong your case is, the outcome of a trial is never certain, and all trials are stressful. While your lawyer can advise you on whether it's wise to settle, the final decision is yours. You'll want to take into account how much money you'll have at the end of the day after paying your legal fees and other expenses.

Last Minute Chaos

Since most personal injury lawyers work on many cases at a time, they often wait until shortly before a trial begins to focus their attention on a particular case. You may have to remind your lawyer to arrange for the necessary assessments early enough to give your experts the time they need to prepare thoughtful, reasoned reports. If he waits too long, he may not be able to hire the experts he wants.

If the ICBC defence team plans to show surveillance videos of you in court, these should be given to your lawyer a few days before trial. You'll need to carefully review this with him. You should also go over the defence lawyer's witness lists to make sure that additional lay witnesses aren't needed to address issues that neither you nor your lawyer had anticipated might arise.

Since your lawyer may give your lay witnesses short notice of when he needs them, you may want to tell them when your trial is supposed to begin. You won't want to lose a crucial witness because she can't re-arrange her schedule to attend the trial. (Your lay witnesses should also be warned that your case may be bumped from the trial docket at the last minute.)

Your lawyer will expect you to be available to him during the week prior to trial. As he re-familiarizes himself with all aspects of your case and re-examines the evidence and documents he's accumulated, he may have a lot of questions to ask you. He may also want to discuss with you how he intends to argue your case at trial.

While you'll want to help your lawyer as much as you can, it's also important to take the time you need to nurture yourself. Exercise, meditate, go for long walks, have a massage — do whatever activities will help you stay calm and relaxed. The days ahead are bound to be challenging and emotionally difficult.

CHAPTER 17

The Trial Process

You should know what judge is assigned to your case a few days before trial. While most B.C. Supreme Court judges are fairly moderate in their rulings, a few seem to make an effort to minimize damages in ICBC cases, while others have the reputation of awarding generous damages. If either lawyer is unhappy with the assigned judge, he may intensify his efforts to negotiate an out-of-court settlement.

ICBC often appeals the rulings of judges whom they feel are too liberal in awarding damages. If your case is assigned to one of these judges — *or* to a judge who typically awards minimal damages — you may want to hire an appeal lawyer early on. He can then advise your trial lawyer on potential grounds for appeal. How your case is conducted in court will determine to a large degree what happens later if either side appeals.

The Adversarial Nature of Our Courts

The Canadian judicial system seems to bring out the best, and worst, in lawyers during trial. Even if you're pleased with how your lawyer handles himself in court, you may be horrified by the defence lawyer's actions. He may make off-the-record remarks about you in the presence of the judge or jury, implying things that aren't true, or rely on biased evidence to support ICBC's position at trial.

The lawyers' behaviour towards each other before and after court sessions may be as disturbing to you as what happens during the trial. Regardless of how hard your lawyer fights for you in court and in out-of-court negotiations, or what tactics the defence lawyer uses to minimize the value of your claim, outside the courtroom they may be friends as well as colleagues. They may joke about how well they're doing in court and how badly the other is doing, as if your trial is a game of one-upmanship between friendly rivals. You don't need to be concerned about this. Once the judge enters the courtroom, the lawyers will "play the game" with the utmost seriousness. Their professional standing rests on the success or failure of their latest case.

The defence lawyer may exploit every opportunity he has to present you in a negative light, whether this involves your past or present behaviour or life circumstances. Your accident-related injuries and disabilities may be belittled or dismissed, and the court told that you've exaggerated your problems, making little effort to recover. While this may be upsetting to you personally, your lawyer is unlikely to be surprised by it. Every ICBC defence is an attack on a plaintiff's credibility in some way, and your lawyer has hopefully prepared his case to respond to any "dirty tricks" the defence lawyer might play. Trials aren't called "courtroom battles" without reason.

As your trial progresses, you may feel that your lawyer isn't doing enough to protect you or that he's dealing with crucial issues in a superficial way. While you can discuss your concerns with him, he'll argue your case however he feels will result in the highest award.

Trial-Related Stress

Sitting in court day every day as the defence downplays your struggles and questions your motivations can be agonizing. You may be enraged by the things that are said or implied about you, worrying that the judge or jury will believe the worst and reject your claim. As your anxiety level increases, you may develop symptoms of post-traumatic stress disorder.

If it's hard for you to be in court every day, you don't have to go unless your lawyer requests this. A relative or friend can go in your place so you don't have to rely solely on your lawyer's feedback.

Whenever your presence in court is required, you should make a conscious effort to try to quiet your mind occasionally, even if you can only do this for a few minutes. Practicing a simple relaxation technique can help you stay sane in a difficult situation.

A trial can place an enormous strain on your personal and professional relationships. Despite everything else going on in your life, you may be so preoccupied with the trial that it's all you can think about. It's important to try to maintain some objectivity, though, and to pursue activities that will keep your life in balance. If you become worn down physically or emotionally, or alienated from the people you're close to, you'll make the situation harder for yourself.

After you've discussed each day's court session with your lawyer, you should try to unwind and forget about the trial until the next session. Briefly describing to a relative or friend what happened in court that day and your feelings about it may help you drop your concerns for a while so you can turn your attention to something else. The key word is "briefly": obsessing over what happened or worrying about what will happen next can make you a nervous wreck. Decide beforehand whom you want to share the court day with — preferably the same person each day — and give yourself a set amount of time to do this, whether it's 15 minutes or an hour. Make it a point to say everything you want to say about the trial within the time frame you've allowed. If other people ask you what's been happening, you can just say that things have been going well and leave it at that. If they want more information, they can contact the person you're discussing the trial with each day.

If there's anything you need to pass on to your lawyer before the next court session, make a note of what it is, then forget about it until you phone or see him. If you want to discuss anything trial-related with anyone else, jot down a reminder to yourself to deal with this later. Limiting how much time you spend thinking about the trial outside court sessions should help reduce your stress.

You'll probably want to cut back on your out-of-court responsibilities as much as possible while the trial is going on. Keep yourself busy with activities you enjoy that will distract you. Also make sure that you eat properly, exercise, and get plenty of sleep. Meanwhile, keep reminding yourself that this, too, will pass, and the trial will eventually be over.

B.C. Supreme Court Hearings

All B.C. Supreme Court trials are conducted in a similar way. In a jury trial, the jury rules on liability when this is in dispute, and the size of the award under each head of damages, but the presiding judge still plays an active role in the court process. She'll question the lawyers and witnesses directly when something isn't clear; make sure the jury understands the facts and issues; and advise them on points of law, explaining how the law applies to a particular situation.

At the start of the first court session, one of the lawyers may try to get the trial postponed if he's not happy with the assigned judge. He may claim that he's grossly underestimated his time requirements, or that he hasn't fully prepared his case. The judge is unlikely to be sympathetic to these arguments if your case was already bumped from the trial docket on one or more occasions.

If the defence lawyer decides that he needs another expert assessment done to support his case, he may request permission for this from the court. Even if you've already been assessed by a dozen defence experts, your lawyer will probably agree to this so he doesn't risk giving ICBC grounds for appeal. If either side wants an additional document submitted to the court as part of the trial evidence, there may be a lengthy discussion about this before the judge rules on whether the document is admissible.

As the plaintiff in the case, your side will be presented first. As each witness is called to testify, he'll be asked to swear an oath or affirm to tell the truth. While you have the right to be in court throughout the trial, your lawyer may not want you there until after you've testified. (The defence might otherwise argue that little weight should be given to your testimony as it was influenced by what other witnesses said.)

Your lawyer's initial questioning of each of his witnesses is known as his examination-in-chief (or "direct"). The defence lawyer then cross-examines (or questions) the witness in what's known as his "cross". Your lawyer can then question the witness again in a "re-direct". A witness' testimony may take a few minutes or continue for several hours. If the court recesses or adjourns for the day while a witness is being cross-examined, she'll be instructed not to discuss her testimony with anyone, and she'll still be under oath when the court reconvenes (or meets again).

When the credentials of an expert witness are challenged, the judge decides whether he can testify. If she doesn't feel he's qualified to provide an expert opinion to the court but he may have relevant evidence to present, she may allow him to testify as a lay witness. The jury, if any, will be instructed not to view his evidence as expert testimony.

During their testimonies, your expert witnesses will be questioned about their assessments and opinions. They may also be asked about the nature of the compensation you're entitled to and what it might take to return you, as nearly as possible, to how you'd have been "but for your accident". Their responses will help the court decide how much money to award you under each head of damages.

While witnesses usually aren't asked to comment on evidence that hasn't been presented in court yet, during his examination-in-chief of an expert witness, your lawyer can question her about the findings of defence experts who haven't testified yet. ("Rebuttal evidence before the fact" is allowed in this situation since few expert witnesses can return to court to refute future testimony.) Your expert should already have reviewed the pertinent reports in her field and had time to form an opinion on them.

Once your lawyer finishes questioning a witness, the defence lawyer will cross-examine her. His "cross" can relate to any subject, not just what was brought up during your lawyer's examination of the witness. The only condition he's bound by is that his questions have to be relevant to your case. If your lawyer objects to his line of questioning, the judge will rule on whether the evidence he's trying to present has a direct bearing on your claim.

In cross-examining your witnesses, the defence lawyer will try to neutralize the impact of what they've said in support of your claim. When he can't do this, he may try to discredit a witness' testimony so it has little impact on the court's decisions. He may also try to elicit information from your lay and expert witnesses to support the defence's position at trial.

After the defence lawyer has cross-examined a witness, your lawyer can question her again. He can't bring up new subject matter in his "re-direct"; he can only discuss issues that were brought up for the first time during the defence's "cross". Once his "re-direct" is done, no further questions are allowed and the witness is excused. (Rather than doing his "re-direct" of a witness immediately, your lawyer can reserve the right to re-call her later.)

When your lawyer has finished presenting his case, the defence lawyer will call his witnesses and the same process will happen in reverse. Your lawyer may want you in court while the defence witnesses are testifying so you can point out when someone isn't being truthful, or suggest questions for him to ask a witness.

After the defence witnesses have all testified, your lawyer will have a final chance to call (or re-call) witnesses. A witness can only be called (or re-called) at this point to deal with matters that were raised during the defence's presentation, which your lawyer couldn't reasonably have anticipated. No new issues can be brought up at this time.

Your Testimony

Unless your lawyer thinks that putting you on the witness stand would be a mistake — or your treating psychologist (if any) doesn't feel you can handle the stress — you'll usually be asked to testify at trial. In most cases, you and your lawyer will go over the questions he intends to ask you beforehand, so he knows how you'll respond and can make suggestions as needed. He should also coach you on your responses to the questions you may be asked on cross-examination.

If there are aspects of your case that you'd like to address in your testimony, you can ask your lawyer to question you about these things. He won't do this, though, if he's concerned about issues being brought up that could weaken your case.

In some situations, your lawyer may not discuss your testimony with you beforehand, just advising you to tell the truth. While this may make you feel vulnerable on the witness stand, this may be what he wants as part of his courtroom strategy.

Don't be too hard on yourself if you're not satisfied with your testimony. You may get flustered and confused, answer questions incorrectly, or not feel you have enough time to say what you want to say. Most people with little trial experience don't feel that they do well on the witness stand, even when they have much less at stake then you do. Not only may you have done better than you think, the court's decisions will be based on the evidence presented by *all* the trial witnesses, not just you.

Closing Arguments

Closing arguments in a jury trial are delivered verbally. In a judge-only trial, they may be verbal, written or both. If the judge wants to reserve judgment on one or more issues, she may request that the closing arguments be written. (The lawyers may also be asked what they'd prefer.)

Your lawyer may want to discuss his closing arguments with you before he presents them. If he feels that your input will be helpful, you may be asked to read court transcripts of similar cases to see whether you can find anything useful that he's missed, including pertinent case law indicating an appropriate award amount under one or more heads of damages.

Your lawyer's closing arguments will be delivered first. The defence lawyer will then present his arguments, which your lawyer will be allowed to respond to. In a judge-only trial, each lawyer will compare your case to similar cases and note what he feels you should be awarded under each head of damages. (In a jury trial, no amount is suggested for pain and suffering.)

While the closing arguments are supposed to be based on the evidence at trial, with each lawyer summarizing what he feels he's proven, they'll each slant the evidence to benefit their side's position. The defence lawyer may ignore evidence that supports your claim; distort it to minimize your damages; or make statements that clearly contradict the trial evidence. In his closing rebuttal (or final arguments), your lawyer will have a chance to direct the court's attention to evidence that disproves the defence's arguments and strengthens your claim.

Handing Down a Judgment

While juries often reach a decision in a few hours in an ICBC case, a trial judge may take a month or more to deliver her Reasons for Judgment. Her Judgment won't just note what she's awarding you under each head of damages, it will explain the reasons for each of her decisions. Which side is to pay court costs will usually be mentioned as well. (Even in a jury trial, the presiding judge rules on costs and disbursements. Unless your claim is denied, you should be awarded these in whole or part. The "scale of costs" may have to be argued after trial. See Chapter 18.)

Receiving your Judgment may not be end of the judicial process. Even when neither side appeals, numerous issues may have to be brought back before the trial judge or ruled on by the Court Registrar.

CHAPTER 18

Receiving Your Money

You may not recover any money until several months after receiving a court Judgment. Unless you and ICBC can agree on the issues discussed in this chapter (and on the present-dollar value of your future economic losses, if any), the lawyers may have to return to court to argue this.

Costs And Disbursements

Since costs and disbursements "follow the event", you'll only be awarded these in relation to aspects of your claim that your lawyer was able to prove at trial. If he argued that you had a brain injury as well as a whiplash injury, but the court rejected your brain injury claim, you won't be awarded costs for trial time devoted to this, nor disbursements solely connected to it. You may also have to pay ICBC's expenses in disproving your brain injury claim.

If a formal Offer to Settle was made for more money than the court awarded you, your costs and disbursements will only be paid up to the date of the offer. You'll be responsible for ICBC's costs and disbursements from the date of their offer to the Judgment date.

Costs: While part of the reason the successful party to a legal suit is awarded costs is to help pay legal fees, court costs rarely cover more than 25% of a lawyer's fee.[70] Court costs are calculated by assigning units (or points) to various legal procedures: each time your lawyer prepared and filed a legal document for you; saw a judge in chambers for you; or appeared in court or other hearings on your behalf, including examinations for discovery, mediation, a settlement conference and the trial itself. Points are assigned for his preparation time as well. The presiding judge determines the value of each point by setting a tariff scale (of 1-5) to your case. The more complex your case is, the higher the scale of costs, and the more each unit (or point) is worth. Lawyers sometimes return to court to argue the scale of costs after a Judgment is handed down. If either side feels the assigned tariff scale is unfair, they can appeal this.

If the court awards you more money than you agreed to accept prior to trial, you'll get "double costs" from the date of your formal counter-offer to the Judgment date. (The court won't learn of the offer or counter-offer until after a Judgment is handed down.) Since lawyers don't earn contingency fees on costs, being awarded double costs can have a significant effect on how much money you end up with. (ICBC is only awarded double costs when the court feels that a case was fraudulent or frivolous.)

Special costs increase the money you get in court costs. Your lawyer will have to return to court to request this. You may be awarded special costs if the trial judge feels that ICBC's conduct was disgraceful or dishonourable.[71] Your lawyer may argue, for example, that the purpose of their defence was to place you in financial hardship.[72] If the judge feels that ICBC tried to mislead the court, you may also be awarded special costs. One situation where this might occur is when the main issue at trial was whether your problems were caused by your accident, and the defence relied on flawed or biased evidence.[73]

Your lawyer may be reluctant to go back before the trial judge to argue special costs. It's his responsibility to represent you in all legal matters relating to your claim, though. If you think that you're entitled to special costs, you should discuss this with him. You'll have to consider how good your chances are of being awarded this money and what your lawyer will charge you for his efforts. If you request special costs and they're not granted, you may have to pay all costs and disbursements with respect to this.

Disbursements are the expenses your lawyer has in conducting your case. These may include court fees and transcripts, mediation costs, experts' assessments and reports, travel and *per diem* expenses for out-of-town witnesses, phone calls, photocopying and courier services. In a complex case, the last two items can come to several thousand dollars, while hiring experts can cost tens of thousands of dollars.

ICBC may dispute paying some of your lawyer's expenses. What they'll cover may have to be negotiated between the two sides or determined by the Court Registrar. Your lawyer may resist going before the Registrar to defend expenses that ICBC challenges, urging you to accept less money than he's billed on his disbursement schedule. You may be told that you'll recover more money through an out-of-court agreement that can't be appealed. He may not feel that he can adequately defend all his expenses, nor want to take the time to do this.

Before you agree to accept less money in disbursements, you may want to ask your lawyer if he'll split the difference with you, *or* at least deduct the non-reimbursed expenses from your award before calculating his contingency fee. (Otherwise, you'll essentially pay a contingency fee on non-recovered disbursements, although lawyers don't see it this way themselves.)

CAUTION! Your lawyer may bill you for offices services at a higher rate than he's allowed to charge on his disbursement schedule to ICBC. Unless your legal contract prohibits him from charging you more than the Registrar's rates for any item or service, you'll be expected to pay this additional amount. (You'll have the right to tax his bill as discussed in Chapter 13.)

If your lawyer doesn't think that ICBC will sign an Undertaking to Pay unless you agree to accept less money in certain areas, it's better to compromise on damages where you'll have to pay a contingency fee, than on costs or disbursements where you won't.

Tax Gross-Ups

If the court awards you $100,000 or more for your future income losses, or $50,000 or more for your future care, it's generally assumed that you'll invest this money until you need it. Since you'll have to pay taxes on your investment income, you may be paid a "tax gross-up" to offset this. All other things being equal, the larger your awards for future income loss and future care (your "futures"), the higher your tax gross-up, if any, will be. Tax gross-up usually isn't brought up until after a Judgment is handed down.

While you won't receive a tax gross-up unless you request one, requesting this money may increase the likelihood of your Judgment being "structured" (or paid out to you over time in the form of an annuity). Since your annuity payments can be made tax-free, a tax gross-up won't be warranted. If you don't want your award structured, your lawyer will have to convince the judge that this isn't in your best interests. (An award is rarely structured when a plaintiff objects to this. See the section on structured Judgments and settlements at the end of this chapter.)

When a large award isn't structured, the BC Law Reform Commission's method of determining tax gross-ups may be used to calculate an appropriate award amount.[74] Among the variables that will taken into account are the size of your "futures", how much of this money you expect to spend each year, whether you're eligible for a disability tax credit, what the anticipated rate of inflation is, and what a reasonable rate of return is on your investments. Unless you and ICBC use the same financial expert to determine your tax gross-up amount, or the lawyers can negotiate an agreement on this, the trial judge will be asked to rule on it. (A tax gross-up can be tens of thousands of dollars. Your lawyer will expect a contingency fee on this.)

Even if ICBC accepts your financial expert's calculations, they may only agree to pay you a portion of the estimated tax gross-up amount. If the suggested reduction is minimal, it may make sense to compromise on this so your lawyer doesn't have to return to court to resolve the issue. You'll have more control over an out-of-court agreement as this can't be appealed.

If your "futures" increase or decrease on appeal, your tax gross-up will have to be re-calculated. Unless an agreement can be reached on the new tax gross-up amount, the appellate court will rule on this.

Any income that raises your tax rate may increase the tax gross-up you're entitled to. Thus, you need to tell your lawyer about any income-producing assets you have and any money you expect to inherit in the future. This can then be factored into the tax gross-up calculations. ICBC or the court may want documentation of your existing assets, investment income, and money being held in trust which you'll eventually inherit.

Management Fees

Most people who are awarded a large sum of money for their future care require professional financial advice. If your combined "futures" and tax gross-up are $250,000 or more, you may be paid management fees as part of your pecuniary damages. (You won't get management fees if your award is structured as your investments will be professionally managed inside the purchased annuity.) Your lawyer may have to argue in court what level of financial help you'll need. Once the trial judge rules on this, if an agreement can't be reached on the size of your management fees, the judge may have to rule on this as well.

The BC Law Reform Commission also standardized the calculation of management fees.[75] While the first two levels of help no longer entitle someone to management fees, if you'll need on-going financial advice, management fees at Level 3 may be warranted. You'll only be compensated at Level 4 if someone will have to pay your household bills and other expenses, as well as assume full responsibility for financial and investment decisions.

The larger your combined "futures" and tax gross-up, the lower the percentage used to determine your management fees. The longer your life expectancy, the higher the percentage used. On combined "futures" and tax gross-up of $1 million, management fees at Level 3 are $22,000 (and at Level 4, $39,000) when you're expected to live ten more years, and $70,000 (or $127,000 at Level 4) when you're expected to live another fifty years. (You'll have to pay your lawyer a contingency fee on this.)

As with tax gross-ups, your management fees will have to be re-calculated if your "futures" increase or decrease on appeal, even though an out-of-court agreement was reached on this. A dispute about the re-calculation may have to be ruled on by the appellate court.

Reviews Before the Court Registrar

Your lawyer may charge you a separate fee to go before the Court Registrar to argue disbursements and other issues after trial. These hearings are fairly informal. The opposing lawyers present arguments, witnesses may be called, and written affidavits may be referred to. If ICBC disputes one of your experts' fees, your lawyer may give the court a sworn statement from her explaining why her fee is warranted. He can also present evidence in his own right.

Either side can ask a court stenographer to be present. If the Registrar's decision is appealed, you may want a transcript of the proceedings. You can also ask the Registrar to provide written Reasons for her decisions or a copy of her court notes.

Since the Registrar's decisions are usually a compromise between the opposing positions, each side typically pays its own costs and disbursements.

Court-Ordered Interest

You're entitled to interest on your award from the date of your Judgment to the date you're paid. (If you're awarded additional money on appeal, interest on this will begin from the date of the appellate Judgment.) Interest rates are set by the court and fluctuate with bank rates. You may get a higher rate than you'd get in the bank during the same time period.

Interest on a large award can be substantial, especially when a case goes to appeal and money is held back pending the outcome. (Your lawyer will expect a contingency fee on the interest paid.)

Deductions for Part 7 Benefits

The court won't learn what accident benefits you've received until after a Judgment is handed down. Any money you were awarded for items or services ICBC has covered as an accident benefit will then be deducted from your award. Total disability (wage-loss) benefits that you've received will be deducted from your award for past income loss, *unless* your wage-loss benefits were taken into account when your past income losses were calculated.

ICBC has the right to ask the trial judge to take a "Section 25 deduction" from your award. This will be based on the present-dollar value of the future care items and services the court awarded you money for, which correspond to Part 7 benefits. A Section 25 deduction can't be made for more money than you have in your accident benefits account. (If you were awarded $50,000 for physiotherapy, but there's only $25,000 left in your Part 7 account, this is the maximum amount that can be deducted.)

ICBC may request a Section 25 deduction for psychological counselling or other services that they've refused to cover as an accident benefit. The reason this is allowed is that the Insurance (Motor Vehicle) Act states that Part 7 benefits include "funds for any other costs the corporation in its sole discretion agrees to pay". If the court awarded you money for psychological counselling, ICBC will now agree "at {their} sole discretion" to pay for this as an accident benefit. (This will reduce the money they have to pay you in damages. They may later appeal the court's decision that you need counselling.) The fewer accident benefits ICBC has provided you with, the more money there will be in your Part 7 account, and the larger the Section 25 deduction can theoretically be.

By requesting a Section 25 deduction, ICBC is agreeing *in principle* to pay for the items and services the court decided are necessary for your well-being. You can no longer require them to sign a "non-discretionary undertaking" that would commit them to provide the relevant benefits. The courts have ruled that this isn't necessary since they're legally obligated to pay for medical and rehab treatment and related health care needs when someone is entitled to Part 7 benefits. If you were denied legitimate accident benefits in the past, you may find the court's faith in ICBC grossly misguided.

While judges have to allow a Section 25 deduction to be made, the courts have given them some flexibility in doing this. If ICBC provided you with few accident benefits in the past, your lawyer can argue that they're likely to continue this pattern in the future. If the judge agrees with him, she may only make a minimal Section 25 deduction. ICBC can appeal her decision if they don't think the deducted amount is large enough.

You may be able to avoid a Section 25 deduction by releasing ICBC from further Part 7 obligations towards you. Your lawyer can advise you on this.

> **CAUTION! You shouldn't be charged a contingency fee on money deducted from your award as a Section 25 deduction. Your lawyer's fee should be based on the money *recovered*.**

To find out how much money is left in your Part 7 account, ask your lawyer to get you a copy of your payment schedule. This should be checked carefully to ensure that it's accurate. Your account may have been billed for benefits that were provided to someone else, for the fees charged by various experts who assessed you — even for the defence lawyer's legal fee! Most mistakes should be easy to correct once they're identified.

You'll want to make sure that all your medical and rehab treatment and related expenses have been deducted from your Part 7 account before a Section 25 deduction is made. You may have more than one active file with ICBC with some accident benefits paid on one schedule and some on another. Your adjuster may also have delayed billing your account for various items or services to make a larger Section 25 deduction possible. If the cost of earlier treatment is deducted from your Part 7 account after a Section 25 deduction is made, you'll have less money to cover future benefits. If you think anything is missing from your payment schedule, ask your lawyer to see whether the judge will make it a condition of her Section 25 deduction that ICBC is *expressly prohibited* from charging your Part 7 account for earlier items or services.

Part 7 Buy-Outs

In closing your claim, you may be able to buy out your right to future accident benefits. Once you and ICBC have agreed on how much money is left in your Part 7 account, a present-dollar value can be placed on this. If you're not satisfied with the buy-out offer made, an economist can calculate what's fair.

Before you have your lawyer negotiate a Part 7 buy-out, find out what, if anything, he'll charge for this. You may be able to negotiate a buy-out yourself at a later date.

The major advantage to keeping your Part 7's open after your tort claim resolves is that the full amount of money left in your account can be used for the items and services for which a Section 25 deduction was made. In some cases, this may mean that ICBC will pay for more treatment than you were awarded money for. (If you were awarded $50,000 for physiotherapy and a Section 25 deduction was made for this amount, ICBC should continue paying for your physiotherapy until your Part 7 account is depleted, even if there was $75,000 in the account when the deduction was made.) If you were awarded less money than you might need for a deducted item or service, it may make sense to keep your Part 7's open.

Once your tort claim is paid out, the only accident benefits you'll get from ICBC are the future care items and services for which a Section 25 deduction was made. If your needs change over time and you require treatment you weren't awarded money for — while you need less of the treatment that ICBC is now supposed to cover — you won't be able to substitute one treatment option for another. It may also be hard to get accident benefits once your tort claim resolves. (If ICBC feels a type of physiotherapy your doctor recommends is unnecessary or too costly, you may have to go though arbitration to get them to pay for this.)

You may want to get a copy of your Part 7 payment schedule once or twice a year until you either buy out your Part 7's or the money in your account is used up. (You can get this through ICBC's freedom of information unit.)

When you're not entitled to damages, closing your claim with ICBC essentially means buying out your right to future Part 7 benefits. (You may also be able to get some of your accident-related out-of-pocket expenses reimbursed.) Your buy-out amount will usually be the present-dollar value of the items and services your adjuster or an ICBC rehab co-ordinator agrees you'll need in the future.

Hidden Legal Fees and Other Deductions

No matter how large your award is, you may be disappointed by how little you end up with after various deductions (and voluntary reductions) are made and your legal fees are paid. In a worst-case scenario, you can win your case in court and end up worse off financially than when you started.

Your award or settlement money will normally be paid to your lawyer. (If another arrangement is made, he'll have a statutory lien on the money to ensure that his legal fees are paid.) Once he deducts his fees, disbursements and the relevant taxes, the rest of the recovered funds should be given to you. You may find out at this point that you've been charged unexpected fees or expenses.

You shouldn't pay a contingency fee on costs, disbursements or Part 7 benefits. However, your lawyer may bill you by the hour or charge you a fixed fee to represent you in a Part 7 legal action; argue costs before the trial judge or disbursements before the Court Registrar; collect your money; or perform other services that you'd assumed were covered by his contingency fee. You may also be charged for consultations he's had with other lawyers about your case. If he bills you for office services at a higher rate than he's allowed to charge on his disbursement schedule to ICBC, thousands of additional dollars may be deducted from the money you receive. (You'll pay taxes on your legal fees, but not on your award or settlement.)

If you disagree with your lawyer's final statement of accounts, set up an appointment to discuss this with him as soon as possible. Unless you can reach an agreement with him on this, you can tax his bill in court. (See the section on resolving conflicts with your lawyer in Chapter 13.)

> **CAUTION!** **Don't agree to a lump sum payment from ICBC without a written statement itemizing how much of this money is for each head of damages, court-ordered interest, costs, disbursements, and a Part 7 buy-out.**

If you have an UMP claim, your award will be reduced by any benefits you've received (or were entitled to) from any source, including Part 7 benefits, payments from the Unidentified-Uninsured

Motorist Protection Fund, government benefits and pensions, and private disability or extended health-care benefits. Any money you get from an at-fault driver or his insurer will also be deducted from your UMP award. Both the $1 million (or more) cap on an UMP award and the $200,000 cap on money from the Unidentified-Uninsured Motorist Protection Fund include court costs and interest. (Your lawyer will expect a contingency fee on the interest, but not on court costs.)

If another insurer provided you with benefits that you'll have to repay when you close your claim, these may be reimbursed directly before you recover any money yourself.

Receiving Your Money

ICBC often delays paying out a claim while they decide whether to appeal. They'll have 30 days to make this decision. Even if your case isn't appealed, they may delay paying you until you agree to accept less money in certain areas. You may have to go to court to get the Judgment "executed" (or paid out).

Once you and ICBC have agreed on what you're to be paid in damages, costs, disbursements and interest, a letter will be drawn up outlining the sums agreed on. This should be followed by prompt payment of the money you're owed — unless part of this is being held back pending an appeal.

Money paid to a minor in B.C. is held in trust for her by the Public Guardian and Trustee until she's 19. The minor's parents or legal guardian may request that funds be released periodically to cover the minor's needs. These requests are normally honoured when appropriate.

If your case is appealed: Even if ICBC decides to appeal your case, they're obligated to pay you the full amount of money you were awarded *unless* they apply to the court for a "stay of Judgment" (or "stay of execution") that will allow them to hold the money until after the appeal. In practice, most "stays" are voluntarily agreed to by the opposing parties. If you agree to accept part of your award money as an advance, ICBC will agree that paying you this money doesn't release them from further obligations towards you.

ICBC usually won't pay you any money that they plan to challenge on appeal. If they don't feel that you're entitled to damages and they appeal the whole Judgment, you may be able to get part of the money you were awarded by agreeing in writing to pay back what you lose on appeal. To make sure you'll have the funds to do this, a lien may be placed on your property, usually your home, or you may have to put the disputed money in an interest-bearing trust account in ICBC's name.

If you're the party appealing, ICBC may not want to pay you anything until after the appeal. While you can "execute the Judgment", forcing them to pay it, what usually happens instead is that your lawyer will ask for a portion of your award to be paid up front, pending the appeal, in exchange for ICBC's agreement that this doesn't end their obligations towards you. Your lawyer may have to ask the appellate court to order that any money not in dispute be paid to you immediately, and the remainder of your award money put into an interest-bearing trust account in your name.

If ICBC was awarded costs and disbursements at trial and you appeal this, you'll either have to pay them the money you owe them up front, pending the appeal, or safeguard it via a letter of credit, a lien on your property, or cash deposited in an interest-bearing trust account in their name.

Structured Judgments and Settlements

Instead of getting all your money at once, it may be paid out to you over time — in many cases, throughout your life. A structured Judgment or settlement is basically an annuity that ICBC purchases for you from a life insurance company. The amount of money you'll receive (usually monthly) will be based on the size of your damages and the terms built into the annuity. While people are sometimes reluctant to tie up their money this way, a properly structured annuity can help ensure that you'll have money when you need it.

Until fairly recently, only minors and people with significant injuries had structured settlements. The courts are now supposed to order that an award be structured whenever the net combined award for future income loss and future care exceeds $100,000, and/or a tax gross-up is requested. The only exception to this is when the judge feels that periodic payments aren't in your best interest, or that an annuity may prevent you from getting the full amount of money awarded.[76]

Structured Judgments are rarely ordered without a plaintiff's approval. If you don't want your award structured, your lawyer can argue that it's not fair to lock up your money this way. Your personal and financial objectives may make structuring your award inappropriate; for example, you may need money for a new home or business, to return to school, or to put a spouse, partner or child through college. When interest rates are low, your lawyer can also argue that a structured Judgment would penalize you financially. (The interest rate will be locked in when the annuity is purchased.) Even when the return on annuities is fairly high, you can usually earn more money with a well-diversified investment portfolio as very conservative investments are made inside guaranteed-payment annuities. If your lawyer backs up his arguments with evidence and legal precedent, you should be able to avoid having your Judgment structured.

It's rarely worthwhile to structure an award or settlement of under $50,000 since your monthly payments would be very small. This being said, even $5,000 settlements have sometimes been structured. Your annuity payments will be guaranteed by both ICBC and the life insurance company issuing the annuity.

Your lawyer's fees and disbursements will be deducted from your award or settlement before an annuity is purchased. You may want additional money deducted as well to use for other purposes. Your lawyer's contingency fee will be based on the present-dollar value of your annuity and any lump sum payments you receive. He'll expect to be paid up front even though you'll get most of your money over an extended period of time.

Deciding whether (and how) to structure your award or settlement requires sound professional advice. Your lawyer should be able to recommend a structure specialist or broker who can provide you with competent, in-depth service. You shouldn't have to pay for this: the broker will earn a commission of about 3% from the insurance company issuing the annuity. If you decide not to structure your award or settlement after consulting a broker, you shouldn't be charged for his time. (If you get advice from a financial professional who doesn't sell annuities, you'll have to pay for his time whether or not an annuity is purchased.) ICBC may consult their own structure specialist.

You may prefer to have your Judgment or settlement structured if you're not confident that you can manage a large sum of money intelligently; you'll have to earn a reasonable rate of return to meet your needs; or your money may have to be protected from outside demands.

Once your claim is close to being resolved, and you have a fairly good idea of how much money will be available to put into an annuity, you can meet with a structure specialist in his (or your lawyer's) office, your home, or the hospital or rehab centre you're in. He'll normally plan on spending several hours with you to help you figure out your future financial needs, and how large your monthly annuity payments have to be to meet these needs.

If you were seriously injured, your case manager or ICBC rehab co-ordinator can set up a budget for you that takes into account the amount of money you'll need each month for your medical and rehab treatment, attendant care, housing, and other needs. She can then consult with your lawyer, a structure specialist, and a member of your immediate family to make sure your needs will be met in the future. A future care assessor can also be helpful in setting up a structured settlement.

Endless variations can be built into an annuity. You may want lump sum payments at specific times to cover anticipated expenses; have your payments increase (or decrease) when you expect your living expenses to go up (or down); continue to get payments throughout your life or only for a specific number of years; start receiving payments immediately or not until a pre-determined future date; receive the same size payments each month or have your payments indexed to inflation; and make your payments fully (or partially) tax free. You may also want to provide for your heirs when you die.

Once the terms of your annuity are set up, you won't be able to change them no matter how much your personal situation changes. This can work to your advantage in some ways: your money will be protected from creditors and can't be given away in a divorce settlement, stolen, used to secure a loan, or lost through bad investments. You'll continue to receive payments according to the terms established.

> **CAUTION! You may want to review all aspects of your structured award or settlement with an independent financial professional before an annuity is purchased for you. Locked-in terms can't be changed later for any reason.**

When a structured settlement is for a minor: A million dollars in damages can translate into a $15 million structured settlement, with tax-free monthly payments spread out over the minor's life. The size of the monthly payments will depend on how much money is paid up front in a lump sum; how old the minor is; what her life expectancy is; and what terms are built into the annuity structure. (The contingency fee paid to the minor's lawyer will be based on $1 million, not $15 million.)

In setting up a structured settlement for a minor, it's common to arrange for a future lump sum payment to be made when she's 19 to pay for her education and again when she's 25 so she can buy a home. The Public Guardian and Trustee will have to pre-approve the terms of the annuity before it's purchased to make sure the minor's interests are protected.

CHAPTER 19

Appeals and Cross-Appeals

The main function of the B.C. Court of Appeal is to determine whether the law was correctly followed at all times during a trial and correctly applied by the trial judge in her rulings. In a personal injury case, an error in law may be little more than an excuse to ask the appellate court to reduce or increase an award.

Either side in a case can challenge what the judge found to be a fact if they don't feel there was evidence of this at trial, or they feel that it's too far beyond the court record to be reasonable. If the appellate judges agree that a significant error was made, they may order a new trial or substitute their own findings for that of the trial judge, altering any rulings based on this.

If ICBC feels that your award was "inordinately high", the court Judgment may be appealed on these grounds alone. One example of this would be a $150,000 award for general damages when the highest previous award for the same injury was $50,000. The B.C. Court of Appeal has also reduced awards under other heads of damages that it considers too generous. (An "inordinately low" award can also be appealed.) While the rulings of trial judges are usually upheld when no clear error in law was made, the B.C. Court of Appeal has shown an apparent bias in ICBC's favour in the past, reducing awards without always having valid grounds to do this.

It's hard to appeal most jury decisions. The only time a jury decision is apt to be reversed in an ICBC case is when the trial judge made an error in law in her instructions to the jury; the jury awarded so much (or so little) money that it's out of line with normally accepted standards; or the jury awarded more than the upper allowable limit in general damages. (A trial judge can declare a mistrial when she feels a jury's verdict contradicts the trial evidence.)

Appeals

All large awards have a good chance of being appealed. ICBC may also appeal a small award that they don't feel should have been granted. When a new legal precedent was set that may be unfavourable to insurers in the future — or for a variety of other reasons — ICBC may appeal part (or all) of a court Judgment.

You can appeal the court Judgment yourself if a legal precedent was ignored by the trial judge or other legal issues are involved. If you're reasonably satisfied with your overall award, though, you may not want to incur more legal costs — *and* give ICBC a chance to cross-appeal at little expense — just because you were under-compensated in certain areas. If you don't agree with your lawyer on whether an appeal (or cross-appeal) is both warranted and likely to succeed, you may want a second opinion from an appeal lawyer.

If your award was "inordinately low" or unreasonable, or you weren't awarded any money in an area where you're clearly entitled to damages, you'll probably want to appeal your case. Your trial lawyer (or an appeal lawyer) can advise you on appealable issues and the consequences of initiating an appeal.

You'll have 30 days from the Judgment date to file a Notice of Appeal. This will preserve your right to have your case reviewed by the appellate court. You can later decide whether to pursue the appeal or drop it. Most appeals take one to two years from start to finish. (The "appellant" is the party appealing and the "respondent" is the party defending the Judgment. When the respondent files a cross-appeal, he's the appellant on this action and the appellate on appeal is the respondent on the cross-appeal.)

B.C. Court of Appeal cases are argued largely through Factums (written arguments and the corresponding documents). The Factums direct the appellate judges to the trial evidence and legal precedent that each side feels is relevant. While a cross-appeal Factum is separate from a reply Factum to an appeal, both are usually submitted to the court (and delivered to the opposing party) at the same time.

The B.C. Court of Appeal has given lawyers a lot of flexibility in how much time they have to prepare their Factums. Delays can't continue indefinitely, though. If months go by without anything happening, the lawyers may be warned that the case will be dropped unless action is soon taken. A respondent can also apply to the court to have an appeal cancelled for "lack of prosecution" when the appellant doesn't file his Factum within a reasonable time. If he promises to do this quickly, the court will usually allow it. Otherwise, the appeal process will end, and the B.C. Supreme Court Judgment will stand as given.

Cross-Appeals

A cross-appeal has to be filed within 15 days of the Notice of Appeal. While many lawyers automatically file cross-appeals, they aren't always pursued.

The major disadvantage to you cross-appealing is that it means you agree there were errors in the court Judgment. If you're reasonably satisfied with your overall award, you may be advised that the best way to defend it is to argue that the trial judge didn't make any errors in her rulings so neither side has grounds for appeal.

If you were awarded a reasonable amount of money in damages, your lawyer may be concerned that a cross-appeal will make you look greedy, prejudicing the appellate judges against you. You should keep in mind, however, that if ICBC's appeal is successful, your award may be reduced to a level that doesn't fairly compensate you. If you can show the appellate judges (through a cross-appeal) that you were under-compensated in one or more areas, they may be less inclined to feel that your award was too generous and should be reduced. Moreover, since the B.C. Court of Appeal often compromises between the opposing positions, a cross-appeal will extend the boundaries of the compromise in your favour.

Appeal Costs

Besides what you'll pay a lawyer to represent you on appeal, your other costs will include filing fees of a few hundred dollars and the legal costs associated with this, which may be another few hundred dollars. Whichever side appeals also has to prepare (and pay for) the Appeal Books. Each Appeal Book can cost thousands of dollars and multiple copies will be needed. When a respondent wants additional material added to the Appeal Books, she usually has to cover this cost. (If an appellant doesn't feel he needs Appeal Books to argue his case, but the respondent wants to place certain material before the court, she'll have to pay for the Appeal Books.) While your lawyer may cover the cost of the Appeal Books or additional material up front, he'll expect to be reimbursed.

Most trial lawyers charge a higher contingency percentage when a case goes to appeal. Or, they may charge an hourly rate or fixed fee to represent a client on appeal. Unless your legal contract outlines how you'll be billed if your case goes to appeal, you'll have to negotiate this with your lawyer. He may agree to only charge a higher contingency percentage on the money in dispute, not your whole award.

If ICBC appeals your Judgment and you don't cross-appeal, your award will either stay the same or decrease, reducing the money your trial lawyer's fee is based on. Since the fee he earned at trial will now be at risk, he'll expect to be compensated for this.

If you hire an appeal lawyer, he may charge you a fixed fee, bill you by the hour, or take a contingency fee on your overall award after appeal, or on the money in dispute. If your trial lawyer's contingency percentage increases on appeal, he should pay the appeal lawyer, not you.

Most appeal lawyers in the province charge $250-$500 an hour, depending on their experience. (Fixed fees vary according to the complexity of the situation and the amount of money at stake.) If you're paying your appeal lawyer on a contingency fee basis, he'll probably expect between 2-10% of your overall award or the money in dispute. The contingency percentage you'll be charged will depend on the size of your award, the amount of money at stake, and whether the lawyer is defending the Judgment or appealing it. Since he'll have to do more work to appeal the Judgment than to defend it, he may charge a higher percentage for this. When a cross-appeal is involved, he'll have additional work to do as well, so the percentage may be even higher. (When a trial lawyer's contingency fee percentage increases on appeal, an appeal lawyer will often charge this increased percentage as his fee under the assumption that the trial lawyer will pay him, not the client.)

Even if your trial lawyer negotiates the fee agreement with your appeal lawyer, you'll want some input in this as you may be responsible for part of the appeal costs. If you lose on appeal, you'll have to pay your appeal lawyer's disbursements; neither ICBC nor your trial lawyer will do this.

Unless the B.C. Court of Appeal rules otherwise, whichever side wins on appeal should have their costs paid by the losing party. When an appeal is successful on some counts and fails on others, or the court compromises between the opposing positions on one or more issues — both of which commonly happen — each side usually covers their own costs. In certain situations, each side may be *awarded* their costs and ordered to pay the other side's costs. The respondent will then pay most of the appeal costs as these are initially paid by the appellant in preparing the Appeal Books. (If you lose your cross-appeal, you'll have to pay ICBC's costs and disbursements relative to this action as well as your own.)

When the appellate court doesn't assign costs to either party, unless an agreement can be reached on which party is responsible for what costs, the lawyers will have to return to court for a ruling on this. (The Appeal Court Registrar will determine how much money one party is to pay the other by translating the court's instructions into a specific dollar amount.)

When to Hire an Appeal Lawyer

While trial lawyers handle two-thirds of the appeals in ICBC cases,[77] you may prefer using an appeal lawyer if your trial lawyer's appellate experience is limited; you're displeased with how he's handled your case to date; or your relationship with him has become strained. If he can't recommend an appeal lawyer to you whom you think you'd be comfortable using, you can ask the Canadian Bar Association's Lawyer Referral Services for a referral.

Since relatively few B.C. lawyers specialize in appellate work, it may make sense to hire someone mid-trial if your case is likely to go to appeal. This will allow you to select the lawyer you prefer before ICBC hires someone to represent them on your case. Your appeal lawyer will also be able to advise your trial lawyer on potentially appealable issues that arise during trial.

B.C. Court of Appeal Hearings

A three-member panel of judges will hear your appellate case. Since most of the case will be argued through written Factums, the hearing itself may take less than a day. Both the appeal and cross-appeal, if any, will be heard on the same date.

By the time your hearing takes place, the panel of judges should be familiar with your Judgment, the trial arguments on both sides, and the Factums on both sides. While some appellate judges read all available court transcripts, most don't do this, assuming that the trial judge reviewed the full trial record in writing her Reasons for Judgment. Only portions of the trial transcripts that are identified in the Factums as being relevant to the issues on appeal may be reviewed, with the appellate judges remaining unaware of the other trial evidence. All they'll know about your case is what's written in the Factums; what appears in the trial transcripts referred to in the Factums; and what they're told at the hearing.

B.C. Court of Appeal hearings are less formal than those in the B.C. Supreme Court. The opposing lawyers argue the positions set out in their Factums and answer questions from the judges, but no witnesses testify. After the appellant's lawyer has presented his case, the respondent's lawyer replies to this (and presents his cross-appeal arguments, if any). The appellant's lawyer then has a chance to respond to the respondent's reply on appeal (and her cross-appeal, if any). Each lawyer draws the judges' attention to the trial evidence and legal precedent he thinks is relevant, explaining how he feels this should be viewed. The judges may interrupt the lawyers to question their positions on various issues or ask them to clarify something.

In presenting his case first, the appellant's lawyer establishes the boundaries of the appeal and the tone of the hearing. If he's brief in presenting his arguments, the respondent's lawyer may feel that he has to be equally as brief so he doesn't appear to be wasting the judges' time. If you're the respondent on appeal, this may make you feel that your award isn't being defended vigorously enough. Your lawyer will follow whatever strategy he thinks is most likely to succeed with this particular panel of judges.

While most B.C. appellate court Judgments are handed down within six months, it may take much longer than this in some cases. Unless the judges' decision is unanimous, the dissenting judge will have to provide written Reasons for her disagreement with the majority opinion.

After the appellate Judgment is delivered, it may still be a while before you receive your money. Determining your new tax gross-up and management fees, if any, the costs and disbursements you're entitled to, if any, and court-ordered interest on your award can delay the final payment of your claim for many months. The opposing lawyers may have to return to court or go before the Appeal Court Registrar to settle one or more pending issues.

Since few ICBC cases are heard by the Supreme Court of Canada, the B.C. Court of Appeal is usually the last court to rule on them. If you lose your appeal, or your award is significantly reduced on appeal, you'll probably have to accept this — even if the appellate decision doesn't seem warranted or fair.

Appeals Before the Supreme Court of Canada

The Supreme Court of Canada (the highest court in the country) only hears about 70 of the 600 or so cases that it's asked to review each year. A case is usually only heard when an important issue of law is involved, or an issue is of national interest and meaningful to the general public, not just the opposing parties. The only time that permission to appeal is granted for the sole purpose of overturning a provincial appellate decision is when the Supreme Court feels that a grave injustice was done.

Leave (or permission) to appeal won't be granted just because the B.C. Court of Appeal made an erroneous or unfounded decision in a case. When a provincial appellate court makes a *gross* error in law, misinterprets the meaning of a law, or interprets the law in a unique way, establishing a new legal precedent, there's a reasonable chance that the case can be brought before the Supreme Court of

Canada. Ignoring a trial judge's finding of fact and reversing her decisions without due cause isn't sufficient reason for an appellate decision to be reviewed. While the Supreme Court has occasionally reversed the rulings of provincial appellate courts when they've interfered with a trial judge's finding of fact, this only happens once or twice a year at most, out of hundreds of similar cases where leave to appeal isn't granted.

Before your case can be heard by the Supreme Court of Canada, an application for leave to appeal will have to be filed, briefly stating the facts in your case, the issues in contention, your position on these issues, and what you're requesting. Your lawyer will have to submit copies of the trial judge's Reasons for Judgment, the appellate court's Reasons for Judgment, and a summary of your arguments against this — along with lists of the authorities and legal statutes he'll rely on, and the documents he'll refer to. (The respondent can oppose your leave to appeal or file a leave to cross-appeal.)

The amount of money involved has no bearing on whether the Supreme Court of Canada will hear a case. A case may be heard when little money is at stake if an important issue of law is involved. In order to get an unfair appellate decision reviewed, your lawyer will have to find an issue to challenge that is legally significant or important to the general public. If the Supreme Court agrees to hear your case, they're likely to reverse an unfair appellate ruling. (Supreme Court of Canada judges tend to take a dim view of provincial appellate court abuses.)

Despite the time and expense involved in trying to get your case heard by the Supreme Court of Canada, there are circumstances where this is necessary. If the trial judge awarded you $500,000 for future income loss, for example, and the appellate court decided that you aren't entitled to damages for future income loss, you'll probably want to file for leave to appeal. (Totally reversing a trial judge's finding of fact in this way can only be done by re-trying the case.) However, if the appellate court didn't dispute that you're entitled to damages for future income loss, but they cut your award in this category in half — for little reason other than the fact that

ICBC felt the award was too high — the Supreme Court of Canada probably won't hear your case. The only way the appellate court could totally eliminate your damages for future income loss is by interpreting the law differently from the way the trial judge did. This raises an issue of law, which the Supreme Court might want to clarify for the provincial courts.

You're more likely to get your case heard by the Supreme Count of Canada when the appellate court decision was split, not unanimous. If one of the judges disagreed with the majority opinion, this may indicate that their decision was wrong and should be reviewed.

The only time ICBC normally asks the Supreme Court of Canada to review an appellate decision is when a legal precedent was set that might have negative repercussions for them in the future.

While the Supreme Court of Canada has the right to ask the opposing parties to orally argue whether leave to appeal should be granted, this is rarely done. Leave applications are usually handled by written correspondence. A few days before the Court's decision, you'll be informed of the decision date by phone. By calling the Court Registry on that date, you'll learn what decision was made. The Supreme Court doesn't give reasons for why it grants (or refuses) leave to appeal, and most decisions on this are final.

If leave to appeal is granted, the opposing lawyers will go to Ottawa for the hearing. While you're not required to be present, Supreme Court sessions are open to the public with several cases generally heard on the same day. A seven-to-nine-member panel of judges will normally hear your case. (Each case is heard by at least five of the nine Supreme Court of Canada judges.)

Few Supreme Court decisions are announced orally. As with leave applications, you should be told when to phone the Court Registry to learn the outcome. (You can also get news releases of Supreme Court decisions e-mailed to you.)

While you're more likely to get an impartial hearing in the Supreme Court of Canada than you are in the B.C. Court of Appeal, it's not the fairness of your case that will be ruled on; it's the legal aspects involved. As the court of last resort in the country, the decisions of the Supreme Court are final. (The only recourse beyond this is direct intervention by the Governor General on behalf of the Queen. This is highly improbable in an ICBC case.)

Timing: It can take several years for a case to be heard by the Supreme Court of Canada. You'll have 60 days from the date of the appellate Judgment to file a Notice of Application for Leave to Appeal (excluding July). A decision on your leave application should be made within six months (again, excluding July).

Once leave to appeal has been granted, a case is normally heard within 12-16 months. Multiple copies (usually 20 or more) of your Factum, records, documents, affidavits and authorities will have to be submitted to the court. A decision is usually handed down within approximately six months of the hearing date (again, excluding July).

Costs: Not only is it expensive to take a case before the Supreme Court of Canada, you may not receive your award money until after a decision is reached. If you insist on being paid before this, ICBC may consider their payment to end their financial obligations towards you. This isn't what you'll want when you're the party appealing.

While the application fee for filing a leave to appeal is only $50, a lawyer who specializes in arguing cases before the Supreme Court of Canada may charge you $5,000-$10,000 for his opinion on whether you have grounds for appeal and a reasonable chance of success. If you decide to have him file a leave application for you, you may be charged $35,000 or more for this.

An appeal lawyer who represented you in the B.C. Court of Appeal may only charge you a few thousand dollars to file an application for leave to appeal. Since he's already familiar with your case, he won't have to study it as carefully as a new lawyer would. (Lawyers sometimes file leave applications on a discounted basis when they feel that a wrong was done which should be corrected.) If your leave to appeal is granted, you'll have high legal fees to pay regardless of who represents you. An appeal before the Supreme Court of Canada requires a lot of legal preparation and specialized expertise, and paying for this is costly.

If your trial lawyer feels that the appellate court ruling was unfair, he may offer to pay the up front expenses involved in taking your case before the Supreme Court of Canada. (The larger your award, the more money he'll earn.) Before you accept his offer, make sure you're clear about how he expects to be compensated for his help — and you get this in writing.

If you lose your Supreme Court of Canada case, you'll still be expected to reimburse your lawyer's expenses, which could be over $100,000. (The Appeal Books alone may cost this much.) You'll only get back this money if the Supreme Court rules in your favour.

Since "costs follow the event", if you lose your case before the Supreme Court of Canada, or your lawyer is unsuccessful in defending an appellate ruling that ICBC appeals, you'll have to pay their costs and disbursements as well as your own.

Should you hire another lawyer?: While an appeal lawyer who represented you before the B.C. Court of Appeal may be qualified to represent you before the Supreme Court of Canada, if he's lost your appellate case you may prefer using a lawyer whose practice is solely devoted to taking (and defending) cases before the Supreme Court. You should be aware, however, that the reputations of these specialists are built as much on the number of cases they argue as on those they win, and you could be given unrealistic hopes of your chances before the Supreme Court. You may want to get a second opinion before deciding whether to proceed. First find out what you'll be charged for this — legal opinions can be costly.

If your trial lawyer is urging you to bring your case before the Supreme Court of Canada, he may be willing to cover the cost of a reasoned opinion from a lawyer he trusts. Make sure he confirms in writing that you won't be billed for this.

If ICBC applies for leave to appeal, you'll want to hire the best lawyer possible to defend your award. Either your trial lawyer or appeal lawyer should be able to recommend someone to you. (You can also contact the Lawyer Referral Services of the Canadian Bar Association.) You may want to do some research to find out how a recommended lawyer's fees compare to those of other lawyers with equal success in defending cases before the Supreme Court of Canada.

PART IV

Managing Your Award Money

CHAPTER 20

Safeguarding Your Future

NOTE: The material in this chapter (and the next) isn't intended to be taken as financial advice. Check with a financial professional before making financial or investment decisions.

Once you've received your award or settlement, your initial impulse may be to indulge yourself and your family. It's important not to waste funds that you'll need later, though. Before you take a holiday or go on a shopping spree, you should pay off your debts, evaluate your future financial needs, and set up a sound budget to ensure you'll have money when you need it. You can also set aside some funds to use in whatever way you want.

Even a million dollars won't be enough to take care of you if you spend it foolishly, lend it to others, or invest it unwisely. As satisfying as it may be to spend money on others or loan it to them, you shouldn't do this without thinking about the consequences. Your damages for future income loss and future care, if any, were based on you investing this money at a reasonable rate of return to replace your yearly lost income and cover your care needs. If you're careless with your money and can't support yourself in the future, it may be hard to get financial assistance from public or private sources.

If you're aware of having a problem holding on to money, your lawyer may agree to hold your funds for you until you can find a financial professional to manage them. You can also put your money into an annuity to protect it from outside demands or misuse, or ask the financial services department of a bank, credit union or trust company to hold your funds and give you a small weekly allowance. This should prevent you from wasting money you may later need.

If you've had little prior experience managing or investing money, or your judgment may be impaired, you may need help from more than one financial professional. Having a comprehensive financial plan drawn up is wise when your ability to earn income is limited. Your plan should show you how much money you have to save or invest each month, and what rate of return you need to get on your investments, to have enough money to meet your lifelong needs.

Financial advisers usually suggest that people put as much money as they can into retirement savings plans. If you earn less than your spouse or partner, she can contribute to a spousal RRSP in your name and take a tax deduction for this at her own (higher) tax rate. As long as you wait three years to withdraw the money, it will be taxed at your (lower) rate. Making investments in the name of the spouse or partner with the lower income can reduce the taxes owed on the profits, provided the investment is held long enough.

If a disability prevents you from working, you may be eligible for a disability tax credit. Both the cost of a personal-care attendant and the repayment of EI benefits should be tax-deductible. An accountant can advise you on what tax deductions you're entitled to and how to claim these.

Paying Off Debts

With the exception of your home mortgage, you should try to pay off all your debts as soon as you get your award or settlement money. You can reduce the mortgage interest you'll owe by tens of thousands of dollars by paying down your mortgage principle, or increasing your monthly payments, while you have the funds to do this. The financial institution that holds your mortgage can tell you how much money you'll save through various pre-payment options. (Paying off a car lease may not be cost-effective if there are early-payment penalties.)

Credit-card debt should always be paid off quickly. Even when your minimum monthly payments are relatively low, annual interest rates are high. When you owe money on several cards, you can spend hundreds of dollars a month on interest without getting rid of your debt load. Unless you can pay off all your credit-card balances right away, a credit officer at your bank, trust company or credit union should be able to help you set up a repayment schedule to do this in the shortest time possible.

To make sure you don't build up credit-card debt as fast as you eliminate it, your credit cards can be replaced with debit cards that withdraw money from your bank account each time the card is used. If you want to hold on to a credit card for emergency use, put it in a safe place (such as a bank safety deposit box) where you won't have easy access to it. By the time you retrieve the card, you may decide that it's not worth slipping back into debt by using it.

You may be able to consolidate all your debts into one low-interest loan through your bank, trust company or credit union. If you have a structured settlement or guaranteed investments such as GICs, your financial institution may accept this as collateral (or security) on a low-interest loan. Posted loan rates usually aren't the lowest available, and you may be able to get a loan for ¼ – ½ % less than the posted rate. Most bank rates are negotiable to some degree. Financial institutions want people's business.

Setting Up a Workable Budget

A budget that incorporates your present needs and desires, and sets aside money for the expenses you expect to have in the future, will help you manage your finances on an on-going basis. The more variables your budget takes into account, the easier it should be to keep. A financial professional can help you draw up a budget that works for you, or review one you've set up yourself, making suggestions to improve it as needed. You may not be able to anticipate all your future needs and expenses on your own, nor place a realistic dollar value on them. (Budget worksheets are available in banks, libraries and on-line.)

You'll probably want to set up both a monthly and annual budget, each of which balances your expenses against your income from all sources. You'll have to consider what your present financial obligations are and what your future expenses may be. How much money do you currently need each month for medical-rehab treatment? Is this cost likely to increase or decrease over time? To what degree and within what time frame? What expenses will you have if you require further surgery or hospitalization? If you need attendant care, child care or household help on an on-going basis, what will this cost? If you don't need this help now, are you likely to need it in the future? When — and for how long?

If you're unable to work full-time (or at all), how much money will you need over the years to get along? Will you eventually want money for a new home, your children's education, or to support ageing parents? How often will you have to replace your car and what will this cost? If you're getting disability benefits from any source now, when are these likely to stop, and how much money will you have to take from your savings or investments to replace this loss? These questions don't have easy answers so you'll need to think carefully about them. You may have to research what a reasonable dollar value and time frame are for your future financial needs.

By setting up a sound budget and following it, you shouldn't have to dip into savings, cash out an investment early, or go into debt to pay your bills.

Professional Financial Advice

If your award or settlement was large, or you'll have to rely on this money throughout your life, you may want a financial adviser to help you set up a workable budget; establish realistic financial goals; and develop an investment program to meet these goals. You may also want him to oversee your investments on a continuing basis. If your judgment or ability to carry out responsibilities is impaired, you may need someone to manage your household expenses and pay your bills, as well as make investment decisions for you.

You should be very careful in choosing your financial advisers. The more complex your situation is and the more limited your financial knowledge, the more training and experience you'll want your advisers to have. Your lawyer, accountant or bank manager may be able to recommend someone to you. You can also check out continuing education courses that are taught by financial professionals, or see whether people who are quoted in the financial pages of the newspaper can recommend someone.

You'll probably want to interview several financial advisers before deciding whom to work with. Unless someone seems open and honest to you, and his responses to your questions make sense, you shouldn't work with him even if he's been highly recommended. You need to feel comfortable with the person you choose; trust his experience and expertise; and feel confident that he'll look after your interests, keep you informed about your investment choices, and see that you're moving towards your goals.

At your first meeting with a financial professional, he should tell you what services he can provide and clarify what his responsibilities towards you will be if you decide to work with him. He'll probably spend an hour or two with you in an initial interview. (While you shouldn't be charged for this, check first to make sure.) You may want to bring a summary sheet with you that shows your household income, current monthly expenses, anticipated future expenses (and when these might occur), and how much money you have available to invest. You can also list your assets and their current value; your liabilities or debts; and details of your life insurance policies, trust funds or business interests, if any.

Before a financial adviser can help you define your goals and priorities, or set up a financial plan or investment program for you, he'll have to ask you some personal questions so he understands your situation. Before you respond to his questions or share the details on your summary sheet with him, find out whether anyone else will have access to this information — and, if so, who this is. If other people in his office may work on your account from time to time, ask to be introduced to them.

Questions to ask: The first thing you'll want to find out from a prospective financial adviser is what his areas of expertise are and what kinds of advice or services he offers. Does he or his firm do tax or estate planning, insurance evaluations, or personal investment management? How long has he worked as a financial professional, what education or training has he had, and what professional organizations does he belong to? Where did he work prior to this and in what capacity? Is he licenced to offer investments to the public? If so, what types of investments is he currently recommending? Does he only sell a limited number of financial products, or will he shop around for the best investments for you? Does he or his firm do independent research on the investments recommended? If he doesn't sell financial products himself, can he refer you to people who do and get you their services at a reasonable price?

If you want him to draw up a financial plan for you, ask to see one he's prepared for someone else. Is it easy to follow and does it suggest a clear course of action to take? What information will he need from you to develop a comprehensive financial plan for your future; establish your investment goals and risk tolerance; and determine how (and where) your money should be invested? How long will it take him to draw up a financial plan, and what will this cost? Will he help you put your plan into effect, or can he refer you to people who will? Before you make any major financial decisions, will you be able to discuss these with him so he can show you how they'll affect your future goals? Will he update your financial plan when there are changes in your life that might affect your financial goals, making new investment recommendations as needed?

You may want to ask a prospective adviser to describe his typical client. Are most of his clients new investors, or do they have a lot of investment experience? How long has he worked with most of them and what's the average size of their accounts? Can you phone a few of his clients? (If you're able to do this, you can ask them if they've been satisfied with him; what they feel his strengths and weaknesses are; whether they've made or lost money through his recommendations; how often they hear from him; how quickly he returns their calls; and whether they'd recommend him to their relatives and friends.)

How would the financial adviser describe his investment philosophy? Is he fairly conservative in his approach or fairly aggressive? What percentage of the money you plan to invest would he suggest you putting into guaranteed investments versus more risky ones? How often will he review your investments and financial plan to make sure you're on the right track? Will he contact you if a new tax situation arises that might affect your investment strategy?

You'll also want to ask a prospective financial adviser how he's normally paid. Will you be charged an hourly rate or flat fee for his services, or will his fee be based on the size or performance of your account? Will he earn a commission, trailer (or service) fees, or get a promotional subsidy from the companies whose financial products you buy? (Trailer and service fees are commissions that are paid out over a number of years. They're most common on insurance policies and mutual fund sales, but they may be paid on other investments products sold to the public as well.)

Does the financial adviser or his firm have a business relationship or ownership interest in any company whose financial products he sells? Are there potential conflicts of interest you should know about? How will you be tied to him or his firm if you make investments through him?

Does he carry professional liability insurance? Will your investments with him be covered by the Canadian Investor Protection Fund, the B.C. Contingency Trust Plan, or the MFDA (Mutual Fund Dealers Association) Investment Protection Corporation? If so, how will this protect you — and if not, will you have any investment protection? Does he subscribe to a code of ethics prescribed by a professional body? Will he give you a written description of the professional guidelines he follows? Has he ever been disciplined by a professional association or regulatory body? If so, what was the outcome?

You may want to ask for a letter that outlines the services the financial adviser can provide, how he's normally paid, and other issues you've discussed. If you decide to work with him, a copy of his letter should be kept in your files for future reference.

What You'll Pay for Financial Advice

A financial adviser who works for a bank, credit union or trust company is usually paid a salary and his clients are charged a fee for his services. He may also earn a commission on the financial products he sells. Some financial advisers allow their clients to decide whether to pay them on a fee-for-service basis, through a commission on sales, or a combination of these options. (The companies whose financial products you buy may pay the commissions, not you.) If it's your choice how your financial adviser will be paid, ask him which payment method would be better for you under what conditions. If he works on a commission basis, will he tell you what he'll earn on the investment products he recommends?

A financial professional who bills by the hour may charge you anywhere from $75 to $300 an hour, depending on his experience and what services he provides. A fee-for-service adviser may charge you anywhere from $300 to $8,000 for a financial plan, depending on how complex your situation is and how comprehensive the plan is. While someone who works on a commission basis may not charge you to prepare a financial plan, he'll try to sell you investment products to off-set this.

When a bank or brokerage company provides discretionary management services, making and carrying out investment decisions for you, they may charge you a flat fee for this. A chartered financial analyst (CFA) who oversees your investments may charge you up to 3% of the assets he's managing. While CFAs usually manage accounts valued at $250,000 or more, they sometimes handle smaller accounts and charge a higher percentage or an annual fee.

Life Insurance

If you have dependants, one of the first things you may want to do with your award or settlement money is take out life insurance. If your spouse or partner is the primary wage earner in the family, it may make more sense to buy life insurance for her with you as her beneficiary.

Assuming you can afford this, you'll want to buy enough life insurance to cover your family's living expenses for as long as necessary after you die. How much money they'll need will depend on various factors. If your spouse or partner doesn't work and you have children, you'll need more life insurance than if she works and you don't have children. If possible, you'll want your family to be able to maintain their present quality of life and for money to be available for your children's education. (If you have a dependant with disabilities, making her the beneficiary of your life insurance policy will help ensure that her needs are met after your death.)

While there are many types of life insurance available, banks and trust companies usually have a limited number of choices to offer. You may prefer using an insurance broker who deals with many different companies and product lines. Once he's aware of your personal situation and has analyzed your income, assets, current financial needs and future financial goals, he can tailor a policy that's suitable for you. He may suggest several options for you to consider, explaining the advantages and disadvantages of each and the relative costs.

Whole (or universal) life insurance — which is also known as permanent life insurance — will cover you for as long as you continue to pay your premiums. Term insurance, on the other hand, will only cover you for a specific number of years, which may be as little as one year or as long as thirty. While you can usually renew your term insurance at the end of the policy period, your premiums may increase substantially. Initial whole life premiums are more expensive than initial term premiums but normally stay the same over time. (Check to your make sure your premiums won't increase before purchasing a whole life policy.) These two types of life insurance can be combined to provide you with the best protection for the price paid. Once the premiums on your term insurance become too expensive, you can cancel this and just keep your universal (whole life) policy. An insurance broker can advise you on the many combinations possible.

Universal (whole life) insurance can be used to accumulate investment income that will go to your beneficiaries upon your death without tax consequences. If you pay your life insurance company more money than your yearly premium amount, the additional money will be invested for you inside your policy. (You may have some choice in how the money is invested.) You should be able to borrow money against the investment component of your policy, or use it to pay future premiums.

Once you decide how much life insurance you need, and which company you want to buy it from, your broker will have you fill out an application form. This will ask for detailed information about your health, lifestyle, and habits. Unless you're totally honest in filling out this form, your beneficiaries may have a hard time getting the proceeds from your policy paid to them upon your death.

When your insurance packet arrives in the mail, you need to review this carefully and have your insurance broker explain anything that's not clear. If you want to cancel the policy after reading the fine print that describes the terms and conditions, you should be able to do this within the first ten days and have your money fully refunded. (Make sure you'll have these cancellation rights before purchasing the policy.)

As your circumstances change over the years, your life insurance policy should be reviewed with your insurance broker and updated as needed. Keep in mind as you do this that he'll earn a larger commission if you buy a new policy from him than if you continue with the one you have. (The commission on a new policy may be larger than your initial premium. Your broker will usually receive yearly trailer fees from the insurance company as well.)

Since most life insurance proceeds in Canada aren't taxable, life insurance often plays a central role in estate planning. (See below.)

Disability Insurance

Disability insurance for the primary wage earner in the family is as important as life insurance. As you've probably seen from your accident, a disability that prevents someone from working can occur at any moment. Being unable to work, in fact, is much more common than premature death.

In most cases, you'll want enough disability insurance to provide you with income replacement of at least 65-75% of your current earnings for as long as needed. (Most people continue to have this coverage until they retire. If you're dependent on someone else for your financial support, you'll want to make sure she has adequate disability insurance.) Your premiums will be based on your age and health at the time the policy is set up and will normally stay the same over time.

Even if you and your spouse or partner have disability insurance through your employers, it's unlikely to cover all your family's needs. Group plans often only pay a small percentage of your gross salary. There may also be a cap on how much money you can receive, and for how long. Moreover, you may only be covered if you're totally disabled from working. If your disabilities prevent you from doing the same job you did prior to your accident (or from earning the same income), but they don't prevent you from working at a lower paying job, you may only get benefits for up to two years. To ensure that you and your family will continue to have a reasonable standard of living, you may have to buy private disability insurance to top up your group coverage.

Estate Planning and Wills

Your estate consists of the assets you have when you die, less your outstanding debts. While everyone with assets or dependants should do some estate planning, it's particularly important to do when you have a dependant with disabilities and lifelong care needs.

Setting up a trust fund to hold assets for your children (or a dependant with disabilities) will reduce the taxes owed on your death. As the trustee of the fund, you'll control the trust's assets while you're alive. After your death, your co-trustee (or the person whom you named in your Will to succeed you as trustee) will take over managing the trust.

Since setting up a trust fund is expensive, you may prefer to make your children (or a dependant with disabilities) the beneficiaries of your life insurance policy and retirement or pension savings plans. The insurance (or plan) proceeds will then go directly to them upon your death. You can also leave money in your Will for the financial support of your children (or a dependant with disabilities), specifying that your assets be used for this purpose before any money is distributed to your other heirs.

Your Will should name the person whom you want as your executor, and where relevant, the person you want as legal guardian of your children (or a dependant with disabilities). You'll also want to leave clear instructions about how your estate is to be divided amongst your heirs. (Life insurance proceeds and retirement savings plans are usually dealt with outside a Will.) You can also mention any conditions or requests you want your executor and heirs to follow, including the kind of burial and last rites you'd like.

While most people appoint a relative or friend as executor, it's also common to ask a bank or trust company officer to serve in this capacity, or a lawyer who is familiar with the family's needs. A beneficiary to your Will can act as your executor, and spouses frequently name one another. (You may want to name a contingency executor as well, in case your executor pre-deceases you or is unable to serve.)

While you may not need an estate lawyer to draw up a simple Will — information on how to do this is available in libraries, bookstores and on-line — if your estate is large, your situation is complex, or you have a beneficiary with long-term disabilities, you'll probably want to use an estate lawyer. He can make sure that your Will says what you want it to say and that your heirs benefit the way you intend. It's also a good idea to have an estate lawyer draft your Will when you own property in different jurisdictions, have joint investments with others, or own your own business.

While a lawyer may charge under $200 to draw up a simple Will, having a complex Will drafted can be costly. You'll usually be billed by the hour for this. At your first meeting with an estate lawyer, he can tell you what his hourly fee is, what he estimates your overall legal costs will be, and what this covers.

A Will is only valid when it's witnessed by two people who aren't beneficiaries to it, nor closely related to the beneficiaries by birth or marriage. While you don't have to register your Will with the Wills Registry in Victoria, doing this will simplify the probate process, reducing the administrative costs to your estate. (Probate is the process through which the government determines that a Will is valid and sees that the terms of the Will are followed.)

For all practical purposes, the moment you die your assets are frozen until the probate court reviews your estate. However, a death certificate may be all your spouse or partner needs for the title of a shared home to be transferred to her. Your bank may also release up to $10,000 to your surviving spouse or partner without waiting for probate.

Unless there are irregularities in your Will, conflicting Wills, or someone challenges your Will, the probate court will generally accept your most recently signed and dated Will. If your estate is worth over $10,000 (excluding life insurance proceeds, retirement or pension savings plans with a named beneficiary, and assets held jointly with someone else), the court will appoint an executor to administer it. This will usually be the person whom you named as executor in your Will. If you die "intestate" (or without a Will), or your named executor can't serve, the probate court will appoint someone to administer your estate, usually a close family member. When this might create family conflicts, a lawyer or trust company officer may be appointed estate trustee.

Your executor or estate trustee will handle all legal and financial matters with regard to your estate. She'll have one year to gather the information she needs to prove to the probate court that your assets will be distributed according to the terms of your Will. She'll cancel your credit cards, re-direct your mail, look after insurance issues, locate and take legal possession of your assets, pay off your debts, and file your final tax returns. Since your assets will be considered to have been sold on the date of your death, capital gains taxes may have to be paid. Before any money is distributed to your heirs, a tax clearance certificate will be needed. (Depending on how much work your executor does, she's entitled to be paid up to 5% of your estate's value for this. This money will come out of the estate itself.)

Probate on a small estate may only take a few months. On a large or complex estate, a year and a half or longer is common. The estate's assets aren't supposed to be distributed until six months after the granting of probate — or one year after death when there's no Will.

The administrative process that's used when someone dies without a Will is more expensive than probate. Both legal and administrative costs usually have to be pre-approved by the probate Registrar. As long as valid receipts are kept, all probate costs should be reimbursed by the estate.

CHAPTER 21

Investing Your Money

Before you make an investment decision, you should make sure you understand the risks involved. In general, the greater the potential rewards from an investment, the more risky it is. In exchange for the security you get with GICs, term deposits, treasury bills and government bonds, their rates of return tend to be low compared to other investment products.

Your financial adviser will probably recommend that you invest in a variety of different asset classes, rather than putting all your money into one type of investment. Based on your goals and risk tolerance, he can help you figure out what percentage of your capital should be in cash, stocks, bonds, mutual funds, fixed-income investments and other investment vehicles. How much risk can you safely handle and what investment time frame do you have? Will you need to get income from your investments right away or not for many years? Your adviser (or broker) should be able to recommend a mix of investments that will maximize your potential returns while minimizing your risks.

Most financial advisers suggest that people keep at least three months' living expenses in a savings account or money market fund where they'll have ready access to it when needed. If the primary wage earner in your family loses her job or can't continue working for any reason, or unexpected expenses arise, you may have to use these savings to support your family.

Annuities

An annuity guarantees you a steady stream of income over time.

How much income you'll get will depend on how much money you put into the annuity, what the interest rate is, and what terms are built into the annuity structure. An insurance broker can help you analyze the options available through different life insurance companies so you can decide what works best for you. You may want to ask an accountant about the tax implications of various types of annuities.

While you can purchase an annuity for as little as $2,500, most annuities are bought for $10,000 or more. A deferred annuity can be purchased with a single payment or through monthly payments spread out over a number of years. You won't start getting income from a deferred annuity until a set future date.

The interest rate on a fixed-rate annuity is set at the time of purchase. You can also buy variable-rate annuities that offer higher potential returns at greater risk. These allow you to invest the annuity principle in mutual funds or a money market portfolio. As the investments in the annuity go up (or down) in value, your rate of return increases (or decreases).

While a fixed-term annuity will only pay you income for a specific number of years, other types of annuities can provide you with income throughout your life. You can also buy an annuity that combines these options. Your payments will be guaranteed for a minimum period of time, and you'll continue to receive payments as long as you live. If you die before the guaranteed period expires, your beneficiaries will receive payments until this time. With a "joint-and-survivor" annuity, payments continue to be made until both parties named on the annuity die.

Annuity payments combine principle (the invested capital) and earned income. With a prescribed annuity, the payments stay the same throughout the annuity's life. Less taxes are owed on early payments as a large portion of this is the return of invested capital.

Before you buy an annuity, you should find out what fees you'll be charged and what withdrawal provisions you'll have. Besides maintenance fees and investment management fees, you may have to pay high surrender charges to withdraw your funds early.

❖

Other Low Risk Investments

GICs (guaranteed income certificates) are issued by banks and other financial institutions. While they generally pay a fixed rate of interest until maturity, there are also variable-rate GICs available. Most GICs have to be held until the maturity date, which is usually one to five years from the date of purchase, but some can be redeemed without a penalty after 30-90 days. (A variable-rate GIC may have to be held for three to five years.)

Money you don't want to lock away in a GIC can put it into a term deposit (TD) for 30-364 days. The interest rate will be guaranteed throughout the selected term. This can be a good choice to make when you think you may need your money in a relatively short time. By buying several TDs and GICs with different maturity dates, you'll have the most flexibility with your funds. You should be able to borrow money against a non-redeemable TD or GIC.

The financial institution where you bank can be asked for a higher-than-posted interest rate on a TD or GIC. A financial adviser or broker can also research the best rates currently available. While term deposits and GICs are very safe, unless they earn enough to keep up with inflation, the "real dollar value" (or purchasing power) of your money may be less than you put into them.

Treasury bills (or T-bills) are issued and backed by the government and typically sell in minimum denominations of $25,000. While they're extremely safe, you may not earn as high an interest rate on amounts under $100,000 as you would with a TD or GIC. Treasury bills mature in less than a year and are sold at a discount to their value on maturity. They're not redeemable prior to maturity, but can usually be easily sold.

Canada Savings Bonds are issued and backed by the government of Canada. They're cashable at any time and can be held as long as you want. (No interest is paid on them when they're cashed in within three months of being purchased.) You're guaranteed a minimum rate of interest, which may increase when market conditions warrant it. Canada Savings Bonds have a face value of $100 to $200,000 and are only sold at certain times of the year. They can be purchased through banks, credit unions, trust companies, investment advisers, and brokerage companies. They're only transferable upon the owner's death.

Canada Premium Bonds are similar to Savings Bonds, but offer a higher rate of return. They can only be redeemed on the anniversary of the date they were issued and for 30 days thereafter. Only Canadian residents can purchase these types of government bonds.

Bonds

Most bonds pay a fixed rate of interest, with the face value of the bond paid back on a specific date. A bond that's "callable" may be paid back prior to maturity. Your financial adviser or broker should tell you if a bond is callable before you buy it. Besides the interest you'll earn on a bond, you can make or lose money on it by selling it before it matures.

The longer the term of a bond, and the less secure the issuing entity, the higher the interest rate it normally pays and the greater the risk. Short-term government bonds have little risk attached to them but usually pay less interest than corporate bonds. While most "junk bonds" have a high rate of return (or yield), they're generally issued by relatively new or unstable companies, making them a risky investment.

Changes in market interest rates influence why bonds go up or down in value. When interest rates drop, the market value of bonds as a group usually goes up. Individual bond issues may go up or down in value for other reasons as well. A bond that isn't traded on the open market, but is only available through select financial advisers, may be impossible to sell. This "lack of liquidity" increases the risk of junk bonds. ("Liquidity" refers to how easy it is to turn an investment into cash. A highly liquid investment can be converted to cash quickly at little cost.)

Bond funds are usually considered a more conservative investment than mutual funds that invest solely or primarily in stocks. While some bond funds invest in high-yield junk bonds, most limit their investments to government bonds and high quality corporate bonds.

Stocks

A B.C. resident can only buy or sell stocks through a broker who is licenced by the B.C. Securities Commission. Before you open an account with a brokerage company, you'll want to find out whether your account will be covered by the Canadian Investor Protection Fund, the B.C. Contingency Trust Plan, or the MFDA Investor Protection Corporation. The B.C. Securities Commission requires all brokers to tell their clients about the contingency programs that are available on their accounts, upon request. You may also want to find out what options you'll have if your broker is negligent or incompetent in handling your account.

Most stocks can be traded quickly, often within minutes of the order being placed. Unless your investment portfolio is being managed by a brokerage company's investment management division, you'll pay a commission on your transactions. Full-service brokers charge higher commissions than discount brokers, but can offer investment advice and make recommendations. You'll pay lower commissions if you trade on-line, but you'll have to do your own research and know when the time is right to buy or sell a stock.

In general, the longer it is before you'll need your money, the less risky it is to invest in stocks for capital appreciation (or growth). Many investment advisers recommend "dollar-cost averaging" — putting the same amount of money into a stock or mutual fund on a regular basis — as a prudent long-term strategy. If the stock or fund goes down in value, your money will buy you more shares, lowering your average price. This doesn't mean you'll necessarily make money over the long term. A stock can double in price one year and be worth almost nothing the next year.

If you can't work or you're close to retiring, you may want to consider stocks that have consistently paid dividends for decades. While this may provide you with a reliable stream of income, no stock is guaranteed to make you money over time.

The more diversified your investment portfolio is, the less risk you're usually taking. If you invest too heavily in one stock (or one sector of the economy), you can incur large losses when business factors (or the economy) change.

Mutual Funds

Mutual funds offer diversification, professional management, affordability, and relative liquidity. (Most transactions settle within three business days.) When you buy shares (or units) in a mutual fund, you're buying a small ownership in a large number of companies. You'll earn (or lose) money when the investments in the fund increase (or decrease) in value from your date of purchase to the date you sell. Dividends and capital gains are also distributed to fund shareholders. You should be able to reinvest these at no cost. Unless your fund is in a tax-deferred plan, you'll have to pay taxes on the dividends and capital gains that are earned, even when your fund shares drop in value due to a drop in the prices of the investments in the fund.

You and your financial adviser or broker will want to look for funds and fund managers that share your objectives and risk tolerance. You'll have to consider what return you need on your money, how long you intend to hold the fund, what fees and expenses the fund pays, the reputation of the fund company and fund manager, and the tax implications. How long has the fund been around and how volatile is it? How many years has the current fund manager been there and what did he previously do? (Few fund managers are right year after year, in all market environments.)

Bond funds and "balanced" funds that hold bonds as well as stocks are usually less risky than mutual funds that only hold stocks. You may want to consider a "segregated fund" that will guarantee your invested capital for a specific time, typically ten years. While paying for this protection is expensive, you won't lose the money you've invested even if stock prices drop substantially.

Before you invest money in a mutual fund, you should be given a fund prospectus to review. Ask your financial adviser or broker to go over this with you, so you're sure you understand it.

Mutual funds can be purchased through brokerage companies, financial advisers and the fund companies themselves. Some funds require a minimum initial investment, usually $500-$5,000.

Most mutual funds in Canada are purchased on a front-load or deferred-sales charge (DSC) basis. A front-load fee is a commission you pay when you buy your fund shares. You can then sell them without paying a sales fee. Front-end fees are usually 3-4% of the amount invested, but can be as high as 5%. Your adviser or broker will decide what percentage you're charged.

When you buy a mutual fund on a DSC basis, you don't pay a fee on your initial purchase, but you may have to pay a redemption fee when you sell. This will be based on the current value of your shares and how long you've had them. If you sell within the first year, your redemption fee could be as high as 6-8% of the share value. Since most DSC fees decrease by about 1% a year, when you hold a fund (or keep your money in the same fund family) long enough, you may not pay a redemption fee when you sell.

"No-load" funds don't charge a front-end fee or DSC fee, but their management costs tend to be high. When you hold a fund (or stay in the same fund family) for several years, you may pay more in management fees than you save on sales fees.

You can usually switch from one fund to another in the same fund family without triggering deferred sales charges. Transferring your money to a different fund company can be expensive, though, unless your financial adviser or broker rebates your redemption fees. If he suggested you make the switch, or you have other money invested with him, he may cover this cost. Not only was he paid a commission (of up to 5%) when you first bought your shares, he's probably been getting on-going trailer fees ever since. He'll also get a commission from the new fund company.

Sales fees are only part of the costs involved in owning a mutual fund. Funds pay large brokerage fees when they buy and sell stocks, and there are management and administrative costs to pay. (A fund manager may receive an annual salary of 1–2½% of the fund's assets.) These expenses reduce your return on your money.

Exchange-traded funds (ETFs) are mutual funds that are traded like stocks. You pay a normal brokerage fee when you buy or sell them. While no minimum purchase is necessary, EFTs are usually bought and sold in blocks of 100 units. You can only buy or sell them through a licenced securities broker.

EFTs are required to distribute capital gains to unit-holders at least once a year. Since portfolio turnover on them is low, though, there are usually fewer taxable distributions made than with other types of mutual funds. Management fees and administrative expenses are relatively low, and you should be able to reinvest your dividends at no cost.

You may want to keep a record of your conversations with your financial adviser or broker, including what stocks, bonds or mutual funds he suggests that you buy (or sell) and when he suggests this. You should also keep file copies of your confirmation and transaction records for tax purposes or in case a problem arises. As soon as you become aware of a problem, phone your adviser or broker about it as soon as possible, following this up with a letter outlining the situation. Most problems are caused by administrative errors and can easily be corrected. When this isn't possible, you may have to file a complaint with a regulatory agency.

Real Estate

Many people use their award or settlement money to buy a house or condo to live in. This may be a good investment to make, as well as providing you with comfortable, secure housing. If you decide to buy rental property, you'll need to learn as much as you can about the local rental market and find a good agent to work with. (Owning residential rental property requires less specialized knowledge than owning commercial rental property.) You'll have to know how to manage your property so it's always rented and well-maintained. While a real estate management company can handle this for you, this may be too costly to be worthwhile.

Real estate can also be purchased through a real estate investment trust (REIT) that owns one or more properties. While some REITs are publicly traded, this isn't always the case. Before you buy shares in a REIT, make sure you'll be able to get your cash out if you need it. (A limited-partnership REIT can tie up your money indefinitely. See the next section.)

A relatively secure way of investing in real estate in most market environments is to purchase mortgage-backed mutual funds. Funds that deal with residential properties or government-backed mortgages are usually safer than those that deal with mortgages on commercial properties.

High Risk Investments

Limited partnerships, tax shelters, high-yield junk bonds, and providing seed money for newly-emerging companies are high risk investments. They usually require a minimum investment amount, commonly $10,000-$25,000 or more. Even if you feel that the potential returns are worth the risks involved, you shouldn't invest money that you may need in the future.

Building and developing shopping malls, vacation resorts, golf courses and apartment complexes, as well as oil and gas exploration and mining operations, are often financed through limited partnerships. The general partners manage the company and control the investment. While there can be substantial tax benefits to limited partnerships, there's no established market to sell your shares. If a deal that's supposed to take two years to complete takes ten years instead, you'll usually have to wait this out. Even then, you may not make a profit nor get back the money you've invested.

Whether you make or lose money in a limited partnership will depend on whether the underlying business succeeds or fails; whether the anticipated tax benefits are allowed; and whether the general partners are honest. Even when a company prospectus or offering memorandum states that the limited partners will receive their dividends before the general partners, the general partners may pay themselves such high management fees that there's no money left over to pay the limited partners. Correcting irregularities can be costly, time-consuming — and is often impossible.

While privately-held companies aren't allowed to sell shares to the public, a financial adviser can sometimes sell shares in a company that isn't publicly traded to "sophisticated investors". (This is usually defined as someone with a minimum net worth of $250,000 or a minimum annual income of $100,000. Minimum net worth and annual income amounts may vary.) If most of your net worth and income is from an insurance claim, you shouldn't consider yourself a sophisticated investor nor take unnecessary risks with your money.

When you invest in a company that's not publicly traded, you may not be able to convert your investment to cash if you need your money. Moreover, since these investments usually aren't sold by registered securities brokers, the B.C. Securities Commission won't protect you if anything goes wrong. At the very least, you should find out what the person who is recommending the investment to you (or his firm) will earn as a commission if you invest in this; what connection he (or his firm) has to the company; and whether he (or his firm) is involved in other business ventures with the company principals.

While investors sometimes make a lot of money in new technologies and cutting-edge products, this takes knowledge, good timing and luck — as well as a willingness to walk away from large losses without regret. For every new company that succeeds, dozens more fail. Even if an emerging company's shares are publicly traded, they may be hard to sell. Long before you realize that a company isn't doing well, company insiders may have sold their shares.

CAUTION! Never gamble with funds that you or your family might need. You're more likely to lose money in a high-risk venture than to make a profit.

Minimizing Investment Losses

No financial professional can guarantee that you won't lose money in an investment. The most you can hope for is that the advice you're given is sound, an investment is appropriate for you, and you have a reasonable chance of making a reasonable return on your money. The higher the potential profits, the greater the risk; there are few exceptions to this.

While financial professionals in the province are legally prohibited from phoning you at home to sell you stocks, bonds and mutual funds unless you already have a working relationship with them, you may be offered other investment products this way. Any recommendation made to you by someone who doesn't know your investment experience or risk tolerance should be looked at with suspicion.

A reputable financial adviser or broker won't use high pressure sales techniques to encourage you to invest in something. Any time you're told that an investment opportunity like the one being recommended doesn't come along every day — or there's no way you can lose money: your capital and return are guaranteed — you're being given a sales pitch. Regardless of how good or bad an investment is, the person marketing it to you (or his firm) will earn a commission if you invest in it. Never let yourself be pressured into making an investment decision, nor base a decision on the fear that you might miss out on a once-in-a-lifetime opportunity. Other investment opportunities will come along with fewer risks involved.

> **CAUTION! Some financial advisers promote and raise capital for high-risk ventures. Anyone who recommends an investment to you should be asked whether this is something he does. If so, proceed with caution. You may be getting biased advice.**

Before you invest in something, make sure you know what the downside risks are and how much money you could potentially lose. A stock may have already increased in value so much that you're unlikely to make money on it now. After researching a company's prospects on your own, you can ask an independent financial professional who knows your personal situation if he thinks this is a good investment for you.

If you're considering putting money into a newly-emerging company, limited partnership or other speculative venture, you'll need to be especially diligent in your investigations. You should be given an offering memorandum that outlines the financial details an investor needs to evaluate the company's potential. This should be reviewed carefully with your financial adviser. Keep in mind as you do this that if he's recommended the investment he may have a vested interest in the company or earn a large commission if you invest in it.

To make sure you understand the risks involved, your financial adviser should be closely questioned. Could any situation arise that might require you to put up additional money? How long will it be before you can expect to get back your invested capital? Is there any guarantee that you won't lose this money? Will you be able to sell your interest in the company at a future date, or use it as collateral for a bank loan? Will the money that's being put into the company through the current offering be kept separate from other funds available to the business?

Write down everything your financial adviser tells you and make sure he knows you're doing this. You can then put your understanding of what he's said in a letter and ask him to sign it. Or, you may want to tape-record your conversations with your financial adviser about the investment. If he's being candid and honest with you, he shouldn't object to this.

You should also check the backgrounds of the undertaking's promoters, principals, and general partners. The B.C. Securities Commission can be asked whether any of them have ever faced disciplinary charges; the Better Business Bureau can be asked whether any complaints have ever been filed against them; and the RCMP can be asked whether they've ever been implicated in a business fraud. You may also want to contact the Business Practices and Consumer Protection Authority for information.[78]

The investment's potential and risks should be discussed with legal, financial and business professionals who have nothing to gain from your involvement. A lawyer, accountant, or independent financial adviser can look over the documents you were given and advise you on whether the investment seems sound. Your accountant can also tell you how realistic any promised tax benefits are and what future tax liabilities you might run into. An investment is only worth pursuing when it can stand up to hard scrutiny by knowledgeable, disinterested professionals.

❖

Pyramid schemes: Even when the underlying business in a pyramid scheme is valid, you can lose your invested capital. In a typical pyramid scheme, new people who invest (or join) essentially pay a profit to the people who are already involved. To earn a profit yourself, you have to get other people to invest (or join). You'll then be paid a small percentage of the money they put in, and an even smaller percentage of any money put in by new people whom they convince to invest (or join). While you may have to buy the company's products wholesale to participate, re-selling them usually isn't as essential to the success of the business as signing up new investors (or participants). Once new money stops flowing in, the pyramid collapses, and the people who invested (or joined) most recently lose their invested capital.

In a *ponzi scheme,* early investors are paid large returns from the money put in by later investors. This makes the investment seem very profitable, encouraging early investors to re-invest and attracting new investors. As with a pyramid scheme, once new money stops flowing in, the business collapses.

CAUTION! Be very cautious about giving anyone full responsibility for your investment decisions. It may be wiser to limit yourself to conservative low risk investments until you've gained enough experience to evaluate alternative options with the help of financial professionals you've come to trust.

Notes

1. In 2003, 46,295 bodily injury claims were made, and 58,866 claims were made for accident benefits. (*ICBC Annual Report*, 2003.) Not everyone who files a claim for damages is entitled to accident benefits and vice versa.
2. *Traffic Collision Statistics Report* (ICBC, 2002).
3. National Spinal Cord Association Resource Center (Fact Sheet 2, 2004).
4. Ibid.
5. High doses of methylprednisilone can improve neurological recovery by about 20% when administered within eight hours of injury — and the sooner the better. ("Acute Spinal Cord Injury" by Wise Young, Keck Center for Collaborative Neuroscience, Rutgers University, 2003.)
6. National Spinal Cord Association Resource Center. (See note 3.)
7. "Prevention: Brain Injury Statistics Sheet" (Newfoundland Brain Injury Association, 2004).
8. *Traffic Collision Statistics Report* (ICBC, 2002).
9. Based on author interview.
10. Based on author interviews.
11. Prolotherapy (or non-surgical reconstructive therapy) may be administered by a physiatrist.
12. "After the Crash: Psychological Assessment and Treatment of Survivors of Motor Vehicle Accidents" by Edward Blanchard and Edward Hickling, 2nd edition, 2003.
13. Ibid.
14. EMDR (eye movement desensitization and reprocessing) was developed through working with shell-shocked veterans. It's widely used in treating trauma survivors.
15. Based on a study by Nancy Kassam Adams and Flaura Winston (*Pediatrics*, December 1999).
16. Based on WCB's *Rehabilitation and Claims Manual*, 2002.
17. WCB's *Rehabilitation and Claims Manual*, 2004.

18. WCB's *Rehabilitation and Claims Manual*, Volume II (December 2003).
19. Ibid.
20. Social Development Canada website (CPP benefits, 2004).
21. Ibid.
22. Social Development Canada website (Employment Insurance, 2004).
23. Amounts from *BC Employment and Assistance Manual* (2003).
24. S.O.I. (structure of intellect) is based on J. P. Guilford's work. Existing capabilities are used to strengthen weaker cognitive areas, "teaching around" a person's disabilities. S.O.I. is most commonly used with learning disabled and academically gifted students, but can also help adults with brain injuries.
25. The M.E. Society of BC (for people with chronic fatigue) and the BC Fibromyalgia Society are now one organization: MEFM.
26. "Facts & Figures at a Glance – August 2004" (Spinal Cord Injury Information Network).
27. Seventy-five percent of the people in Canada with TBI are unemployed. (Newfoundland Brain Injury Association. See note 7.)
28. *Traffic Collision Statistics Report* (ICBC, 2002).
29. "Sharing the Road with Motorcyclists" (ICBC information update sheet). Almost half of all motorcycle collisions result in injury or death.
30. *Traffic Collision Statistics Report* (ICBC, 2002).
31. Ibid.
32. Prior to 2003, 70% of all LVI claims were denied, and 25% of the denied claims went to court. Now that accident benefits are being paid, fewer people with LVI claims may sue for damages.
33. See note 1.
34. Gordon Adair, "Public Review of No-Fault Insurance in Saskatchewan" (June 10, 2000).
35. Examples from the *Law Student's Legal Advice Program Manual* (2003).
36. *Traffic Collision Statistics Report* (ICBC, 2002).
37. Case C, *Annual Report of the Fairness Commissioner* (March 2002).
38. Amounts from *Insurance (Motor Vehicle) Act – Revised Regulation* (1984).
39. Ibid.
40. Autoplan brochure.
41. Based on author interviews.
42. In 2003, ICBC's net income was $225 million and their investments totaled $6.4 billion (*ICBC Annual Report*, 2003).
43. An estimated 87% of the people injured would lose their right to fair compensation under a no-fault system. (Coalition Against No-Fault news release, March 2002.)
44. "Is ICBC Using 'Hired Guns' to Win Cases?" by Jeff Lee (*Vancouver Sun*, January 21, 2002.)

45. In 2001, for example, ICBC paid one doctor over $350,000; four other doctors over $200,000; and another 12 doctors over $100,000. (*Statements and Schedules of Financial Information*, ICBC, 2001.)
46. Jeff Lee. (See note 44.)
47. Miller and Miller (1992) in "Issues in Malingering" by Jeffrey Barth (National Academy of Neuropsychology, 2004).
48. Canadian Coalition Against Insurance Fraud (2004 fact sheet).
49. In 2000, criminal charges were filed against 99 people in B.C. for auto-accident fraud, and 41 people were convicted. (*ICBC Annual Report*, 2000.) There's no indication that any charges or convictions were for fraudulent bodily injury claims.
50. *ICBC Claims Procedure Manual.*
51. In 2001, private detective agencies accounted for more service-provider dollars than anything except auto-body repair shops. (*Statements and Schedules of Financial Information*, ICBC, 2001.)
52. *ICBC's Claims Procedure Manual.*
53. Ibid.
54. Ibid.
55. Based on author interviews.
56. Bernie Simpson & Company (*Vancouver Yellow Pages*).
57. Based on author interviews.
58. From contract supplied to author by Murphy, Battista.
59. An articling student is a law school graduate interning at a legal firm.
60. A 30-minute consultation with a referred lawyer shouldn't cost more than $10.
61. *Legal Profession Act Review Process* (B.C. Supreme Court Registrar).
62. Summons forms available on-line or at Small Claims Court Registry.
63. Of the auto accident claims that go to mediation, 70% settle there. Another 10% settle after the Notice to Mediate, without mediation. ("The Management of Civil Litigation" by Justice Duncan Shaw, *The Advocate*, July 1999.)
64. Based on author interviews.
65. *Brown v Golaiy* (B.C. Supreme Court, 1985).
66. *Hill v Church of Scientology of Toronto* (Supreme Court of Canada, 1995).
67. *Warrington v Great-West Life Assurance Co.* (B.C. Supreme Court, 1995; B.C. Court of Appeal, 1996).
68. *Infant Settlement Submissions* (Public Guardian and Trustee of B.C.).
69. Ibid.
70. "The B.C. Supreme Court . . . is considering an increase in reimbursement of legal fees from 25-30% to 50%." (*ICBC Annual Report*, 2003.)
71. *Anson v Karoway* (B.C. Supreme Court, 1997): special costs are to be awarded "when the conduct of either counsel or client [is] . . . reprehen-

sible." This was said to include scandalous or outrageous conduct.

72. *Garcia v Crestbrook Industries* (B.C. Court of Appeal, 1994): special costs were awarded when the defence tried to place a financial burden on the party with "significantly weaker resources".
73. *National Hockey League v Pepsi-Cola Canada* (B.C. Court of Appeal, 1995): special costs were awarded when a deliberate attempt was made to mislead the court. *Heppner v Schmand* (B.C. Supreme Court, 1996): special costs were awarded when the argument against the main issue at trial came from clearly flawed reports and expert testimony.
74. *Report on Standardized Assumptions for Calculating Income Tax Gross-Up and Management Fees in Assessing Damages* (Law Reform Commission report 133, 1994). (See B.C. Law Institute.)
75. Ibid.
76. Future economic losses are usually discounted to a present-dollar value that takes into account anticipated interest rates and inflation rates. If your award is structured, the interest rate on the purchased annuity will be fixed at the time of purchase.
77. Based on author interviews.
78. Prior to July 2004, the B.C. Ministry of Public Safety and Solicitor General oversaw business practices and consumer protection.

Resource Directory

Disability-related organizations

BC Coalition of People with Disabilities (BCCPD)
#204 – 456 W Broadway, Vancouver
(604) 875-9746
www.bccpd.bc.ca

BC Paraplegic Association (BCPA)
780 SW Marine Drive, Vancouver
(604) 324-3611
Chapters throughout B.C.
www.canparaplegic.org/bc

Cowichan Valley Disability Resource Centre
225 Canada Ave, Duncan
(250) 746-3930
www.cvilrc.bc.ca

Nanaimo Independent Living Resource Centre
2122 Northfield Rd, Nanaimo
(250) 758-5547

Vernon Disability Resource Ctr
107 – 3402 27th Avenue, Vernon
(250) 545-9292; (877) 288-1088
www.vdrc.ca

Victoria Disability Resource Ctr
1990 Fort, Victoria
(250) 595-0044
www.vrcvictoria.com

Richmond Disability Resource Centre
160 – 5726 Minoru Blvd, Richmond
(604) 232-2404
www.drcrichmond.ca

BC Living Independent Service
205 – 2006 W 10th Avenue, Van.
www.independent-living.ca

Brain Injury Resource Center
212 Pioneer Building, Seattle
(206) 621-8558
www.headinjury.com

Vancouver Island Head Injury Association
#201 – 651 Queens Avenue, Victoria
(250) 598-9339
www.biasvi.org

MEFM Society of BC
Box 462 – 916 West Broadway, Van.
(604) 878-7707; (888) 353-6322
www.mefm.bc.ca

Chronic Pain Society
c/o Comox Valley Nursing Centre
961A England Avenue, Comox
(250) 338-5453

Active Living Alliance
720 Belfast Road, Ottawa
(613) 244-0052; (800) 771-0663

S.O.I. Systems
Vida, Oregon
(541) 896-3936
www.soisystems.com

Social Planning and Research Council of BC
#201 – 221 E 10th Avenue, Van.
(604) 718-7733
www.sparc.bc.ca

Legal organizations

Lawyer Referral Services
(604) 687-3221; (800) 663-1919

Canadian Bar Association of BC
(604) 687-3404 or (888) 687-3404
www.bccba.org

Law Society of BC
845 Cambie Street, Vancouver
(604) 669-2533; (800) 903-5300
www.lawsociety.bc.ca

UBC Law Students' Legal Advice Program (LSLAP)
(604) 822-5791
www.lslap.bc.ca

Continuing Legal Education Society of BC
#300 – 845 Cambie, Vancouver
(604) 669-3544; (800) 663-0437

Legal Services Society
#1500 – 1140 W. Pender, Vancouver
(604) 601-6000
Offices throughout B.C.

Disability Law Program
(604) 685-7611; (888) 685-6222

Government agencies

Human Resources and Skills Development Canada (HRSDC) & Social Development Canada (SDC)
www.hrdc-drhc.gc.ca

EI Benefits (and local HRCC offices)
(800) 201-7218
(See above website.)

CPP Disability Benefits
(800) 277-9914
(See above website.)

Federal Income Security Program
for Trustee of Gov't Pension Income
(800)277-9914

B.C. Ministry of Human Resources (MHR)
www.mhr.gov.bc.ca/fs.htm

BCEA Appeal Tribunal
(250) 356-6374

B.C. Ministry of Health Services
(250) 952-1742; (800) 465-4911
www.gov.bc.ca/healthservices

Home and Community Care Branch
www.hlth.gov.bc.ca/hcc

Office of Assisted Living
(866) 714-3378

Public Guardian and Trustee
(604) 660-4344
www.trustee.bc.ca

Health care

George Pearson Centre
700 W 57th Avenue, Vancouver
(604) 321-3231

G.F. Strong Rehab Centre
4255 Laurel Street, Vancouver
(604) 737-6291

G.F. Strong Sexual Health Services
(604) 737-6411

Provincial Health Services Authority
700 – 1380 Burrard, Vancouver
www.phsa.ca

UBC School of Nursing
T 206 – 2211 Westbrooke Mall, Van.
(604) 822-7420

UBC Chronic Pain Program
St Paul's Hospital, Burrard St, Van.
(604) 822 -7314

Caregivers Association of BC
306 – 1212 W Broadway, Van.
(604) 734-4812
www.vcb.bc.ca/cabc2000

WCB

Head Office
6951 Westminster Highway, Rmd
Offices throughout B.C.
www.worksafebc.com

Claims Call Centre
(604) 231-8888; (888) 967-5377

Disability Awards
(604) 276-3076

Disclosures Department
P.O. Box 5350 Station Terminal, Van.
www.claimsdis@wcb.bc.ca

ICBC

Head Office
151 W Esplanade, North Vancouver
(604) 661-2800; (800) 663-3051
www.icbc.com

Dial-A-Claim
Lower mainland: (604) 520-8222
Elsewhere: (800) 910-4222
(See above website.)

Out-Of-Province Claims
(604) 520-8800; (800) 667-7740

Other internet sites and links

When someone is in a coma: www.waiting.com
US Brain Injury Association www.biausa.org
Newfoundland Brain Injury Association www.nbia.nf.ca
Computer software for people with TBI www.parrotsoftware.com
National Spinal Cord Injury Association: www.spinalcordinjury.org
SCI information network: www.spinalcord.uab.edu
SCI resource directories: www.makoa.org & www.paralinks.net
Disability resource directories: www.disabilityweblinks.ca; www.enablelink.org
Parents with disabilities: www.disabledparents.net
Disability healthcare products and books: www.blvd.com
Disability-related products: www.abledata.com
Disability-related films: www.disabilityfilms.co.uk
Disability and sexuality: www.sexualhealth.com
Canadian Association of Financial Planners: www.capf.org
Canadian Investors Protection Fund: – www.cipf.ca
***Globe and Mail* mutual fund information**: www.globefund.com
B.C. Securities Commission: www.bcsc.bc.ca

Books

I Can't Get Over It: A Handbook for Trauma Survivors by Aphrodite Matsakis; *Protect Yourself in the Hospital* by Thomas Sharon; *The Ragged Edge: 15 years of the Disability Rag; The Complete Product Guide for People with Disabilities* (800) 833-8735; *Spinal Network: The Total Wheelchair Resource Book* (Nine Lives Press); *Life on Wheels: For the Active Wheelchair User* by Gary Karp; *The Sensuous Wheeler* by Barry Rabin (800) 543-4116; *Enabling Romance: A Guide to Love, Sex and Relationships for the Disabled (and the people who care about them)* by Ken Knoll and Erica Levy Klein. **SCI memoirs:** *Moving Violations* by John Hockenberry; *He Can't Get Far on One Foot* by John Callahan. **TBI memoirs:** *Conquering Darkness* by Deborah Quinn; *Where Is the Mango Princess?* by Cathy Crimmins; *Over My Head* by Claudia Osborne; *I'll Carry the Fork* by Karla Swanson.

Children's books on disabilities: *Mama Zooms* by Jane Cowen-Fletcher (ages 3-6); *Don't Call Me Special* by Pat Thomas and Lesley Harker (ages 4-8); *Susan Laughs* by Jeanne Wills and Tony Ross (ages 4-8); *The Berenstain Bears and the Wheelchair Commando* by Jan and Stan Berenstain (ages 9-12); *The Road Back* by Harriet Sirod (young adult). **Children's books on bereavement**: *The Fall of Freddy Leaf* by Leo Buscaglia (ages 4-8); *When Dinosaurs Die* by Laurie and Marc Brown (ages 4-8); *I Miss You: A First Look at Death* by Pat Thomas and Lesley Harker (ages 4-8); *Help Me Say Goodbye* by Janis Silverman (ages 4-8); *When a Friend Dies,* edited by Marilyn Gootman (young adult).

Magazines

Abilities Magazine; *New Mobility Magazine*; *Special Living*; *The Ragged Edge* (formerly, *The Disability Rag*).

Disability-related movies

The Other Side of the Mountain (1975); *Waterdance* (1992); *Frida* (2002, Salma Hayek); *Frida Kahlo* (1983, award-winning documentary); *Good Luck* (1997, Gregory Hines); *The Bone Collector* (1999, Denzel Washington); *Coming Home* (1978, Jane Fonda & Jon Voigt); *The Terry Fox Story* (1983, Robert Duval); *Passion Fish* (1992, director John Sayles).

Disability-related videos: *Here: A Poetry Performance* by Cheryl Wade (1613 – 5th Ave, Berkeley, CA); *Vital Signs: Crip Culture Talks Back* and *Dancing from the Inside Out* (award-winning movies from www.fanlight.com or (800) 937-4113); *Sexuality Reborn* (`Kessler Institute for Rehabilitation, West Orange, New Jersey)

Index

Additional copies of this book may be purchased through your local bookstore or directly from the publisher. Please see our website at **stonemountainbooks.com** or write to

Stone Mountain Books
P.O. Box #41128
2529 Shaughnessy Street
Port Coquitlam, BC
V3C 5Z9

Discounts are available on bulk orders to professional organizations and disability or non-profit groups. Contact Stone Mountain Books for more information.